CW01476801

Bierton Strict
and
Particular Baptists

my Testimony and Confession

Alternatively

Set for the Defence and Confirmation

Of the Gospel

By David Clarke

SBN 978-0-9539473-7-9

First Edition 16th January 2012

Abshott Publications

Trojan Horse International (TULIP) Phils. Inc.

11 Hayling Close,

Fareham,

Hampshire,

PO14 3AE

UK.

E mail: **SecretaryDolores@yahoo.co.uk**

www.BiertonParticularBaptists.co.uk

ISBN 978-0-9539473-7-9

A True Story

This is a true story of David Clarke, born in Oldham Lancashire, in 1949.

During the 60's he and his older brother Michael began to enjoy lives of crime, promiscuity and infamy during their teenage years, whilst living in Aylesbury, Buckinghamshire and they lived with their parents and younger sister in Aylesbury and became criminals. They were both sent to prison in 1967 for malicious wounding and carrying a firearm without a license. David served his time in a young persons Borstal Training Institute at Dover, and Michael served his time in Maidstone Prison.

On leaving Borstal in 1968, David was determined to have a good time living a life of crime, with no fear or belief in God, respect for society, parents, or the wider family. He proceeded on a three-year career of undetected crime until he met a Christian woman who informed him that his life style was wrong.

It became David's opinion that Christianity was for people who could not enjoy life, or stand on their own two feet.

On the 16th of January 1970 David was arrested whilst he experienced a bad trip on LSD but not by the Police. It was by Jesus Christ who spoke to him after he had cried out to God for help. Jesus said to David that the horrors that he had experienced were nothing compared to what hell was like.

David turned away that Friday night, from a sinful life of crime and immorality to follow Christ as best he could.

David began to read the bible immediately, and other Christian books, and attended a wide range of churches. He finally confessed to the police to 24 crimes that he had committed during his release from Borstal in 1968 and conversion in January 1970.

David eventually joined the Bierton Strict and Particular Baptist Church in 1974. And then trained as a Lecturer commencing teaching electronics at Luton College of Higher Education, and taught for 22 years in both higher and further education colleges, until 2001.

The Bierton Church, which was founded in 1831, became a Gospel Standard listed cause, and in 1982 David was called by the Lord and sent by the church to preach the gospel where ever the the Lord opened up the door for him to speak.

David then sought to reach his old friends from the past, and organized a preaching meeting at the Bierton chapel in 1983, inviting all his old friends to come and hear of all what the Lord had done for him. Providentially that preaching meeting was televised on video and is available on YouTube under the title:

"David Preaching at Bierton Strict and Particular Baptist" 5th June 1983" (Click to view).

David recalls that it became apparent after this meeting his real troubles began, and he seceded from the Bierton Church in 1984. An account of this secession was written by David's own hand entitled, "The Bierton Crisis".

This story is a complete account of David's early life, experience of conversion from crime to Christ and life in the Bierton Strict and Particular Baptist Church. He concludes that men may begin well in their faith towards God, trusting in the person and finished works of Jesus Christ alone for their salvation, but then **fall from grace falling** into the error of seeking to please God by works according to their own inventions or distortions of the Law of Moses. They fall into the trap of making themselves **"perfect in the flesh"** and then judge others who do not act like them.

4

The story continues to the time of Michael's arrest in the Philippines, in 1995, and his 16-year prison sentence.

The story goes on through to Michael's own conversion from crime to Christ, in New Bilibid Prison some 30 years after David own conversion to Christianity. This occurring after he was convinced that Jesus was the Christ, the son of the living God, through reading CS Lewis's book, "Mere Christianity". It tells of his baptism as a Christian in an old oil drum in that prison in September 2000.

This story demonstrates the manifold grace of God, in saving two brothers from a life of sin, crime and immorality, through the person of the Lord Jesus Christ.

This book is really David's confession and testimony written for the **defence and confirmation of the gospel**. David also believes the things that have happend to him have fallen out rather unto the furtherance of the gospel. Phil 1. verse and 7 and verse 12.

David's solution to help and assist in the promotion of the gospel of the lord Jesus Christ is the creation of the Bierton Particular Baptist Open College (an Internet Cloud). This is outlined in the last chapter of this book. Those wishing to be trained and educated In the doctrines of grace can enrol and obtain all the assistance they need.

Contents

1   Confession to 24 crimes

(The court case)

It was real, absolutely real, but none of my friends really believed me. All I could do was tell them what had happened to me, and that was what I did. I told them all, the long, the short and the tall. As many of them as I could. They thought I had gone mad after taking LSD.

Jesus Christ had spoken to me and rescued me from a bad LSD trip on Friday evening, 16th January 1970. He had said that what I had been going through was nothing compared to what hell was like. I now knew the way and was determined to tell the others. I had become a Christian and no longer needed to live the life style that I had adopted, which had involved crime, drugs, promiscuity, flash cars and fame. I had been born again.

I was now responsible for sorting out all my stolen gear. What could be done with a builder's shed and stolen cars? I still had in my possession many stolen goods, which included the 48-foot by 24-foot. builders shed, which we had stolen one night from a building site at Berkhampstead, and a lovely "G" reg. mini, stolen from Hemel Hempstead, which was in the process of being "rung". Ringing meant replacing and old mini with legitimate registration documents and number plates with a new one. My new mini was being used to replace it. This was to be my new car. I also had a Morris Minor Traveller, which had been "rung" and was being used as a hire car. I had stolen garage equipment, which included an air compressor, electric welding equipment, spray guns and a trolley jack. I also had several pieces of electrical test equipment, which included oscilloscopes, AVO meters and Colour TV's. I had all the garage equipment I needed to repair and spray cars.

I had a lovely Citroen DS car in the builder's shed, which was being repaired. I obtained this car through swapping it for a colour TV set. The only problem was that I had stolen the TV set from an old people's at Redfileds old peoples home in Winslow, Buckinghamshire.

I also had two nice speedboat engines, getting ready for the summer of 1970. All in all I had had a real good time full of excitement and fun.

In fact I had been stopped in the midst of my career, which involved stealing all kinds of goods to have a good time. I had intended to have a caravan, a speedboat, water skis, aqualung diving gear, flash cars, motorbikes, and clothes and so on, all through stealing. I was in fact stopped whilst in the midst of my career but not by the police. It was Jesus Christ who had called me by name and I followed him.

What to do with stolen goods after one becomes a Christian

I thank God he intervened again a year later and His hand was clearly seen once more. I had no one else to help. As I write this I take encouragement in the faithfulness of God to me in never leaving me or forsaking me. I realize now I was kept through the power and grace of our Lord Jesus Christ to bare witness today, to many people of the goodness and mercy of God.

The problem was solved by a visit from the C.I.D.

I was sitting at the table in our kitchen at 37 Finmere Crescent one evening in late 1971, when a knock came on the door. I had two visitors, a detective constable Robson and a younger man. I was greeted quite politely but with sure and certain words " You are charged with stealing a colour television set " and "would you accompany us down to the police station to make a statement".

I knew instantly what I must do and say. I saw the hand of God and believed this was all his doing but I did not know the outcome. Leaving the outcome to God I asked the two men to sit down in the kitchen and I admitted the charge. At this DC Robson seemed most relieved, for he said to me later, he had thought I would be very difficult and awkward and deny the charge.

I explained I would certainly come with them to the police station and make a statement but I wanted to speak to them about other things first. I said I had many crimes I wished to tell them about but wanted to tell them first of all why I was informing them.

I wanted it to be known that they would not have been able to find out about my crimes unless I confessed to them and I wanted to testify to the saving work of Jesus Christ that he had saved me from my former criminal way of life a year previously and that I did not wish to get off lightly with this confession but rather bear testimony for Christ. For in no way could my crimes be discovered unless I tell them and owned up to them. I had a lot of property, which could be returned.

I went with them to the police station and spent the rest of the evening making writ ten statements giving details of my crimes. I was detained that evening in the police cells at Walton Street police station in Aylesbury, not that I was a stranger to prison cells. My shoelaces were removed but I was allowed my New Testament (Authorized Version, working mans pocket addition).

I had to appear in Aylesbury's Magistrates Court on the 9th February 1971 and answered two charges of burglary and one of theft. I also asked for 21 other crimes of theft to be taken into consideration, all of which had been committed since I left Borstal, between September 1967 and 16th January 1970. I had decided I did not need legal representation, as I would speak for my self.

With my past record of probation and Borstal training it was quite expected that I would be sent to prison. I was quite OK with this because I deserved it and I believed God was in this and had a definite purpose in this event. I prepared for this by setting my affairs in order at home and gave directions that my Mini Traveller, which I had rebuilt, was to be given to Barry Crown, if I got sent down. I believed that whatever happened to me the outcome was of God and there would be good reason for it. I thought I might be being sent to prison so as to preach the gospel to inmates. A friend of mine Mr Peter Murray was concerned about my court appearance and suggested I get some written testimonials from some of my Christian friends and he felt he ought to appear in person and speak on my behalf. The friends who wrote were Barry Crown, Cyril Bryan, Tom Thompson and Eric Connet. I am including these letters, which were sent to court. These people all testify to the saving grace of God in changing my life. These are some of the written testimonies:

1 Testimony of Barry Crown

R.B Crown 45, Mitcham Walk, Aylesbury. Buckinghamshire

To the Clerk to the Magistrates

Dear Sir,

6th February 1970

I am a graduate of Salford University, and hold a B.Sc. in Civil Engineering. I am at present an employee of Aylesbury Borough Council, working under Mr. Hanney, the Borough Engineer and Surveyor. I have held this post since September 1970.

Shortly after taking up residence in Aylesbury I befriended Mr.

David Clarke whom I met at the Full Gospel Church, Rick fords Hill. I found David to be a true and sincere Christian seeking to spread the Gospel of Jesus Christ and to give personal testimony of the salvation through Jesus Christ, which he himself had experienced.

David told me how he had been miraculously converted on January 16th 1970. And have the subsequent change in his whole manner and outlook to life. Before his conversion he confessed to a life of drugs and theft, but now he no longer had any desire or pleasure in such things, since Christ destroyed the power of such in his life.

For the six months I have known David I have been a witness to the truth of his testimony and I know him as a person who is a completely honest and trustworthy follower of the Christian faith.

Yours Sincerely,

R. B. Crown.

2 Testimony of Cyril Bryan

176 Cambridge Street Aylesbury

To the Clerk to the Magistrates   2/2/71

Dear Sir,

I am privileged to write a testimony to you concerning David Clarke, and I count it a privilege because it is to the glory of God.

I have known this young man through conversations and meeting with him, through the church I attend in Aylesbury. The Full Gospel Testimony Church at Rickfords Hill.

What I wish to bring to your notice is the wonderful change that has taken place in him as a result of him believing the gospel and receiving the Lord Jesus Christ as his personal saviour, according to the scriptural instruction and ordinances.

The change of character and speech is miraculous, as are all the works of God, and as a believer in the Lord Jesus Christ for 30 years; I know that David Clarke is a transformed person, by the grace of God. As are we all who know the reality of the new birth as taught by Johns Gospel.

You will know his past life, I testify to his new life in Christ Jesus. Yours Sincerely,
C Bryan.

3 Testimony of Mr E Connet

E.H. Connet
125 Park Street,
Aylesbury,
2nd February 1971

TO WHOM IT MAY CONCERN

This is to certify that I have known Mr. Clarke for a period of approximately 9 months since his conversion to Christianity. I am fully persuaded that he has turned his back on his past life and changed for the better.

He is now earnestly endeavoring to make amends for his past mistakes and even influence others to turn their lives over to God, as he has done.

My object in writing this testimonial is that it may help to throw some light on David's character from one who knows him as a Christian.

Yours Faithfully,

E Connet.

I Speak In Court

I appeared in court on the 9th February 1971, dressed in my dark blue (Mod) suit. I pleaded guilty and then a report from the police was read and I was given leave to speak for myself. I spoke extempore (without notes- trusting in the Lord for all the help I needed) describing my preconvention days up to my conversion. I also spoke about life since being a Christian explaining my difficulties with respect to the stolen goods that I had in my possession.

I was able to speak of what Jesus had done for me in a way that only God could have worked.

After this Peter Murray spoke on my behalf confirming my testimony.

This happened on Tuesday 9th February 1971, a date that proved significant to me 3 years later.

I was amazed, so were all my Christian friends. The magistrates thought I was trying to be a martyr. I do not know how or why. They obviously thought I should be sent to prison but part of my punishment would be I was not going to get what I wanted. God smiled. We smiled with him. It was good to be a child of God.

News Head lines

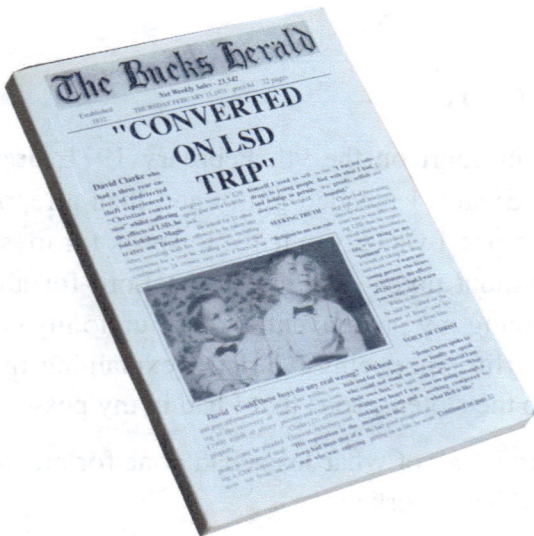

The Bucks Herald Weekly Paper

The whole court appearance was reported in the local newspapers and in the national Evening Standard.

The news headlines of the Bucks Herald read, " Why he confessed to 24 crimes" and " Converted on LSD trip". Whilst the Bucks Advertiser read " Man speaks of horrors on LSD".

The following are copies of those headlines all of which were fairly accurate.

Bucks Herald Script

The Bucks Herald 11th February 1971. David Clarke, who had a three-year career of undetected crime, experienced a "Christian conversion" whilst suffering from the effects of LSD, he told Aylesbury magistrates, on Tuesday. After wrestling with his conscience for a year, he confessed to 24 crimes, and gave information leading to the recovery of over £1000 worth of stolen property. In court he pleaded guilty to charges of steeling a £300 colour television set from an old peoples home, a £20 spray gun, and a hydraulic jack. He asked for 21 other charges to be taken into consideration, including stealing a builders shed, two cars, and an electric arc welder, two other TV sets, two compressors, and a road trailer. Clarke (21) of Finmere Crescent said that his reputation in the town had been that of a man who was enjoying himself. "I used to sell drugs to young people, and indulge in permissive sex" he declared.

Seeking Truth

"Religion to me was rubbish, and for sissy people who could not stand on their own feet", he said. "Within my heart I was searching for truth, and a meaning to life". He had good prospects of getting on in life he went on but "was not satisfied with what I had, I was greedy, selfish and boastful." Clarke had been using pep pills, and marijuana since he was 16 he told the court, but it was after taking LSD that he experienced, what he described as, "a major thing in my life". He described the "torment" he suffered, as a result of taking the drug, and went on "I warn any young person who hears my testimony, "The effects of LSD are so bad, and I warn you to stay clear". While in this condition he said he, "Called on the name of Jesus" and his torment went from him.

Voice Of Christ

"Jesus Christ spoke to me as clearly as I speak here today saying, "David, I am with you". Mr Murray, of Manor Crescent Wendover said he was habitually sceptical of sudden conversions, and preferred to put them to the test of time. The time, which had elapsed, since Clarke's profession of faith had convinced him that this young man would now be salt and light to society". "He is in truth, a new man, and had experienced what Christ called a second birth". Murray said Clarke now put himself out to be of assistance, read the bible intensely, always carried a New Testament, attended a wide circle of churches and would spend hours in discussion on spiritual things.

Difficulty

Clarke's difficulty during the months spent deciding how to make amends for his past had been the problem of accusing himself, without informing on others.

Passing sentence the chairman of the magistrates, Colonel I. Tetley, told Clarke, "You have pleaded guilty to three offenses and asked us to take into consideration 21 others, and except a record over a short period of time, which is quite the worst we have ever seen, we have considered what we aught to do and have come to the conclusion that your evident desire to become a martyr is one we are not going to gratify".

He gave Clarke a conditional discharge for three years pointing out that the sincerity of his conversion could be shown by his behaviour during that period.

The outcome of the court case was a complete surprise to us all, and we were overjoyed. A Christian friend, Mrs. Chapski of Broughton Avenue Aylesbury, invited us all back to her home for coffee.

DC Robson informed me that they had discovered I was the person who had stolen the television from Mike West. An enemy of Mike West had tipped them off about the stolen Television. Mike West appeared in Court on the same day as myself and was fined £25. He nearly lost his job with the insurance company that he worked for. His encounter at court, to his embarrassment, also appeared on the front page of the newspaper alongside the article about my conversion.

After this I gave Mike West his Citroen car back that I had swapped for the colour TV. I had re sprayed it a bright Banana yellow, and replaced the engine. At lease he was able to sell it and get some money back. I now know, and take encouragement that God works well and sorts things out when we cannot do so.

As far as the other stolen goods were concerned the police managed to take away most of them but the firm who owned the builders shed sent a trailer. The ironic thing is that I could get no help to load the shed on the trailer. In the end Mrs. Knight was the only one to help. This was very hard work but between us we managed to load it on the trailer late one night. To give you some idea of the value of the stolen items. The shed was said to be worth £400. The mini was brand new and worth £672. The price of a terraced house at that time was £2000.

I Tell My Story

I wish to tell my story starting when I was born (natural birth) and lead the reader until my conversion when the Lord Jesus spoke to me (second birth).

I then wish to speak about being a Christian and seeking to follow the Lord and meeting with the many and varied Christian groups and people. I wish to share with the reader how I learned the distinctive truths of the distinguishing doctrines of grace and sovereignty of God, which led me to joining the Bierton Strict and Particular Baptist Church.

In this account I relate my call to preach and I list the many churches I share the gospel with until the very sad occasion of my secession from the Bierton Church due to a departure for the truth. The church fell into the error of allowing general redemption being taught and a falling away into the error of the Law of Moses becoming their rule of life and conduct, rather than the Gospel. My secession being fully recorded on my publication, **"The Bierton Crisis"**, which I now believe could serve as a real help to many churches as in this account I name the many errors that I found to be prevalent, in those days amongst believers, and I point out the truth and scriptural view, which opposed those who held differing views.

It is my desire that this will serve to help and edify fellow Christians, and those seeking the truth as it is in Jesus Christ.

2   My Early Life

I was born on the 16th February 1949 at 9.50 AM, in Boundary Park General hospital, Oldham, Lancashire. My mother's name was Elsie Dyson Clarke who was married to my father Thomas George Clarke some time after the war. She informed me that this hospital was next to Oldham Athletic football ground.

Boundary Park Hospital

This Is Where I Was Born

We lived with my mother's father in his house at 26 Fleet Street, Clarksfield, Oldham. My granddad's name was Watts Ormrod and he was a retired craftsman and senior member of a Trades Union. His hair was white, which I am told happened due to an accident at work when a large rivet was pushed through his hand. I had a brother, who was two and a half years older than me, Michael John (spelt Michael instead of Michael due to my mother's stubbornness when he was named at the registrar's office. The official informed her that the way she had spelt Michael was in fact wrong, and my mum reacted at being corrected and insisted it would be spelt just as she had written it.

My mum and dad were both in the armed forces and were very proud to be British. Dad was in the Army and mum was in the Royal Air Force.

My Parents

Thomas George Clarke (Dad)   **Elsie Dyson Clarke (Mum)**

I was christened at Christ's Church, Glodwick and my Godfather was David Maltby of 382 Barton Road; Stratford and was a sides man at the Church on Barton Road. He gave me at that time a bible with a text of scripture written on the inside cover. Prov. 3. 6 "In all thy ways acknowledge him and he shall direct thy paths ".

I have found a baptism certificate dated 3rd April 1949, where it states I became a member of Christ the child of God, and an inheritor of the "Kingdom of Heaven". This however is wrong, as I did not become a member of Christ until I was born again on The 16th January 1970, which I speak about later.

My Baptismal Certificate

Holy Baptism

'A member of Christ, the child of God, and an inheritor of the Kingdom of Heaven.'

Name David Clarke
Place Christ Church
       Clodwick, Oldham
Signed G. Mornes
Date 3rd April 1949

David's Baptismal Certificate 3rd April 1949

I remember attending the church and Sunday school at Christchurch, which was just along the road from our house in Fleet Street. On one occasion I was so cozy, sitting on the pew, I fell asleep and woke up with a jolt wondering where I was, just as the vicar had finished his sermon. I had been lulled into sleep by the stimulating sermon. I haven't changed even to day. I must have been about 3 or 4 years old. It was my mother's idea to take my brother and I to Sunday school.

Barnabus Sunday School

St. Barnabus Sunday School Building

At Sunday school I remember we painted pictures of houses and still remember wondering why did the teacher draw the house with the door in the middle of the building and windows either side of the door. This was because I knew we lived in a house in a terrace and our door was to one side, just like the other houses in the street. I had no spiritual impressions of the Lord Jesus Christ from these times.

Just across the street from our house there was a great Roman Catholic Church building, and living accommodation, surrounded by a high wall. It was built of red engineering bricks and several stories high with stained glass windows alone the long church building. I remember looking up at the crooked lightening conductor and I still get the feeling of austerity and awkwardness when wondering what was behind that wall. It produced the same feeling in me when I had the story of Toby Twirl red to me. In that story he meets a giant who lived behind a great high walled castle. I was afraid to go near, or to even think of climbing the wall, or trespass in the grounds. I did not know it was a Roman Catholic Church building until about 25 years later when my mother informed me.

Roman Catholic Building

The Roman Catholic Building

At that time I knew of no other religion than that of the Church of England, I assumed my mother was right in all such matters and so the Catholics were wrong.

The Back Of Our House

Back Yard of 26 Fleet Street (Where I lived)

I remember the street lamps because a man use to come around each night to light them as they were gas and he had a small ladder, which he carried with him, pointed at one end. He climbed the ladder and lit the lamps each night. I assume they were gas lamps.

I remember my favourite sweets were what was called Kylie, it is called sherbet now. We could also buy a very small loaf of bread called a penny loaf.

At that time when I was about 4 years old I wanted to go to another Sunday school (I did not know at the time it was at a church building), which was at Lee's Road. My mother must have taken me there before. On this occasion it was Saturday morning and I did not believe there was no Sunday school that day. After being dressed I think my mother must have humoured me and did not take me seriously. I said I was going to Sunday school. I left home, I do not think my Mum realized and I walked at least two miles along Balfor Street and along the busy Lee's Road and found the building, to my disappointment it was all locked up. On my return I wandered off and got lost and ended up asking for help from a Laundry Shop. They put me in the window as a lost boy and called the police. I was soon returned home. I think my Mum was horrified how far I had been.

Back Alley

Back Alley at 26 Fleet Street

I commenced my school days at "Clarks Field" Infants' School. My brother Michael John was already attending and was in the third year when I started.

Clark's Field Infants School

Clark's Field Infants School (David bottom right)

I remember my first day at school in the classroom with other children. The ceilings were high and there were things like sandpits and black board easels and old fashion classroom desks and tables.

The girl next door, Vivian Butler, began school with me and I can remember her crying for her Mum. I remember not feeling the need to cry and I tried to comfort her and assure her all would be well.

My Auntie Edith was very good to us boys and we would visit her every Saturday. She lived with my Granddad's sister. She was called Auntie Alice. Auntie Edith would take us out to a great park in Oldham and on the way home we would call in at the chip shop. In those days chips were real chips, cooked in real fat. One of our favorite meals she would cook was potato pie, with red cabbage. In the house there was a cellar, which I always liked to visit. I think at one time washing was done in the cellar.

At that time my brother was probably the only close friend I had, although we were not too close. He was just there. We use to go swimming on a Saturday morning to the "Waterhead Baths". This type of swimming baths was typical of the old-fashioned baths of the time. They were small, the water green, and walls tiled cream. At the side of the pool there were slipper baths where you could sit up to your chin in hot water and carbolic soap was supplied to wash with. It was very cozy. In fact the whole atmosphere was warm and cozy, not like the cold clinical swimming baths of modern times. Next-door was the washhouse where mum used to go at the same time to do washing.

One Saturday morning I nearly drowned and was saved by the attendant called Norman. I had tiptoed backwards and as the pool got slowly deeper and deeper I found I could not touch the bottom. It was through the providence of God that the attendant turned to see me reaching upwards out of the water. I couldn't speak. He dived in to rescued me and I can still feel the fear today of nearly drowning.

Across the road from the swimming baths was a slaughterhouse, next door to inhabited houses. We were very curious and would look through the slatted windows and see the men kill the pigs, sheep and cattle. This was awesome and ghoulish and a fearful thing, but we were very curious and wanted to see how the men slew the animals. There was blood, animal intestines, animal heads bones and blood. The smell was awful and not pleasant at all, and it seemed as though the pigs knew they were going to be slaughtered, and their end was come. I have wondered about my brother since then, as he was two and a half years older than me and how this may have affected him. Later on in life he demonstrated a callous way, which was characteristic of killing without mercy just like these slaughter men.

About this time I remember coming home from school and in the dusk of that day the house seemed unusually quiet. I noticed some blood on my brother's book and my mum told me there had been an accident. My brother had fallen down a basement stairway shaft at school and landed on his back. He was concussed and I remember then feeling how precious life was. My brother could have died through the fall. It was awesome. I still had no recollection of God during this time.

Oldham

Oldham is a town in the north of England, not far from the city of Manchester, and during the 19th century was an industrial community famous for its cotton mills. In fact, my grandfather was a great supporter of the Trades Union.

As a child I remember the old mills, red brick built with huge chimneys towering high above the buildings. Also the water reservoirs, which we were always warned to stay away from. My mother had spoken about children being drowned in them and this was sufficient for me to obey her.

An Oldham Mill

Typical Old Mill Oldham

3   Garston Infant School

We moved from Oldham to Garston, Watford when I was 5 years old and my mum took me to my first day at school, which was at Garston Infant School. I was in the second year of the infants. My mum had arranged for me to walk home with a girl called Vivian who apparently lived in Coats Way where we lived. Not that I knew my address because I didn't. All I knew was we had move to a place called Garston, so I assumed we lived in Garston Road.

When it came to walking home I had to follow Vivian, but she took me by a way I had never been before. A completely different way, and across a park to what was the other end of Coats Way. She left me there and I had no Idea where I was, as I did not recognize anywhere at all. Feeling uneasy about all this I realized I was lost. So I made my way back towards the school and began to ask people where Garston Road was. There was no such place but I insisted I lived in Garston Road. A man with a red Bedford dormobile offered to take me back to school to find out where I live so off we went. The schoolteacher said I lived in Coats Way where Vivian had took me but I said I didn't live there, as I could not recognize the place. The man took me back to Coats Way but I could not recognize where I lived. He drove from one end to the other. It was quite a long Way with a Council estate on one end and private houses at the other end. This was where I lived 149 Coats Way. I saw my Mum in the front garden - so I arrived home after being lost on my first day at school.

German Teacher

My classroom teacher was a German woman called Miss Kitchinger. She spoke with a German accent and I spoke with a broad Lancashire accent. We did not hit it off and I was hopeless at reading the flash cards. It seemed as though I was singled out and proved to be a dunce, as I could not really read. Being small I think I messed about to divert attention from my inability to do class work.

One day when I arrived at school I found a pair of pumps (they called them plimsolls now), which I later found out belonged to Vivian on my desk and I did not like them being there. Feeling rather indignant I place them in the dustbin. I think I might have asked the teacher, "please Miss, whose are these pumps?", but was ignored, as she did not understand me, so in the bin they went.

The next day Vivian's mother came to school wanting to find out where her plimsolls had gone. The caretaker said he had found them and placed them on my desk. When I was questioned I was in trouble and Miss Kitchinger said my mum would have to buy a new pair as I had thrown them away. I felt this unfair and felt really picked on. I know my mum came to the school and had an argument about the pumps and the fact that a German teacher was trying to teach English. This was only few years after the war with Germany had ended.

David And The Hampster

At that time my mum had to work late and it was arranged for me to wait in the classroom after school until my mum came to pick me up. This was shortly after the event with the plimsolls. The class had a pet hamster and this little creature got all the attention from every one. I was the one that got no attention but rather got into trouble. One evening whilst I was waiting in the classroom for my mum to collect me, the teacher left the classroom for a short while.

I went towards the hamster cage and thought to my self why do you get all the attention. I know what I am going to do with you. I took the hamster out to the cage and closed the door. I looked at the hamster in the in the eyes and went over to Vivian's desk and put it inside, shutting the lid quickly thinking that will pay her back for getting me in trouble over her plimsolls. I sat back in my chair before the teacher returned and went home with my mum as though nothing had happened.

The next day I went into class as quiet as I could and keeping out of the way. I waited patiently for the eruptions. Then suddenly, Oh Miss, screamed Vivian, the hamster is in my desk. It had weeded and messed everywhere through out the night. Every one gathered around the desk to see at the same time. I felt very guilty. One boy tried to suggest the hamster had escaped and climbed up the table leg and got through the whole drilled for the spilled ink to drain. A good idea I thought so keep thinking that thought. Then some one asked how did it get out of the cage as the door was closed. I was feeling very, very guilty now and wondered if Miss Kitchinger was thinking had I done the deed the night before. I kept quiet and to this day they do not know how that hamster got there. During this time my brother was attending the Lea Farm Junior School, the school I was to attend the next year or so.

Congregational Sunday School

My mum use to take me to Sunday school from time to time and I didn't mind going. One day (about 1958) on the way home from normal school I would walk past the Congregational church building, rather a modern building, and the vicar lived in a Gypsy stile caravan in the church grounds.

Garston Congregational Church Building

Congregational Church Building

The church building was always left open and we often went in the church building on the way home. I saw, on one occasion, some boys took the money out of the collection box, which too was left unlocked. I could not understand this. Why where things left unlocked for boys to steel from. One day after school I met the vicar when I was looking around the church building and I asked him why is the building left open and why it the collection box not locked. His reply puzzled me. He said the church should be always open for people because God was like that if people fell they need to steel the collection then they must need it badly. He did not feel the box should be locked. I was puzzled and said but why? The vicar was sure it was the right thing to do. That stayed with me to this day and people get angry some times with me for not locking up my house.

At this same church I can remember the Easter services. I had no Idea what the gospel was nor did I understand the Easter story.

I remember sitting in the pew during the Easter service listening to how they crucified Jesus wondering why Jesus did not come down from the cross. I felt he could have done so and confounded all them

Pharisees, but why didn't he do so. I knew the story about his death and resurrection but did not know what it all meant. I never did find out until 14 years later when I was 21 years old when I learned to read the bible for my self. It was then I learned that Jesus had to die to take away my sins. That he died in my place to set me free from sin, self and death.

It was about this time (1959) that my mum encouraged me to play the piano. My mum's favourite artist was Perry Como and "Side Saddle" was a piece of mum's favourite music, which I learned to play. I had music lesson with a Miss Mary Lee, a music teacher in Garston and eventually I graduated with a merit Grade 1 (Primary) RSA in Pianoforte. This was July 1960.

The sort of music, which was popular in those days, was. "Yellow Polka Dot Bikini, My Old mans a dustman, by Lonnie Donnigan, Living Doll by Cliff Richards. Also the Hula-Hoop was a craze at that time.

Cecil The Sissy And Air Pistol

Living not too far away from us in Coates Way, was a boy who my brother nicknamed Cecil, as this sounded like a suitable name for a sissy. He was a cripple in the sense that his feet were curved inwards and he walked awkwardly. He must have been about 10 years old. My brother poked fun at him and I too soon followed suit. We would sing about him a song called Cecil, Cecil a Cecil feet. He would try and avoid us.

One day Cecil came on his bike down to the woods that we called the dell. We were playing up the trees and had made a catapult out off one of the great branches of the trees. One person would sit in the branch and two or three other kids would pull on the rope till the branch was fully bent. The rope would be released and the person would be catapulted up in the air. They would have to hold on tightly other wise they would end up in the trees.

On this day my brother had it in for Cecil. We took his bike and put it into the catapult making sure it was catapulted up into the trees. We thought this was great fun but Cecil did not.

His mother came to our house and complained to my mum about our bullying Cecil but my mum seemed to have no mercy. She said Cecil had got to learn to look after himself and he was a sissy. I felt mum was wrong as I knew how bad we were and my mum seemed to have no mercy. I felt bad however.

Shortly after this incident my brother encouraged me to take our newly acquired air pistol to school, and Cecil was the one who my brother bullied and threaten to shoot in the playground. On reflection my brother seemed to have no mercy at all. My brother must have been in the final year and I in the first year of Lea Farm Junior School.

David at Lea Farm Junior School

David At Lea Farm Junior School

It wasn't long however before my air pistol was found and confiscated. After assembly one of the boys had taken it out of my desk and was running around the classroom with it when the teacher walked in. I was in trouble again with the Headmaster and this would have been another time I got the cane for bringing a dangerous weapon to school.

Wrexham Holiday

Michael and I must have been about 7 and 10 years old and Mum and dad had renovated an old Ford convertible car whose number plate was BBU.

Mum had bought the car whilst we were living in Oldham and dad was working in Watford. Dad had moved to Watford to get a job, and was living with his mum (our grandma at Ash Tree Road Garston, Watford). Mum and dad were able to by a house at 149 Coats Way Garston and it was mum who decided to buy the car to get Michael and I down from Oldham to Watford.

It was this car that I often fell out of when the breaks were hit. It caused me to move forward and push open the door lock and the door opened the opposite way round. I would end up on the road outside the car. Dad eventually was able to put a safety chain on the handle to stop this happening.

Dad had rebuilt the engine and painted it black and green, Mum made a new convertible top using her sewing skills. It was a bit like Noddy's car it was really good.

In this car we went to Brixton for a holiday and it was there mum and dad bought Michael and I a fishing rod each. I had a wooden cane one and he had a metal rod. I remember I was always jealous of what he had as I always thought his things were better than mine.

Keen to try the rods out near the sea harbor Michael rushed to the waterside just around the corner and soon came back crying. He said a man had taken his rod and thrown it into the sea. Dad rushed around but no one could be seen. We looked for the man on his bike but no one was to be seen. It is only now that I look back that I believe Michael had quickly put the rod together pretended to fish by casting an imaginary line and the rod top had gone straight into the see. He probably felt he would have been told off by our dad and be in trouble. So he invented a story about a man on a bike.

When I look back it is incidences like this that I learned about the way Michael thought and worked and in later life it made one wonders at the tales he told.

The Fair Ground Paper Round Stolen Bike

Every year the fair would come to Garston and I really looked forward to ride the dodgem cars. All the kids would go to the fair and spend lots of time watching. I can remember two brothers who worked on the fair and these were like heroes, and we would wonder who was the strongest and speculate which one could lift a dodgem car above his head. We would also listen to the latest pop music, which played through large loudspeakers. This was before any one had personal radios or cassette players. There was no Top of the Pops on TV. So the fair was the place to hear pop music.

I was probably about 11 or 12 years old, and this year I remember stealing £3 from my mum's purse. I felt very guilty and bad at the time and I still feel the shame as I write about it now, but this was spent on the fair. I am thankful for the truth that the blood of Jesus cleanses us from all sin. This became my only way of me dealing with my sin when I became a Christian and still is.

My brother at that time had a paper round and use to get up early each morning and so he began to earn his own money. I remember him obtaining all sorts of new things like writing cases, pens, pencils, ink cartridges, etc. all the little things one would like but could not afford. I soon realized that my brother was not buying them but stealing them from the shop where he worked.

On the odd occasion I would go and help him deliver the papers. I enjoyed this as it took me to places I had never been before.

On one occasion we had to deliver papers to a hospital or residential home, and around the back of the building we could see the kitchens and we helped our selves to the cakes, which had been freshly cooked. I learn from my brother how easy it was to get things I wanted.

I always looked up to my brother and often envied the things he did and had. I remember him going to Switzerland, with the school and him coming home with all kinds of goods. Like a walking stick, flick knives, and badges etc. Flick knives were illegal and to have a flick knife was a good thing.

My brother soon got in to bows and arrows, and air rifles and pistols swords and sheath knives, which seemed good to me. In fact we use to hide all these weapons under the floorboards in our shed, which was at the bottom of our garden.

At this time I remember my mum and dad buying me a new bike. It was a red Californian, with curved crossbars etc. I thought it was great and was ever so pleased with it. One day the bike went missing, and I knew some one had taken it, so I was very upset.

When I went out looking for it I noticed up the road an accident had taken place, as there were cars stopped and people milling around. To my horror I saw my nice new bike crumpled and just lying at the side of the road. The boy who had taken it had been knocked off the bike and was lying in the road awaiting an ambulance and every one was trying to take care of him.

I thought to my self never mind about him, as he had stolen my bike, but look at my new bike, all bent. I was very upset. No one however took any notice of me, neither were they concerned about my bike being damaged. The boy's name was Michael Abbes and we had been friends until recently and I seem to remember that he had broken his legs in the accident.

A Stolen Crystal Set

My interest in radio, which we now call electronics, started the day I heard a crystal set operate. I must have been 10 or 11 years old.

My mum and dad belonged to the Camping Club of Great Britain and every weekend we would go camping to Chertsey, where we had a tent pitched.

One weekend my brother stole a crystal set from a camper's tent. It consisted of a small tuning capacitor in a blue plastic case and a crystal diode, together with a set of headphones. I was amazed as it worked and became interested in radio from that day forward.

Camping at Chertsey

Dad at Chertsey Campsite Dad By Our Canoe

I sent away for a set of parts to build a two transistor reflex receiver, and put the thing together as best I could. I wired the circuit as I thought the diagram showed, and crushed it all together to fit inside its plastic case. It didn't work and I was most disappointed. I didn't realize that all the wires were shorted together when I crushed it into the plastic case. Another friend of mine's dad helped me out. He was a radio technician in the Royal Air force and he rebuilt the receiver and showed me how to wire circuits up. From that time I began to learn about how things worked and taught my self-many things with the help of others.

Another friend of mine had a dad who had a radio workshop and I was very envious of all the equipment that he had in his garage. I remember the boy being confident enough to take apart out of an old radio for me, without any sense of fear. I was quite impressed. I taught my self quite a lot and began to learn about transistors.

One day on the way home from school we climbed over the fence of someone's back garden and discovered a shed full of radio parts, and equipment. There were valves, tuning condensers, transformers etc., we took what we wanted and thought no more of it.

This hobby was to last me a long time and helped me to get a job in radio and television servicing and to Technical College at a later date. During this time I had no sense or knowledge of God and I had stopped going to Sunday school.

Francis Coombe Secondary School

My first senior school was in Garston, as I had failed the 11 plus. It was at this school I first heard a boy play a tune called , "Apache" by the Shadows, on an acoustic guitar and I was very impressed. Michael had already started at this school and did well at cricket, boxing and basketball. I was not good at any of these things but rather was interested in my radio hobby, which led me to trips to London on the train, from Watford Junction, to buy components in Tottenham Court Road.

My Visit to Soho

It was towards the end of my first year, at Francis Coombe Secondary modern school, that I ventured out to London on the train, with a friend of mine, Paul Dorrington. This was to visit the second hand electrical shops, to buy radio parts. I loved visiting Tottenham Court Road for this purpose and it was on one of these visits that we stumbled across Soho and noticed the strip clubs.

These aroused our curiosity. Paul and I plucked up courage and paid to go in and sit at a table. We could see a nude lady sitting on a chair and were given a sketchpad and pencil and encouraged to draw her picture. I felt I was growing up. Afterwards we paid one or two more visits and became wiser.

When we moved to Wilstone, a village near Tring in Hertfordshire, my radio and television hobby helped me pass the time and kept me out of too much trouble

Our Move To Wilstone

In 1961 we finally moved to Wilstone a village near Tring and Michael and I went to Tring Secondary modern school called Mortimer Hill. I can remember my brother wearing winkle picker shoes and some of the girls from the next village couldn't help but say oh look at those shoes. They were just different and I suppose they felt threatened.

It was during this time that I taught myself more about Radio and amplifiers and became absorbed in this hobby. I met a man in the village called Cluck Turney, who was the man to know about televisions and radios and he gave me a lot of help. He taught me about valve amplifiers and allowed me to build a power amplifier, from all the spare parts that he had. It was a push pull amplifier using two PX4 valves and a triode driver. I had to rewind the driver and output transformers in order to get it working. I learned a lot from Cluck Turney.

On one occasion I was able to connect a microphone up to my amplifier and I directed the speaker out of my bedroom window and spoke to people out side our shop. On this occasion I saw a woman in her rear garden called Ethel. I called out with the amplifier as loud as possible saying Ethel, Ethel I am watching you. I heard many years later that she thought it sounded a bit like God speaking from the sky.

Stolen Shot Gun

I later had a visit from the local policeman as I had stolen a 12-bore shotgun from an old barn and brought it home. When I showed it to my next-door neighbour he recognised the gun and realised who it belonged too and so he informed the local policeman to get it returned to its owner.

Whilst at Tring School a friend of mine Duncan Miller found a baby fox cub in a wood, and I wanted to keep it so I took it home. Unfortunately my Grandma, who had come to stay, freaked out when she saw it as she was frightened and to my dismay my brother killed it and to this day I felt he was callous.

It was during this time at Wilstone my brother got sent to his first spell in Detention Centre. He had made a knuckle-duster at school, in the metal work classes, and tried it out by hitting some boy in the village. What happened was some lads had found our moped in the field and had a go at riding it without our permission. Not that they would know whom to ask, but my brother felt he would sort them out for riding it. I think it was an excuse to use the knuckle-duster he had made.

When the police were called in he made out the knuckle duster was made as a part for the moped and my mum was certain this was true and she defended my brother to the hilt. I knew it wasn't true and my brother did a spell in Detention center for 3 months, for grievous bodily harm. I did not go along with my brothers' violence and could not understand it. His reputation spread and at school the teachers began to identify me with my brother and I think they began to be wary of me too.

My brother mixed with all the lads who had bad reputations and no one would dare up set them.

Village life proved too much for my mum and she became

depressed, due to they way things were, and the trouble Michael had gotten into so it was decided to sell up and move to a new house in Aylesbury.

4 The Big Freeze 1962

Once we had sold the village shop mum and I moved to Oldham whilst Michael and my dad moved into lodgings in Aston Clinton. This was while the house they had bought off plan was being built. Mum and moved to live with my aunt Edith at 26 Fleet Street, in the town where I was born and had to go to school. This was Clark's Field Senior School and I became a bit of a celebrity simply because I was from "London". This status increased when I told the "lads" about my trips to Soho. It was here that I first heard of the Beatles as they were playing in Oldham at that time. The song I remember that was popular, "Love me do", by the Beatles, which came out in October 1962.

During my time in Oldham we were there for about three months, I built a balsa wood, controlled line, aeroplane, a radio transmitter for a remote control aircraft and learned to ice skate. We had a very cold winter, the coldest on record and the snow fell and the streets froze over. My mum bought me a pair of second hand ice skates and I learned to skate on the frozen streets in Oldham.

Short Stay Back To Watford

After staying for while in Oldham we moved back to Watford and lived with my Dad's mum. On this occasion I had to go back to Francis Coombe Secondary School and I renewed acquaintances with my former friends. It was during this time I made my own transistor radio set. This was before printed circuit boards were available. It was a two transistor reflex receiver and I was very proud of it, as it was the size of a matchbox. I also missed riding the moped and so I got up very early one morning and walked into Watford where I knew a motorbike was parked and stole it. I drove several miles to a secret place and parked it up and went home. I later used it for joy riding with my friends. I walked miles that morning and my mum never knew about it.

Michael also would visit us at Watford and see his old friends who played in a pop group and on one occasion he gave me a pair of bell-bottom trousers and a shirt, with a long pointed collar. Michael and his friend wanted to take me to tthe dance that was held at Leavesdon, on a Friday or Saturday night. I really enjoyed myself there and wanted to go again. I met some of my friends from school there and one boy noticed my clothes and said that I was a Mod.

Unfortunately for me after this I began to get bullied at school by a group of boys who were what you might call "Jack the Lads". I learned afterward the reason and it was to do with Michael. One of the boys was from Australia and was the ringleader of this gang and he had a girl friend at the school called Pat Petty. She was every boy's dream of a girl. Well Michael had met her at the Leavesdon dance and chatted her up. This Australian boy was jealous and a soon as they realised that I was Michael's brother they had it in for me.

My First Matchbox Radio

It was during this time (13 years) I obtained a circuit diagram for a Two transistor Reflex Receiver and with the components I obtained from Tottenham Court Road, London, I built this on a small paxolin board. This was before printed circuit boards were readily available. I was very pleased with this as it had good sensitivity and selectivity and was about the size of a matchbox.

My Two Transistor Wireless Receiver

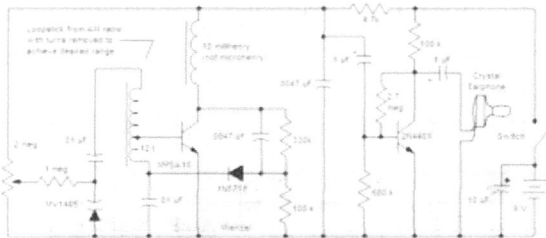

Here IS The Circuit Diagram

5 Aylesbury: Our new Home

Our new house was situated on the Bedgrove Estate, in Aylesbury and was ready for us to move in, in April of 1963. However before we left Wilstone I had enjoyed riding a moped in an old orchard, in the village. It belonged to a friend of Michael and I was allowed to ride this moped. It was a 50 cc NSU Quickly and was kept in his orchard.

Once we had moved into out new house in Aylesbury I was able to return to Wilstone and take the engine from the moped frame and put the engine in a home made go kart. I made this go- kart from builder's wood that I took from the building site. I use the moped engine, a set of wheels from a child's three wheeler tricycle, and various parts from a cement mixer. I then began to ride this machine around the new roads on the housing estate. However I was eventually stopped by the local police and warned that it was illegal to ride this Go Kart on the roads and soon after that the local newspaper came and gave me a write up in the Bucks Herald.

David's Do It Your Self-kart

An Aylesbury boy was able to return to school after the Easter holidays and proudly tell his friends, " I've made a Go Cart in the holidays." He is 14 years old,

Bucks Herald news article My Go Kart

David's Do It Your Self Kart 1963

On Sunday of last week a friend gave David (pictured above) and old moped. As he was unable to ride it he - he is too young he dismantled it. He then made a Kart frame from some pieces of wood, four old wheels and a set of handlebars and the moped engine.

My NSU Quickley Moped

My Moped

Within three days it was in working condition and David estimates it will do 20 miles and hour.

Incidentally David, who has lived in the town for only a month has very little real interest in engines. His main hobby is in radio construction work and one of his proudest possessions is a transistor radio, which he built that is slightly larger than a matchbox.

I Steel Push Bikes

It was during this space of time, before starting my new school; I met another lad called Ian Motrem. We encouraged each other to steel push bikes. In fact the first day that I went to school I stole a bike to come home from school.

I eventually got a Francis Barnet 150 CC motorbike, which my brother had stolen from Aylesbury College, with some other lads. I kept this in a field on the Bedgrove Estate near our home. It was great fun to have a motorbike and I would ride across the fields to school and return home during my lunch hour. However one day some one stole my motorbike and Ian Motrem informed me that he thought he knew the person that had taken it. I went to this person's house early one morning, during my paper round, and found a motorbike in his garage. This wasn't my bike but I took it anyway. This ended up in me being charge with garage breaking and being put on probation for two years.

Stolen Francis Barnett 150 CC Motor Bike

My Francis Barnett Motor Bike

Leaving School Teenage Years

My first recollection of any religious person having any effect on my life was when I was about to leave school, at the age of 15 years old.

My mother had spoken to a Mr K H Knight who was the proprietor of Central Bucks TV and had arranged for me to have a part time job working after school and on a Saturday. This was until I left school and took up full time work as an apprentice to Mr Knight. I am told years later that my letter of job application was so badly written and the spelling so awful it was laughable. However I was taken on despite my inability to write, spell or use correct grammar, or read properly. This was during my last year at school.

I first met Mrs Grace Knight, one Saturday morning, whilst working for her husband Ken. She was in hot pursuit of her husband and shouting at him for doing some thing she disapproved of.

I was in the workshop, with Norman Garret the other apprentice, and I thought- wow what an awful dragon of a woman and pitied Mr Knight from that moment on.

Through Mr Knight (Ken) I was introduced to the Radio and Television servicing trade and often went with him into customer's houses to repair TV's and install television aerials.

I spent many hours with Ken going to peoples homes and soon learned that he was not faithful to his wife. Not that it bothered me, as I knew what Grace was like from our first meeting. The idea of sexual promiscuity was very attractive to me. When we went out enjoying our selves Mrs Knight would be left at home or in the workshop minding their two children Allison and Mark. They also had a big dog called Rufus.

By this time I had left school and was interested in our band, as we wanted to make music. Ian Myers was the bass guitarist and he built his own guitar amplifier from a circuit design and published in Practical Wireless. He built the amplifier I helped him with the speaker cabinet and it was used in all our future gigs.

I soon began to realize the things I enjoyed were not the things Mrs Knight approved of, or found interesting. I thought she was a right "kill joy" and was boring. She was a Christian what ever that meant and I soon realize her values were not the same as mine. What I considered good and enjoyable she would call it sin and sinful. She would also complain to her husband that I was always with him and he gave her no time. It seemed she was often driven to despair by him never being in on time and being very unreliable. He would often leave her for hours whilst we were at work out on jobs.

Conversation On The Intercom

On one occasion Norman Garret's mum complained to Mrs Knight the Norman her son, was not getting the training he needed because Ken was always taking me out with him. I heard this conversation over the shops intercom. Mrs Knight said yes I was a nuisance and she did not like me one bit and it was not good that I should be out with her husband all the time. Upon hearing this I felt angry and went down the stairs to where they were and confronted them both saying that I had heard what they had said about me. They were embarrassed and I am sure this did not help our relationship. I really thought Mrs Knight was an ogre.

I began to attend Luton College of Technology, to learn about Radio and Television Servicing, and travelled by bus, one day a week, from Aylesbury to Luton; it was about an hour's and a halfs run. I think it must have been due to Mrs Knight and her religion that I began to notice the texts of scripture put up out side churches as I past by on the bus, they were called "Way side pulpits". I began to memorize the verses such as:

" Righteousness exalteth a nation but sin is a reproach to any people"

And also another:

" Jesus said if you find life difficult learn of me and the burden I shall give you will not be too difficult to carry".

At that time I had no idea of the meaning of these texts of scripture but found it amusing to quote them to Mrs Knight at any in appropriate moment thinking it would embarrass her.

On one occasion I remember being dressed in an old blanket made into an undercoat from my brothers Mod anorak. I was standing on the corner of the street near to the workshop one Saturday morning with Mr and Mrs Knight. I quoted at the top of my voice these two scriptures in order to embarrass Mrs Knight. I am not sure how they felt about it but little did I know that one day I would learn the truth of these texts and become a preacher of the Gospel myself.

A Confident 15 year old

I enjoyed working for Mr Knight because he seemed to appreciate my help and abilities and would trust me to drive the van at 15 years old. On one occasion he was short of a driver and had to deliver a television. So he dressed me up in a sheepskin coat and gave me dark glasses to wear with instructions to deliver a TV to a house in Quarendon. I was very pleased to do this even more when it turned out that I was delivering the TV set to one of my school friends called Gillespie.

On another occasion I was given the job of replacing a complete I.F. board on a new Ferguson 850 T.V. receiver in a customers home. A qualified engineer in a workshop setting normally would have done this but this unconventional approach was normal to me. Mr Knight had complete confidence in me at the age of 15 years old. I am sure the customer was not at all happy at this 15 year old repairing their lovely brand new Television receiver.

During this time I was still making music in the group and when I was 16 Mr Knight's business failed and went into liquidation so I found myself another job. I got an apprenticeship with Sale and Mellor at Radio a TV shop in Aylesbury. I worked there until I got in trouble with the police when I was sacked at the age of 17 years.

It was shortly after this time that I got into trouble with the police for breaking into a garage and stealing a motorbike. I had a Francis Barnett 150 CC, which had been stolen from the field where I kept it and a friend of mine told me that it was in this garage, along the Tring Road. At first I was just interested in getting my bike back but when I opened the garage door I was disappointed not to find it - just a 125 BSA Bantam.

I thought well its better than nothing so I decided to take it any way and wheeled it out of the garage and back to our field, to use it later. The police later caught me and for this first crime I was charged with garage breaking and put on probation for two years.

6   Our Rock Group

It was after this that decided I wanted to play the electric guitar and I remember a lad called Alan Lawrence, from Tring Secondary Modern School, having an electric guitar and bringing it to school. He plugged it into the schools record player and it sounded great. I wanted to learn to play like him. The first guitar I owned was an electric Hofner Futurama Two and a friend called Steve showed me how to play Twist and Shout and it was this that got me really interested to play properly. I put together my own guitar amplifier, using the P.A. amplifier that I had stolen from the Catholic Church.

Stolen BSA Bantem

My BSA Stolen Bantem 125 cc

My First Guitar Stolen Amplifier

Liner Concorde 30 Amplifier

Top View using EL34 Output valves in push pull

Underneath the Chassis

Hand Wired Main Chassis

(I had inherited a prejudice against the Catholic Church, from my mum, and so when I took the amplifier I ignored my conscience by saying to myself they were wrong any way).

I then began to get more interested in making music and during my last year at school we formed a band and we played at the end of term school dance. Our Gym teacher, Mr Pottinger, organized this event.

The Fowler Mean our Rock Group

Ian Myers was the base guitarist and later Robby Woods became our lead guitarist. On that occasion though, at the school do, Willie Barrett was lead guitarist. He was the only one of us to make musical fame. He became known as Wild Willy Barrett and played music with John Otway.

My Vox A.C. 30 Amplifier

My Vox AC 30 (Cost Second hand £60)

I had a new amplifier that was a Vox AC 3.0. and replaced the amplifier that I had stolen from the Catholic Church. One of our regular spots, on a Saturday night, was Courts Dance School, just off Kingsbury Square. Here is our music play set:

The Fowler Mean (Play Set) Click to view and listen

After leaving school we reformed the group and began to play music at various dance halls and I named the group "The Fowler Mean".

The Fowler Mean

Dave Clarke from the 60's, with Robby Woods (top) Ian Myers

We would play all cover music by groups such as, The Rolling Stones, The Who, The Small Faces, The Kinks, Ottis Reading and John Lee Hooker. We played, "My Generation", but I knew it was not quite right and I never did find out how to play the right cords to this day. The opening chords we played were four down strokes on G followed by four downward strokes on F but that is not right. I always thought if ever I met Pete I would ask him to show me how to play those opening chords. I really enjoyed playing with the band but was eventually sacked and it was then that Malcolm Kirkham and I began to knock around with each other.

Our Favorite Band The Who

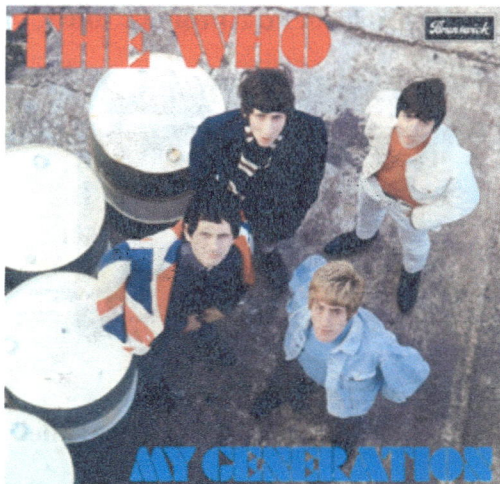

John Entwhistle, Pete Townsend, Keith Moon, Roger Daultery

My favorite band was The Who. This group introduced something to music that was new. It was volume. My Generation was the real hit that made the Who. I can remember hearing them, at the Grosvenor Dance Hall, in Aylesbury. Pete Townsend was the lead guitar, John Entwhistle on bass, Keith Moon on drums and Roger Daultary lead singer. There was not a band to touch them they were brilliant. We saw them on a number of occasions including places like Borehamwood and the Bedford Corn Exchange.

The Who (Click here to go to Wikipedia)

I remember the amplifier line up (being interest in amplifiers) Pet Townsend had:

Pete Townshend Amplifier line Up

Two A.C. 100 Amplifiers in Parallel

John Entwhistle Amplifier line up

4 X A.C. 60 watt Vox Bass

Amplifiers and their PA system was Vox columns and Shure microphones.

The volume added another dimension to the experience. I call it Rock and Real Music, It added depth to the sound and none of us had experienced anything like it before These are just some of the songs:

Click the link listen to the following Who songs:

 My Generation

 I can see for Miles

 I'm a Boy

 I can't Explain

These were all classic Who numbers and none forgettable pieces of music

Malcolm Kirkham use to be one of our singers which made 5 in the band and we use to go out together on our scooters. I had inherited my brother's Lambretta TV 175 CC and Malcolm had a 150 CC new Lambretta and we began to mix with the Mods in Aylesbury and district.

He had been sacked from the group because he messed about. Malcolm would always arrive late and never be in time to set up the equipment. He was always comb ing his hair or having to press his trousers, and he general fooled around. He was nicknames Cocoa the clown.

After mixing with the other lads in Aylesbury I soon found out my brother was well known and when it was made known I was Mike Clarke's brother it was like having a license to or say any thing, I was accepted. I was one of the boys. I recalled the times my brother had told me of the parties they use to have and I began to want to get involved in all the fun. Pep pills, scooters, Mod fashions, dances, girls and permissive sex. All of which I found positive and attractive as we were looking for a good time in the world.

The image I had of my brother was that he was quite a character and had a way with girls. I remember that was how I wanted to be and follow him in fame. I remember one impressive occasion I must have been just 16 and met one of Michael's friends who was a Mod. One Saturday night out side the Grosvenor he came dressed in brightly coloured trousers and a black plastic mac wearing girls make up around the eyes. This was the in thing to do and I thought this is good and liked it.

The normal mode of transport was either a Lambretta or Vespa scooter with crash bars, back rests, spare wheel carriers and mirrors. The scooters would be custom sprayed and generally a world war green Parker or black plastic cape was the uniform. All of this became the world I wanted to be in.

Oxford Bags

I remember my brother coming to see us at Rockley Sands, in Bournemouth when I was away with my parents on holiday. I must have been 15 years old. He came dressed in a brown suit with 22 inch, Oxford Bag trousers, with small turn-ups. His top was a white crew necked and red stripped tea shirt. Also brown brogue leather shoes. This was some fashion that I had not seen before. It was the Mod fashion.

He told me he had to return to Aylesbury to do some repairs and tidy up mum and dads house as they had a party and the place had been wrecked. Apparently all the Aylesbury Mods and from the district had been to his party held at Mum and Dads house. They had rolled up the carpets and put them in the garage but the bathroom sink had been pulled off the wall as some girl had got drunk and sat in it. He told me of the promiscuity and it all seemed good fun. This was the year 1963 or 4 when the Beatles and Rolling Stone came to fame. Also Gerry and the Pacemakers had a hit records at the time called, "I Like it".

My First Girl Friend

I met Susan, at a Friday night dance being organized at the Aylesbury College; she was 15 years old and looked great. She had blond hair in a Bob style. I was 16, wearing my navy blue Mod suit. I had arrived on my Lambretta.

I asked her to dance and later asked if I could take her home. I was feeling great when she agreed and so I covered up my learner plate, which was just under the rear, number plate and took her home. This was the beginning of my first love. The relationship only lasted a few months. When she told me she wanted to finish the relationship I was heart broken and she sought to encourage me by saying I would find some one else. I never did and had no interest in finding any one else. My only interest in girls after that was for sex alone- not friendship or anything else.

Love is Strange

Love is Strange (Click Here)

I first heard this song, by The Who, at Borehamwood

Another Who song that expressed my emotions at that time and I first heard this at Borehamwood.

The Mod Image

Lambretta Scooter Blond Girl Friend Sue

The Who Play list (Click here)

During this time Malcolm and I mixed with the Mods in Aylesbury we were both 16 years old and we began to meet with these older lads and were curious to try pep pills (purple hearts, black bombers and Dexedrine) and smoke hashish, or grass, so we began to make some inquiries where to get some. In the mean time we would experiment smoking crushed codeine tablets and dried banana skins. This was purely to satisfy a curiosity and to experience new things. The was a pub in Aylesbury called the, "Flee Pit" situated in Kingsbury Square and it was there we understood we could buy hash. However at 16 years old I went in this pub and became very embarrassed as on the wall behind the bar were displayed ladies knickers in various styles and colours. I felt embarrassed because the sight aroused me as at that time there was very little pornography and the sight of a woman in a short skirt and legs was very provocative for a 16 year old, On reflection I had a very high libido. Which led to a very promiscuous life style.

Carknapping (Steeling Cars)

Shortly after this I remember my brother coming home about 9.30 pm in a hurry. He had not long been released from Detention Centre. Our parents were away and I had a girl friend there. In came my brother and told me of his narrow escape from the police. About six of his friends had been out in a stolen car, not taxed or insured, when the police had stopped them along the Tring Road. They had all jumped out and made a run for it. It was soon after this that my brother got sent to Borstal Training for some crime or other. Never the less it all seemed a good life style and I wanted more of it.

I had discovered I could buy chloroform from a chemist and this was much better than sniffing carbon Tetrachloride or the glue substances people began to experiment with. Shortly after this Malcolm Kirkham, after trying something like, this took it in his head that he could fly on his scooter. He broke his arm and smashed his scooter in the process but fortunately not his head as he was wearing a dear stalker crash helmet he had stolen a few days before.

The names of some of the lads we knew and come to mind were: Stuart Knight, Keith Guntrip, Ian Wilton, Dill Dorwrick, and Terry Tatem (Now dead), Phil Davis, Brian Collier, Mickey Coil, Roy Miles, John James, Dave King, Jimmy Findlay, Phil Davis, and the like all of which had one thing in common. They wanted fun and were the lads of Aylesbury. (Time of writing this is the year year 2000).

My Lambretta Scooter

Lambretta TV 175 CC

At that time after being sacked from the group we began going to a nightclub called the Banbury Gaff. Here we would stay up all night taking pep pills (we use to say getting blocked) dancing and talking and in the morning end up in a cafe eating toast before driving back to Aylesbury. Soon after this Malcolm began to mix with the lads from Oxford and he was later sentence to some time in prison, for some crime or other. During this time my brother was in Borstal and at the Gaff, I met Alan Dodd. He was my brother's partner in crime and had escaped from Borstal and was living on a barge in Oxford. He told me at the time he had a gun and all this type of living impressed me as it seemed rather exciting. We would spend time at the Gaff talking with other lads about the crimes we had done and planned various schemes and bragged and boasted about things we had done.

Mods Scooters, Bikes Bubble Car

Shortly after my brother came out of Borstal a form of transport was required for two. A solution to this came through my brother who persuaded me to swap my scooter for a two-seater, Issetta 350 cc bubble car. I had inherited the scooter from my Michael when he was sent to Borstal but by now it had been renovated. I had rebuilt it in the spare bedroom at home and re sprayed it British racing Green. It was a Lambretta T.V. 175 cc. The fuel tank and tool compartment was stove enamelled gold. It had a dual seat with a passenger back rest with very little extras. There had been crazes whereby crash bars, wing mirrors, wheel racks and anything made of chrome were generally attached to such machines, but not mine. I was proud of this Lambretta. It had to go to make way for the sky blue Bubble Car.

Pete Townhsend Gives Us A lift

Before this time we had to thumb lifts, to get to where we wanted too if the scooter was out of action. On one occasion we were keen to get to Bedford, as The Who were playing at the Corn Exchange. We were dressed in our Mod mohair suits and carried a small suitcase with our night things in. We got as far as Ampthill and were stuck at the corner of the Ampthill to Bedford road and were about 20 miles from Bedford. We were stuck and Michael went into a pub to get a drink whilst I stayed on the corner trying to thumb a lift. as my brother needed a lift as well. To my relief and just after Michael had gone to the pub, a two seater red coupe Jaguar pulled up to offer me a lift. I rushed up to the window of the car, carrying our small suit case, feeling very relieved that I had a lift, but at the same time anxious as my brother was still in the pub. I said to the driver cheekily would he mind waiting a minute, The driver was fine and said OK. However to my surprise and amazement I realized whom the driver was it was Pete Townsend, the lead guitarist of The Who. Of course that made our day. By this Time Michael had arrived and we both squeeze into the front seat of Pete's Jaguar. We told him who we were and that we were off to Bedford to their gig at the Corn Exchange.

Pete Townsend's Jaguar

Pete Townhsend MK1 Jaguar

(Click here listen to Road Runner by The Who)

You can imagine listening to this song driving Pete's Car.

As we drove into Bedford we stopped and Pete asked me to ask some girls the directions to where The Who were playing. Sure enough they knew and pointed us in the direction of the Corn Exchange. It was a great evening.

The Bubble Car

The bubble car belonged to David Ness of Chiltern avenue in Aylesbury, who had been given it by his brother. There was only one thing wrong with it. We had to bump start it as the starter motor did not work. (Push it and the put it in gear and jump in once the engine had started).

In this vehicle we had many adventures because we were liberated from the two- wheeled scooter and could cram four people in this vehicle, if we wanted. Neither of us had passed our driving test to drive a normal car but I had past my test to drive a motorbike and my license allowed me to drive the three-wheeler bubble car. We were able to carry blankets spare clothing etc. all in the dry. We carried all that we needed for a night out in that case. It was ideal for catching girls. The front opened up and it could be driven with the front door open. All we did was drive up to the bird we wanted to catch and stop in front of her. Open up the door and drive forward. She had no option but to fall in and we would drive off with her in the car. It was questioned was any girl safe with us around. On one occasion we set off to Margate, on one Bank holiday. This was a custom amongst our generation of Mods. We all seemed to migrate to Yarmouth, Margate or Brighton. This was Whitsun bank holiday.

David's Issetta Bubble Car

1966 and Mod and Rocker riots were common. On this trip to the coast my brother was true to form he had borrowed a 22 Webley air pistol from Pat Jones and was determined to have a good time. He had fired the occasional pop shot at one or two girl's bottoms, which cause many amusements to us all. This was not what I would have normally done because I remember how shocked I was at 11 years old a boy I recalled boys having air gun fights in the woods on the way home from school. I thought then how dangerous and stupid it was. However her was my brother older than I acting fearlessly. I just went along with it suppressing my natural cautiousness.

As we past through the various towns in London the air pistol was used to cause alarm. (As I write I shrivel up at the thought of what was done) We found it amusing to shoot at ladies bottoms as their reactions of shock was funny. As we passed through Lewisham several people must have reported the mystery air gun shooter and at least one lady was wounded.

Caught By The Police

Traffic police on route to Margate stopped us. These men briefly searched our car but found nothing suspicious and let us go. My brother had hidden the pistol just in time and we did not allow this close shave stop our adventure. Persons (girls) bathing at night were targets for our folly and we found it amusing to see and her scream from a female. It was not intended to wound or harm but that really was inevitable.

Our BMW Bubble Car

Looking back: the BMW Isetta bubble car

300 CC Bubble Car

During this weekend we moved on to Ramsgate and again moved with a spirit of naughtiness decided to steel a tray of peaches from a fruit and vegetable shop. The bubble car was to be used as the get away car. The shop was half way down a hill with houses on either side of the road, it was decided I should take the peaches and my brother to drive the get away car. I lifted the tray of peaches and jumped in the car as it rolled down the hill making a chug, chug, noise-attracting attention. Naturally we were spotted and reports were made to the police but we did not know this.

Our foolishness was brought to an end when the same traffic

police that had stopped us in London, on the way home, picked us up. I could tell from their faces that they had it in for us.

A quick search of our vehicle revealed a stolen handbag. If only we had got rid of it, I thought. Then the air gun pellets and finally the air gun itself. That was it we were arrested, the policemen having a snarl on his face and almost laughing as us. We were charge with malicious wounding and two cases of stealing. A woman in Lewisham had been travelling in a side car and been hit in the neck by the air pistol by my brother.

I was granted bail but my brother detained in custody. We had decided that I would say I had done the shooting and my brother was a sleep. This was to get my brother off a prison sentence as he had already done two spells in detention centers and two years in Borstal. I had only had a probation order and had an apprenticeship. I thought I would only get a fine but I was wrong.

Our Mum managed to obtain bail for my brother and we appeared in Kent Quarter sessions several months later.

On recollection I can remember a prison officer, at the Rochester Borstal, where I had visited my brother a year previously, had said to me that I would be sent to Borstal if I didn't watch out. I said. "You must be joking". I was sent to Borstal just as he said I would be for confessing to this crime. We were charged with malicious wounding.

On reflection I think my brother was not being a good brother to me. He should not have let me do it.

Bubble Car Blows Up

During the time we were awaiting our court appearance we went one night to Bedford in the bubble car. On the way home the bobble car caught light and blew up as the petrol tank was above the engine. We managed to walk to Woburn Green and decided we would have to sleep the night there. After routing through some ones garage we found an old mattress and blankets and there was a newly piled mound of grass on the village green. This was where we made our bed and it was very comfortable. We put up our umbrella that we had rescued from the bubble car and slept soundly until the morning. The police, who wanted to know what we were doing - as if they could not see, waked us up. When we explained the bubble car had blown up they said oh yes they had seen it up the road. So they let us go without any further questions. I arrived at work that morning but was soon to be dismissed because I was due to appear in court and they were not prepared to trust me any more. This was the last of the bubble car as my parents managed to sell it when we were in prison.

7   Canterbury Prison

When my brother appeared in the Kent Quarter Sessions court I pleaded guilty to the charges of malicious wounding and carrying a fire arm without a license and my brother pleaded not guilty on all accounts.

The Fire Arm

The Offending Weapon

Canterbury Prison together

I was sentenced to Borstal Training, which meant I could do any time between 6 months to two years. That would depend on me to some degree on how I behaved.

My brother was detained in custody until he appeared in court a month later during, which time we were both detained in. Our time in Canterbury Prison was in one sense a time of continuous fun and just another of our good times together, even though I had just received an awful sentence.

Upon arrival at Canterbury Prison we were taken into the reception hall. Here we were with other newly sentenced young persons and being with my brother made it that much easier for me, and it gave me confidence because he had been to Rochester Borstal, and detention center on two occasions, before and he knew

Canterbury Prison in Kent

This housed young persons who must have been typical of the criminal population of England at the time. In this prison we shared our experiences with others who had been sentenced to three, four and six months, and many had already been to approved schools, detention centers and Borstal before. Some were on their second or even third visit to prison. There was an element of excitement and curiosity about what made people like they were?

Canterbury Prison

Canterbury Prison Gates

In the reception hall we were issued with prison clothing. Our fingerprints were taken and photographed and we were each given a number. After this the medical officer (all prison officers were called screws) had inspected us and we were taken to our cell (called a Peter). At that time we were three's up. My brother and I and a lad from Liverpool. In this cell we were to remain for a few days until we were issued work. The cell was approximately 12 foot by 9 foot and housed a bunk bed and a single bed. A table, chair, water jug and urinal pot.

At half past six each morning our sleep was broken with a bang on the door and words saying "Slop out". This meant we had to get up make up our beds and empty the urinal pot. We then could get hot water for a wash in a jug for a shave and return to our cell. A razor blade was issued and collected after and then we were banged up until breakfast.

At breakfast time we were unlocked and had to line up in single file to collect our food. This was served up on a specially shaped metal tray, which was recessed in three places to retain the food.

A typical breakfast would be a scoop of porridge, four slices of bread, a knob of margarine, a sausage or piece of bacon with beans and a large mug of tea.

The bread dipped in porridge became one of my favorite meals but on one occasion this practice of dipping bread in my porridge offended one inmate (when I was in Dover Borstal) he expressed he thought what I was doing was a disgusting habit. I just ignored him with contempt.

One of the ways we past time, when locked up in the cell, was to play "Blind Mans Buff". One of us would be blindfolded whilst the other two crept about and hid from the other, while the blind man tried to catch the others. There were all sorts of places to hide in such a small cell. We enjoyed this game we would jump from bed to bed which made the game that much more fun.

During this time I found time killing boring so I tried to read one ore two books. The books I found I could read were James Bond as these were about my level and the Beano and Dandy comics. Any other reading would be too difficult to me.

On the days we were not working, each morning and afternoon was exercise. This was where all the inmates walked as a body around the prison yard. No doubt each prisoner looked at the high walls and every building looking for a possible way to escape. During this time we could talk with whom we pleased, those that attempted an escape were made to wear yellow patches so they could be spotted easily. These times became a time of communication and formed the prison grape vine

Hair Style Change

On one occasion I decided to change my hairstyle. So during the wash period my brother removed the safety edge from the Government Issue razor and was able to shave my head. It was much easier to wash in the mornings with no hair and much fresher. However I had gone against the prison rules and was put on a Governors report and put in solitary confinement for a period of time.

At the meal time it cause an amusing stir and I was to get laughed at when one of the cooks slapped a handful of strawberry jam on my baldhead. After this when my hair grew a little I was able to razor a parting in my hair which was really the beginning of the hair fashions for the skin head.

What Sentence Have You Got?

I could not help but notice the various characters and the first points of conversation were "What sentence had you got and what was your crime, or crimes". After this an inquiry would be made as to your previous convictions and prison sentencing.

Our time at Canterbury came to and end when my brother was found guilty and was sentence to two years prison at the Kent Crown Court.

I was a witness at his trial and was detained in the cells below the courtroom. When my brother was brought below, handcuffed to a prison officer, I was shocked and disappointed that he had been found guilty. In fact all our plans had come to nothing and I was to do a stretch in Borstal. He was found guilty of malicious wounding as well and was sentenced to 2-year prison.

On that occasion my mother was not allowed to see either of us and we were taken from the cells in Kent back to Canterbury prison that dark wet night. As we approached the prison gate I saw my mum with tears in her eyes out side the prison gate. We both waved and motioned to the prison officer to say she had come to see us and his reaction was, "So what, she can't see you because you are now prisoners". She had not got a visiting permit. She had travelled from Kent to Canterbury late that night to try and see us but she was rejected.

From that time we hated that prison officer called Titmouse. He was about 6 foot 7 inches tall. My brother, weeks later, after we were separated laid into this screw because of the hate. He head-butted him (nutted) and of course was on a governor's report and put in solitary confinement. This I heard through the grape vine when I was at Wormwood scrubs awaiting my allocation to Dover Borstal.

Wormwood Scrubs

I was moved from Canterbury Prison to Wormwood Scrubs in London, which was a Borstal allocation centre. After a period of four weeks it was decided I was to go to Dover Borstal. A closed Borstal called the Citadel. For the first time I was on my own and was moved from one cell to another having to share some times with others. I did not really enjoy things here, as it was lonely being on my own.

The Scrubs

Wormwood Scrubs

Dover Borstal (The Citidal)

We were allowed to go to church on a Sunday, which I did to break the monotony. How ever I remember being horrified by the fact that I saw some inmate tearing pages out of the bible to role cigarettes. This was probably the first sense of me acknowledging the existence or fear of God.

When at Dover Borstal I was placed in an open dormitory with five other lads. Here I had to learn to survive. There was a 6 foot 6 inch Lad nicked named Te Oh who was bullied mercilessly by a 5 foot 6 spectacled bottle job, called Vince Bowker. I saw this bullying the moment I arrived and Te oh was made to do this, do that, and he would say yes Vince, no Vince and so one hoping to get off lightly. In the end Te oh turned and lashed out on Vice Bowker and that put stopped to that. I was determined I was not going to let that happen to me. I stood my own ground whenever I sensed any one trying to bully me. I was in fact nick named Flash Clarke because I had all kinds of goodies like, cocoa, coffee, milk and sugar and even Ovaltine and had one of the senior green ties make me Ovaltine in the morning.

Borstal Boy

This is a film made about life in Borstal featuring Ray Winston. This is a real to life story here ins the link Borstal Boy

(This is a classic movie click here to view)

One bully, 6 footer, was moved into our dormitory because he had mercilessly bullied another inmate. We got on well until I tied his shoelaces together one morning for a joke but he didn't see it that way. When he realized who it was that did it he threw these tied shoes at me in anger and this gave me a black eye. As he came at me to hit me I was quick enough to hit him on the jaw bringing him down to the ground. After that he kept out of my way and the screw that could see my black eye ignored it. I think they must have known how to deal with bullies.

Electrical Installation Course

Whilst at Dover I went on a six months training course doing Electrical Installations and I worked really hard obtaining top marks every week and I use to be rewarded half an ounce of tobacco for coming top of the class. I traded this with an inmate for his ration of milk each morning and cornflakes and an egg each Sunday morning.

Dover Borstal

Dover Borstal (The Citidel)

We had to attend church on a Sunday and were would be marched to church in whatever the weather. We would have to be dressed in our best gear after Sunday morning inspection. I remember I had no sense of respect for God or anything like that. In fact when the vicar Rev. Whally took us for talks before we were to leave Borstal I can remember ridiculing him in front of all the inmates. I thought it was a huge joke.

Paternity Suite

Whilst serving my time in Borstal I was served with a summoned to appear in court to answer a paternity suit. A former girl friend was pregnant and I presume the Social Services had made her declare whom the father of the child was in order to get the finances but I am not sure as I never spoke to her about it. In fact I do not remember knowing any thing about it until I had to appear in court. The first time in court I admitted I was the father because I could have been even though I knew she had been with other men. At the time. I was ordered to pay maintenance out of my three shillings and six pence a week, at the rate if one shilling and three pence per week. I had no idea of the serious nature of being a father or bringing up children or any idea of taking responsibility for my actions.

My mother how ever was very anxious and after listening to the evidence given by the girl, she maintained it was not possible for me to be the father, as the timing of the events did not fit. She encouraged me to appeal and she really fought the case for me. This I did and with the aid of a Solicitor the girl had to prove I was the father of the child. When I look back it must have been humiliating for the girl because she had to explain when and where these events took place. My defence solicitor asked where the event or events took place. With incredulity he questioned her how could things take place in a bubble car, in the daylight. This I think on reflection was humiliating for her.

The suit was not proven and I was release from the charge. My probation officer Mr Moorland Hughes asked me many years latter, when I became a Christian and had to appear in court over my confessions to many crimes, "Was I the father of the child", I replied I might have been.

The child was called David and my mother say's he had ginger hair. She had seen him out with his mother in Aylesbury whilst I was still in Borstal. He must be around 33 years old now.

I met all kinds of lads here in Borstal, car thieves, burglars, forgers, and gamblers. None of us had any idea for the reason of our existence but were probably looking for the best in life never finding it.

When I was released I was determined to have a good time. I wanted the best clothes, a good car, a speedboat, and a caravan. You name it I wanted all these things and intended to obtain them by one means or another. I had learned many criminal ways and had no intention going straight. I just had no intention of getting caught at any crime I may choose to be involved in.

8 My Release From Borstal

I was released from Borstal a year later and it was during this time I began to get into all kinds of things and criminal activities in Aylesbury.

My Gold Mini

My first car 850 CC Mini

I bought my first real car for £100 when I came out of Borstal. It was a gold mini 850 cc.

I decided to visit my brother who was now in Maidstone Prison and I visited him when I could. Whilst he was there he met an inmate senior man from Cyprus who told him some fantastic story, which we both believed. We had ideas of being involved in gold smuggling.

It led to my brother absconding from prison and being on the run from the law for a year. He was offering us the opportunity to make money by smuggling gold. The idea was we had to pretend to be just married, we would have a suitable partner and we would carry the gold strapped under our clothes making out we were newly weds. This would reduce the chances of being stopped by customs and so get the gold through. We were prepared to take the risk. It sounded exciting and that was what I wanted.

The plan was that when my brother came out on home leave we he would go to Greece. We had to a contact in London all set up by the Greek man and take it from there. We were all hyped up but the was no such person or arrangements and we felt really let down.

However my brother decided he could not face going back to prison so he just did not return. He changed his name to Kenny? And managed to stay away from the police for a whole year before being picked up whilst working on a building site in Aylesbury.

At this time I was doing a Government training course in Enfield Middlesex and Michael got some work with a shop filling company and worked in London. He decided he would live above the shop, which was near Kings Cross, where they were working and so I was able visit him during the week.

For a bit of fun one morning we decided to go to the cafe down the road dressing in our pajamas and dressing gowns bringing with us our own cornflakes. We went into the shop and asked for breakfast bowls and milk and sugar. This seemed a funny thing to do and it all went down well.

Michael soon got fed up being there on his own so he decided he was leaving.

So one night we took all the companies tools and equipment and returned to Aylesbury where our parents lived.

During this time I renewed friendship with Pat Jones and we did many things together. My brother had got a girlfriend now and I was seeking to have a good time.

On one occasion I showed Pat Jones the powerful effect of chloroform and knocked him out so he was unconscious. Moved by my strange sense of humour I cut several chunks of hair from his head and when he came too he had no idea what I had done. I found it great fun when I took him home and saw his mother's face. Of course he had no idea what she was upset about. I just left and got out of the way laughing to my self.

It was after this that Pat Jones got the first skinhead hair cut in Aylesbury. No one would normally cut all their hair off it just was not yet fashionable. He did it and I was proud of him. I am sure he set the trend of the Skinhead fashion.

Mods, Skinheads, Greasers at Yarmouth

On one bank holiday weekend in 1969, when I was working for Radio Rentals in Hemel Hempstead, Pat Jones and I decided to go to Yarmouth and meet with the Aylesbury Mods, later called skinheads.

I took my firms Ford van in which we would sleep the night. On this particular weekend I was sleeping in the back of the Ford van that Sunday afternoon and Pat Jones was out with some of the lads. They had a run in with a crowd of Greasers.

Greasers were motor bikers who would fight with knives and motorbike chains. It was a very similar to the Mods and rockers you see in The Who film Quadraphenia. They were the sworn enemies of skinheads.

Mods On a Bank Holiday Weekend

Mods at Margate and News Reports

This company of Greasers had come across Pat Jones and his crowd when out on the sea front in Yarmouth and they were combing the area for skinheads, to pick a fight with. There were too many of them and Pat Jones and the crowd was on the run and I was happily asleep in the back of the van quite safe. Or I would have been had not Pat Jones came running up to the van shouting and screaming to get out and run or do some thing. He ran off just having just called attention to these Greasers. As I looked up and came too and looked out of the van window I could see a crowd of Greasers grinning and running towards the van. They knew they now had a victim in a van. I was concerned it was the firms van so had to get away. There wasn't much I could do so I locked the doors quickly and jumped into the driver's seat hoping to drive. Unfortunately I was awkwardly parked. As I tried to start the engine a great whack came from the roof of the van. The van was hit a number of times with motorbike chains and I heard shouts of glee. Then they began to rock the van seeking to turn it over. They lifted it and rocked it as I tried to drive forward then backwards. I must have hit one or two as I managed to gut get away in time for a beating. That was all thanks to Pat Jones!

This how ever was all part of our fun getting into scrapes of one kind or another. On the way home that week end we decided to tow a four wheeled sea side bike back to Aylesbury so I got Pat Jones to ride the bike whilst we towed this bike all the way from Yarmouth to the outskirts of Norwich before deciding to lead it outside a pub as I began to realize we would be captured by the police going through London. It was all good fun and it made us laugh.

Newquay Here We Come

It was the summer of 1968, shortly after my brother had been released from prison and I had served time in Borstal. We had decided to go on a holiday. He had become friendly with a girl called Karen Mead but that did not stop our plans. We were going to go off with no plans to return. Michael had a nice red Bedford, long, wheel base van. This was fitted out with our equipment to live and we fitted a double mattress on the roof with a tarpaulin like tent. This was to be our sleeping arrangement. It was decided we would make our way to Newquay in Cornwall as I remembered going there with my parents when I was 16 years old. That year the sun was hot, the surfing was good and a really nice summer. We were off to seek the sun.

Our Holiday to Newquay

Newquay The Place Of The Sun

Our first mischief that we planned but fail to do was the stealing of a speedboat, moored in the water at Barnstable. That evening we had planned to swim out to the boat and cut its moorings and float it down river to load on a trailer. That after noon we borrowed tools from a workshop and got some welding done to make a tow bar fo the van. We needed a tow hitch to drive away with the stolen speedboat and trailer that night.

All went to plan until that night when we got the trailer ready but when we looked at the cold dark water, it being pitch black, we both lost our bottle and decided to call it off. We left Barnstable disappointed.

I Am A Waiter At The Gull Rock Hotel

Our first bit of work, which we did, was to work in "The Gull Rock Hotel" in Newquay. I was a waiter and my brother was a kitchen porter. I had never been a waiter before but soon picked it up.

We were given sleeping quarters but we soon realized this kind of work and life was not what we wanted. The hours were unsociable hours. So the next morning we decided not to go to work, just stay in bed. We made a huge joke of it and expected to get the sack.

Sure enough we were knocked up when it was realized we were late but still we did not surface. When we decided to get up we went to the chef believing we had got the sack and so to collect or pay. To my surprise they hadn't sacked us but had just thought we had too much to drink the night before and were prepared to over look the sleep in. I said no we would leave and we each got the £1 each we had earned for the day's work.

In or mischief we went back to the sleeping quarters the next day where the girls were sleeping and jumped into bed with two of the girls. They didn't want this really and made a bit of a protest but before we left the manager's wife had been informed and came to see what was happening. As she came into the bedroom we were seen in bed with Angela the chambermaid. The manageress screamed, "Oh! Angela how could you". The girl got the sack and I felt really bad about that afterwards.

Shortly after this we decided to rob a petrol station to get some money. My brother tried to disguise him self by wearing a long girls wig but this made him stand out even more because he was flat chested and had no hips like a woman and this attracted attention rather than do the opposite. That idea was discarded so I decided I would take the money. When the attendant was looking after a motorist I crept up to the till and took the notes and ran away behind some building. Then quickly dressed in an old overall coat and then walked slowly away without being noticed.

We Return Home To Aylesbury

In the end I noticed my brother writing to his girl friend and somehow we decided to return home to Aylesbury.

After this I began to spend time with Pat Jones as my brother got more involved with his girl friend. Pat Jones and I got into all kinds of things, which I will mention later on. I was 20 years old and he was just 16 years so he began to learn many things off me, all which was probably bad for him.

It was after this I managed to get a job with Radio Rentals in Hemel Hempstead

This was a good job and at 20 years old I was the only Colour TV Engineer in the Hemel Hempstead branch and with a company car.

Our Trip To Shoreham

About this time we went on a sailing trip to Shoreham near Brighton. This weekend we were invited to go sailing with Ken and Grace Knight. I took Mary Bilton a girl friend of mine, Bernie Gilbert and Alison Knight. Whilst we were there Mrs. (Grace) Knight went off to stay with a Christian friend in Brighton. Not that I knew that at the time I just thought she did not like sailing and it was a Sunday and she wanted to go to church.

The History Of The Jews And 1967

We were all invited back to this Christian mans home. He was called Tom and was a manager of an insurance company in Brighton. That afternoon he sat and talked to us all about the bible. I was almost convinced by his talk and began to believe there was more to the bible message than I had ever really liked to admit before. He told us about the history of the Jews and all future events. It was all foretold in the scripture. The history of Israel was recorded and the return of the Jews to the land of Israel in 1967 was clearly a sign of the last days.

I was very impressed at what he said. So much so that I began to tell my friends at college the very next week all about it. This made me readi parts in Deuteronomy about the curses that would come upon the Jews if they forsook Moses Law and reject the Lord Jesus Christ.

Pat Jones And The Bully

At this time Pat Jones was in his final year at school and he informed me of a bully who would relentlessly give him grief at school. The school was the Grange Secondary Modern School in Aylesbury. The school I had attended until June 1966.

One day at the evening youth club held at the school I decided we would sort this bully out so I instructed Pat ' Bones" to do as I said. I was dressed in my long Crombie over coat, which my mum had altered for me, and inside I kept a large long rubber torch, which was ideal for use as a cosh. Not too hard to break the skull and not too soft to do no harm. Just about right to knock some one on the head and possibly knock them out.

This was the plan. We were to go to the youth club and search out this bully. The Grange youth club was held behind the school buildings in some prefabricated buildings. It was early evening and not too dark and a few people were around. Here we looked out for the bully.

I gave Pat Jones the large heavy rubber torch and said to him when he sees the bully he must call out to him, " Come here" and walk towards him. When he came right up close he was to shout at him the words, " I have had enough of your nonsense and if you don't watch out I am going to set Dave Clarke on to you". He was then to point in the direction away from him so at to make him turn around and say' " look he is over there". When he turned around he was to hit him on the head, as hard as he could with the torch. Then say, " Now I am going to do it again and roar at him.

The plan went perfectly. We saw the bully dressed in a Denhim Jean jacket he had slight ginger hair. I am sure his nickname was Ginger) .I had never met him before. Pat Jones shouted out to him and sure enough the bully came walking like a gorilla with his arms swinging by his side. Almost running to get at Pat Jones eager to get him. I was happy because this was where he was going to get the treatment. Pat did exactly as instructed. He said look over there and as he turned around Pat walloped this bully hard on the head.

Every eye was on the two in conflict. The bully was stunned and his hands went up to his head to hold it as it hurt. Then Pat shouted at him to say he was going to give it to him again and sure enough the bully ran away as predicted. I encouraged Pat to chase after him to make sure he now knew his place. Every one looking on looked in amazement.

From that day forward Pat Jones had no more trouble from that bully. I felt quite satisfied in dealing this way with the bully.

How would Jesus have us deal with bullies today? This is a real problem to parents in a world of violence like to day. I was not a Christian but this remedy actually worked in Pat Jones's case.

9 Conversion from Crime to Christ

Having worked through and experience many things I often thought about life and its meaning. I could recall the absolute emptiness of my soul after going out for the evening and coming home. All was empty and what was the point to it all. I was seeking an answer to life, the universe and every thing.

A Bad LSD Trip

The following is an account, taken from memory and notes made of my experience of conversion to Jesus Christ on Friday, 16th January 1970.

Towards the end of 1969 I was continuing my studies at Luton College learning Radio and Television Servicing. We would often engage in discussions and it was quite easy to divert our lecturer onto subjects like spiritualism and the like. We would discuss what we would do if another world war came. We would talk about the future as portrayed by Nostradamus, drugs and our experiences. At that time I was informed of a new film called Easy Rider and wanted to see it. On one occasion I obtained some hashish mixed with opium and smoked this during our break time. This was so effectual I made use of the sick room at college to sleep and enjoy the illusionary effects of the drug, which amused my student friends.

On another occasion in January 1970 I had obtained 4 tablets of LSD from Peter Coppenhall, a student friend from Bedford, he was one of my fellow students at Luton College, and I decided to take them the following Friday night 16th January 1970

On this Friday night the 16th of January my brother I decided to each took half a tablet and Pat Jones had a quarter. He had been a close friend of mine (he was only just 16 years old) for some time and I use to think of him as my apprentice. I taught him all my bad ways. There was little we did not do together. I had known him whilst he was at school and encouraged him in crime, sniffing chloroform, smoking (marijuana, hashish, weed etc.) drunkenness, violence and permissive sex. He was known amongst our friends as "Bones", Patrick Bones.

My brother was going out that night with his girl friend Karen Mead so Pat Jones and I decided to walk up town and not risk driving for we did not know the effect this drug would have on us. I was dressed in my old clothes deliberately for I did not know what might happen too us. We tried to thumb a lift but eventually caught a bus and got off at the bottom of the High Street. As we walked past the "pictures" I noticed the film "Easy Rider" was being shown so we decided to go and see it. We wanted to take some one else with us, some one who was in their right state of mind, so we went up the billiard hall and found Bernie Gilbert and Mike Ellis but they said they would only come and watch the film with us if they too had some acid. I decided this was OK, and so we got a taxi back to my house to get the rest of the Acid. Bernie had half a tablet and Mike Ellis the other quarter. So all four of us were about to trip on acid whilst watching the film Easy Rider. We arrived back at the "pictures" about 8.45 PM and I fumbled a bit with my ticket as the acid had begun to take effect. Bernie and Mike suggested we go and sit up in the balcony but I thought to my self, what if we decide to jump off? I was tripping now and just followed them up the stairs. We sat two in front and two behind, but Mike and Bernie's trip had not yet begun as they acted and spoke normally.

I did not realize how tripped I was until the film had finished in fact the film records Peter Fonder and his friend actually on an

LSD trip. During the film the acid had taken me on a very pleasant trip in time with the music.It was almost as if the film crew had deliberately filmed the film for me. They seemed to know how to give the correct lighting and sound effects. How ever Bernie and Mike seemed to be jumping about all over the place and it was irritating. I still was sitting in my seat when all the people had gone, before I decided there was nothing more to do. So we decided to up and go but Mike and Bernie were annoying me because they were mucking about.

All my thoughts and feelings began to reverberate four times over and thought patterns were being reflected and at the same time building and snowballing.

We walked outside the cinema and I said to the boys, "Man you are all on the wrong scene you can't be turned on". Then I heard Mike and Bernie say he's turned into a wizard (Hippie) and there was a club room for wizards like me (The Dark Lantern Pub in Aylesbury). I then began a downward trip, which ended in the horrors. I began to feel paranoid thinking they were now sorry for me and were being polite in hiding their feelings from me.

As we went further up the road Mike Ellis asked if I wanted a scrap with some blokes across the street. It was as if he was testing me out to see if I was the same person he knew. I said no I didn't. I thought they had thought I had gone mad and they wanted to test me out. We went further up the high street and Bernie began to mess about and pull faces at me and make noises. I hid in a shop door way and told him to stop it and Pat Jones pulled Bernie away saying don't do it as he didn't understand. My horror began when I could not face the thought that they thought I had cracked up and gone mad. This feeling was too much for me to bare. More was to come.

We decided to go to the Crown pub and Brian Sale came up to me and spoke but I was out of my mind by now with this feeling of paranoia and could not speak sensibly and came out with a load of nonsense, so I had to say quickly I was drunk because I didn't think he would understand other wise.

I then saw my Michael sitting with his girl friend and I went up to him and told him what was happening. He laughed and motioned to wined me up like a clockwork toy and then my mind began to distort so much so I had to run out of the pub to get away. Pat Jones followed me and I kept thinking the others were following us. I kept looking back as I didn't want them following me as they annoyed me. We left the Green Man and walked towards Mount Street, via Richford's Hill and along Friarage Road. On the way down it seemed like a scene from a picture book and was like Alice in Wonderland with all the street lamps lit up.

The torment of my mind had grown so much that I could not bare the pain but I could not get rid of the torment. Ken and Grace Knight lived at Mount Street. We went down there with no real aim and as I arrived just outside their house Jock Macallion, another friend of mine, was about to leave and drive off. I jumped in besides him and told him my situation. After telling him I was tripped out of my mind I was thinking he would take me home and as I was about to ask him he said, "Dave you are a worried man". I knew this and I now though so did every one else and being told that did not help me at all. My mind was about to blow so I had to run again. I jumped out of the car and into 24 Mount Street where Ken and Grace were. I wanted to escape and so I told them my plight but I could not explain to them what was happening to me. Grace Knight recalled she thought I was in serious trouble and began to question me. This didn't help so I had to say forcefully I must have peace so

they took me out to the summerhouse to lie down in peace.

No one seemed to understand the torment of mind I was in and no one could help me at all. I told Mrs Knight to leave me alone to work it out on my own and let me lie down. Then the torment got worse. I knew it was only the LSD doing it but I could do nothing about it I would have to wait till it had taken its course. I thought it could be 12 hours or so but to me each moment seemed like an eternity of torment and I could not endure this any more.

I lay down and tried to settle my mind by thinking good thoughts and different things but my mind would not be controlled. The thought came, " I may be driven to kill myself to get rid of the pain", but I was horrified at the thought and the more I tried to stop thinking like it the more I thought about it. I looked around to see if there was a mirror or glass in the room and wanted to get rid of it just in case I cut my throat or wrists. I just did not know what to do I was at the end of my self.

In this condition it was evident I could not help myself. My friends could not help; my brother had not helped. Mr and Mrs Knight couldn't help and I could not help myself.

In this desperation it came to me to call out to God for help. So I cried out calling on the Lords name saying, "Jesus please help me". At that moment my mind went blank and his name appeared in the imagination of my mind but the torments soon came back again. I called out again and his name appeared twice and the happening repeated. I called four times in all and his name appeared four times and formed a square in complete emptiness.

I then began to feel emotional and wept but I didn't know why and at that moment Mrs knight came to the chalet door to see if she could help. It was then, at that, a flood of guilt overcame me. I was convicted of the sin of Adultery and did not know what to do. I beckoned Mrs Knight to come in and said to her did she realize how bad I was and what I had done. I asked her to tell me the way what could I do.

Mrs Knight had spoken to me about Christian things and some how I knew she knew the way. Mrs Knight sat down and quoted the scripture saying, " For God so loved the world that he gave his only begotten son that who so ever believed on him should not perish but have everlasting life." (John 3 verse 16).

Dave I Am With You

After this Jesus spoke to me, I heard his voice as clearly I am writing this he said, "Dave I am with you, you have been searching for a long time, this is what our Father says. What you have been going through is nothing compared to what hell is like. I replied with thanks giving saying thank you, Jesus thank you.

Mrs knight I think thought that I was speaking to her she but she did not know what was going on.

It seemed that the words that Mrs Knight had spoken, were in fact the way out and pathway to my escape. It appeared as though I was at the bottom of a pyramid and the words were the way to the top and if I were to follow the words I would escape. I replied thank you Jesus thank you.

I then thought of hell and my thoughts were about the Pat Jones, Bernie Gilbert and Mike Ellis and I said what about the others. Jesus spoke again and said, " all I could do was tell them".

I replied feeling it an impossible thing to do to convince them "but what more could I do" I was feeling the agony of the LSD horrors and knew I wanted to warn my friends of the hell to come. I reasoned within my self they will think I have gone mad on LSD how could I convince them, I wanted to do more than tell them. I asked what more could I do.

All I could Do Was Tell Them

In order to answer my question the Lord took me back in time to show me all I could do was tell them. A number of weeks earlier I had reason to read about the curses that were to come on the children of Israel if they forsook their God. Deut. 28 v 53. And though shall eat the fruit of thine own body. (I knew nothing about the back ground to these things) I thought it was saying people would be so hungry and having no food to eat a woman would be driven to eat her own after birth. Which of course was shocking. With this in mind these weeks earlier I was trying to shock this girl at work. I was working for Radio Rentals as a Colour TV engineer and I said to this receptionist how would she like to be so hungry to have to eat her own after birth? She responded with expected repulsion " How could you say such a thing". I simply said I hadn't said it but God has. This thing repulsed her and she did not want to know anything about what I was saying (Not suppressing). However to this incident Jesus took me and asked me, " what did the girl do when I spoke to her"? My answer was she shut her ears, as she did not want to know. It was repulsive to her. His reply was to me that, " if I tell people about Hell and what I had learned and they screw their faces up and do not want to know I could do no more." The condition of the person listening is not my responsibility but theirs. All I could do was tell them. So tell them I would.

To these questions Mrs. Knight thought I was asking her, because I was speaking aloud, but before she could answer I had been answered directly from the Lord.

When Jesus stopped speaking I felt as though I was falling back into my torment and I prayed again, "Please don't leave me". My reply was, " I will never leave you".

Why Boast

Jesus then questioned me and asked me, "Why boast". This is because I was naturally prone to boasting amongst my friends just to make a good impression. I reason within myself now and now knew I had no need to boast of anything. So from that day I have always avoided boasting.

My torment ceased from that time and the rest of the night passed with various thoughts going through my mind. I do not think Mrs Knight was fully aware of what had taken place.

The next day was Saturday and I was due in to work but I decided to take the day off. I phone in briefly saying I was not up to work.

10 What after Salvation

Pat Jones had spent the night in the caravan parked at the side of the Knight's home, together with Paddy who had no where else to live. We spent that day together and I told them both of my experience. I assumed and expected them to fully understand and see what had happened.

Instinctively things were different with me. An internal change had come about and by it I had new desires. I no longer wished to live as I had lived and wished to be rid of my bad ways. No one told me I had to give up any particular way of life, I found within me an internal desire to choose the good and refuse the evil.

Evidence of the New Birth

Upon reflection I say this was the evidence of the new birth and I later found this experience spoken of by the Lord Jesus Christ in Johns gospel. John 3. Jesus answered and said unto him, Verily, verily I say unto thee, except a man be born again, he cannot see the kingdom of God. The Apostle Paul also writes the same in Cor. 5 17. Therefore if any man were in Christ Jesus, he is a new creature: old things are past away; behold all things are become new.

I knew also there was a part of me which was just the same and when I would do good evil was also present with me. The Apostle Paul in Romans also expressed this. Rom. 7 verse 21. I find then a law that when I would do good evil is present with me.

Whilst this was my experience I found it impossible to convey this to my friends even thou I tried ever so hard.

What To Do With Stolen Goods

I had in my possession much stolen property. In fact hundreds of pounds worth of stolen goods. I was no longer prepared to live off the benefits of stolen goods. What should I do? I had involved others in my crime of stealing and these could not help me now. In fact Mike West came to see me the next day and when he heard me explaining Jesus had spoken to me he began to fear I might go to the police and confess my crimes. I did not actually say to him I wanted him to return the Colour TV set, which I had stolen and swapped for his Citroen car but he was concerned, as he did not know what to think.

Poor Mike he must have panicked thinking I was about to go to the police, as he was concerned some of the stolen goods that I had left in his garage were a stolen including the mini engine sub chassis. I don't remember what happen to these parts but I asked Mike to dispose of them. I was later informed they had been dumped in the reservoir.

That Saturday evening both Pat and I decided to go to the Social Club at Park Street.

This was the usual thing for us to do on a Saturday night. I had determined to go and see my mates to explain what had happened to me. We walked down there but did not go in. After seeing one or two people I broke my news to them. I cannot remember what I said. I had no desire to stay so went back to the Knight's home. My inclination to live it up as normal was no longer with me. I now seemed at a loose end not knowing what next to do. From that time forward Pat Jones began to realize things had really changed for me.

The next day, being Sunday, Mrs Knight took both Pat Jones and I to the local Baptist Church in Southcourt, in the evening. I distinctly remember the passage of scripture the preacher spoke from. It was in Exodus where the whole nation of Israel was about to enter the Promised Land. However they listened to the evil reports of the 10 spies and did not take heed to the voice of the two good spies. Who gave encouragement to go in and possess the land? I remember also I saw, whether he preached this or not, that this was a picture of the body of Christ - the church of that day.

I Seek To Tell Others

After the meeting Mrs Knight introduced me to a Martin White who gave me a copy of the New Testament called the Good News for modern man. I began to read this straight away. This I received gratefully and began to read it every day

Southcourt Baptists

South Court Baptist Church

The following days were spent in the after glow and certainty of this new life that had opened up to me. I thirsted for knowledge, the knowledge of God in Jesus Christ. I told the folk at work about my experience and could not remain silent about the things I was learning.

My evenings were spent at Mrs Knight's home discussing the scripture with some of her Christian friends. Both Pat Jones and Paddy all seemed interested to hear.

My own ignorance I had never read the Bible

I am now amazed at my own ignorance then for until then I had never read the bible for myself. I did not know what the Acts of the Apostles meant. Within two weeks I had read the New Testament and thought I understood it all. I soon learned from the scripture that in the economy of Salvation it was the blood of Jesus Christ shed on the cross at Calvary that was the means of me obtaining a free pardon for all my sins. And also that I was given freely a righteousness to justify me before God.

In this respect the Lord Jesus was a true substitute and he died for me without cost at all to me. These were the things, which I learned and as it were drank in like water from the well of salvation. I learned them by reading the scripture and did not know them from the night Jesus spoke to me.

Difference at College

I attended college that week but there was a difference. I had decided I would not dress in my usual clothes to show off. Which would have been Levi jeans, white boots with red toe caps (or whatever colour I chose to spray them), a Ben Sherman shirt and loose leather jerkin. I felt I must not only be more sober but dress more soberly too i.e. not show off as I use to do.

So I dressed in my best trousers, which were from my Prince of Wales cheque suit, shirt and normal pull over and normal shoes. O course I had to tell all my friends about my experience. I protested to them look I even dress differently. They could not believe me. I told one of the lecturers, Mr. Jones, in front of them all but I was just given a smile of wonder.

I tell Rupert

That same week I felt constrained to go and tell my friend Rupert, a West Indian from Jamaica. He lived in a room, at 14 Bicester Road Aylesbury so Pat Jones and I went to see him. As soon as I met him I told him what had happened in front of his new girl friend but Rupert's reply was, " I told you Dave not to take LSD ". Again they were none plus, they could not believe even though I tried my best to convince them.

Turning From The world

Being in the world but not of it. It was now wrong for me to continue in the way of life that I had lived in the past. My back was now turned from the world that I once laid hold on, and had built for myself. I was self-seeking (ones own glory), asserting self without considering others, stealing, and thoughts of adultery, fornication, drug taking, drug selling, boasting, drunkenness, violence and worldly ambition. I say worldly ambition because I believe we all have worldly ambitions but when we are converted and come to Christ we are called to forsake it; that is forsake the world and its ambitions.

We all have our own worlds to forsake when we become a Christian. Some have a religious world to turn from; as a person may have been born in a religious family or have a circle of religious friends but in their world they have their own natural fallen nature to contend with. Fallen human nature seeks to gratify its desires and as such sin the whole day long. A religious person still has all the workings of a natural man as those who have no religion. Any thought or act, which is born out of selfishness, greed, pride, avarice, thinking evil of others, back biting, slander and prejudice may all be practiced by those in a religious or none religious world. So to forsake the world means to forsake all those thoughts and actions, which are natural to us, and are contrary to the way of Christ.

Religious and none religious persons

need to turn from their world

Some persons have no religion or religious friends, yet they too have natural desires and a fallen human nature, which they seek to please. Ambitions of fame for its own sake, the love of money, selfishness, the practice of gossip, evil speaking of others, are all to be turned from. It doesn't matter whether you be in a religious or none religious person we are to world are to be forsaken the world from which we come from when we seek to follow Christ. We are called to be in the world but not of it. This is really what John Bunyan sought to express when he told his story of the man who turn his back on the city of destruction. One of the problems how ever was that his story only described the picture of those who were none religious and the pattern of their life styles. In reality a religious person, one who is not born again, has a pattern and life style, which is equally wrong and such need to be turned from. It is very easy for such a person to think because they do not do certain things that they see people in a none-religious world do, to look down and judge them thinking they are better than them. Not so, we all have a world to turn from. When a person is born again they have an ordinary life natural to them and are part of the natural world but we all must turn from our world in order to follow Christ

Being kept By The Power And Grace Of God

I now had an inward and real desire not to continue in those ways, which I have just mentioned, for they just perpetuated my former sinful self, of which I had, had enough. A change of heart had taken place. This was the fight. That is not to say I could not be tempted to find pleasure in such sins there was a part of me still the same but I had a desire to put to death sinful thoughts and actions. Should I allow wrong affections to move me I was self-condemned with an accompanying self-abhorrence and I knew was not pleasing to God. By the grace of God I was able to resist and fight against sin.

What To Do With Stolen Goods

I was now moved by a new set of principles but here in lay a problem. I had erected a 48-foot by 12-foot wooden builder's shed on waste ground belonging to the Water Board next door to the Knight's home at 24 Mount Street. This became my garage and workshop. I had stolen the builders shed from a building sight in Berkhampstead. I had persuaded Mr. Knight to drive his lorry whilst me, Pat Jones and Paddy lifted the shed panels from the building sight late one night.

In this shed was my newly acquired Citroen DS car, which had formally belonged to Mike West of Wendover. I had swapped it for a colour TV that we had stolen from old peoples home called Redlands, in Winslow. I had some lovely garage equipment which included a trailer, ark welder, trolley jack, air compressor, spray gun, tools, speed boat engines even a stolen car and various other items all of which by one means or another I had stolen or burgled.

My Citroen DS Car

What could or should I do now. I was responsible for at this stuff. Conscience would not permit me to continue to make us of all this stolen gear. What should I do? Should I just dispose of it all and brush the past behind me? How should I dispose of it if

I decide to do so? I could not sell the goods for what would I do with the money. Conscience would not allow me to use it. I had in fact so much stolen property go through my hands, which had been disposed of by one means or another, none of it could be recovered anyway.

My Citroen DS what I acquired

Citroen DS except mine was Banana Yellow

I had only just stolen a nice new Mini car, which was about to be used to make me a lovely new car.

1968 Mini Stolen from Hemel Hempstead

The body had been cut up and disposed of in my parents' garage in Finmere Crescent Aylesbury. (Whilst cutting up the body with the arc welder the hydrolastic suspension fluid caught light a nearly burnt the car and garage to pieces).

The Stolen Mini

My Stolen Mini

I had also another stolen Morris Minor Traveller, which I had swapped the number plates and disposed of the old body. This was and used it as a hire car. I think on reflection with hindsight and the faith I now have in God I would have been able to act differently than I did.

I was able during this time to return one or items of stolen goods. Late one wet night in February 1972 Pat Jones and I loaded the trolley jack into my firms van. I am not quite sure what Pat Jones thought about all this but I drove up to the garage from where I had originally stolen the trolley jack and parked on the forecourt.

Returning The Trolley Jack

The garage had been closed for the night (next to the Broad Leys pub on the Wendover Road, Aylesbury) and whilst no one was about I opened the van door and swiftly and quietly lifted the jack and placed it down on the forecourt. We then drove off as fast as we could. I often wondered what did the owner think when it was returned several months later.

The Broad Leys

The Broad Lees Wendover Road

I had no real advisers or any one who really knew the depths of my crimes and the amount of acquired stolen goods I had. I was faced with this problem what ever happens to me was no real concern but I did not feel I could involve others and get them into trouble. Mike West was very fearful in case I confessed all to the police and he must have been puzzled by what was going on. I had hoped he would have offered me the colour TV back and I would have given him the Citroen back but he wished to keep the Colour TV so I gave him the Citroen any way, as I felt I could not use it.

Dealing With Sin and Temptation

I did not need anyone to tell me what was right and wrong. I knew the difference and in particular the sin of fornication. This is sexual activity out side of marriage. Sexual temptation was really fierce and strong to me, but by the grace of our Lord Jesus Christ I fought the fight against them. So much so that I had to avoid meeting girls because of a natural inclination, which had I given into would not have been good for them or me. The words of Jesus are clear that the very thought of sex with another mans wife was to commit the sin of adultery and I agreed. This area of my life was really difficult to me and would be to any new believer.

Hippies In The Shed

Pat Jones began to acquire new friends and some were what we called hippies. They smoked pot, took drugs and generally did nothing but think about life etc. We invited them down to Mount Street as I felt it would be right to speak to them about Jesus Christ. About five or six came and they ended up sleeping in the shed.

The Shed at Mount Street

Whilst trying to speak the gospel to them I saw no real effect so I was disappointed. Perhaps one day I will see some fruit. I felt it OK to use the shed to house the hippies. About six lived in the shed for a number of weeks until they moved on. I thought I was putting it to good use.

My problems were solved by an intervention of God and his hand was clearly seen by all one year later.

The Hippy Shed

The stolen builders shed on Water Board Ground

This solution came by the knock on the door. It was the C.I.D when I was arrested for stealing the colour TV set from "Redfieds" old peoples home in Winslow. See part 1.

11 Going to Church

During the first few weeks of conversion unto Christ, in February 1970 there were a series of meetings held at Limes Avenue Baptist Church. The person speaking was Mr. Lance Pibworth and a girl called Geraldine Dunbar was being baptized.

Limes Avenue Baptist Church

Limes Avenue Baptist Church Aylesbury

I saw my first baptism here. After the meeting a man informed the congregation that if any one wanted to talk about any thing or ask questions they could stay behind. On this occasion I had brought Pat Jones and Paddy along to the meeting. I was dressed in my overalls and leather jacket, which I always wore when working on cars- I wasn't dressed up at all. I knew God did not look on the outward appearance but man may do so it did not bother me that we were not dressed for the occasion. I asked to see the minister Mr Sibthorpe and we three were invited into his study. I explained to Mr Sibthorpe about my conversion and wanted him to confirm that what I was saying to Pat Jones and Paddy was in fact true. On that occasion I half expected him to baptize me, there and then. I was under the impression, from reading the scripture, a minister of Christian were under direct command to baptize new believers as soon as they believed. I was very disappointed that he did not command me to be baptized that night. I knew nothing of church membership, modes of baptism, doctrinal distinctions and the like only that I should be baptized.

Shortly after this I met a man called Charley Tweedy, of the Church of Christ meeting (it is now a Seventh Day Adventist Church) at Stoke Mandeville Road, Aylesbury. He maintained that unless you are baptized you couldn't be saved.

He held some kind of responsible position in this Church so I explained to him about my conversion after which he gave me his telephone number to ring him if I needed too. I knew he was wrong about baptism but felt constrained to speak to him as I reasoned according to him, " I shall be damned if I die today if I am not baptized". I felt the need to reassure him that was not the case and he need not worry. When I rang him he seemed non plus nor moved with concern that I was not yet baptized. Again I was disappointed.

I Attend Various Churches

I had not been accustomed to go to any particular church but did go to a Sunday night meeting with Mrs. Knight. This was the Assemblies of God; Pentecostal church meeting at Rickford's Hill and Pastor Baker was the minister. Here I was received without any question and made to feel welcome. This was also the church Cyril Bryan went to and where I met Barry Crown.

Church of God near Stoke Mandiville

The Church of God, Mandeville Road Aylesbury

Rickford's Hill Assemblies of God

Assemblies of God Church Building.
(They referred to Five points)

Giving A Testimony

On one occasion I was asked to give an up to date testimony as to the Lords dealing with me that week. So dressed as I was, in my working clothes (overalls) not knowing a difference between working days or Sabbath days, I went to the front of the congregation and gave a clear and detailed account as to how I had combated the devils suggestion to steel a car battery that week.

I had some trouble with my car battery and I needed a new one. The temptation was this. Here was I, passing Adam's Garage, on the Tring Road in need of a car battery. Just over the fence belonging to the garage were several car batteries. All I had to do was nip over the fence and help my self. This was the way I had thought in the past and would have done just that all one time. Not now. This kind of thinking was the old man of whom I had to continually combat and I knew Satan had a hand in the matter. To avoid this temptation I rebuked the devil and told him to clear off in Jesus name. On that occasion I told them the exact language I had used to the devil. I said to the devil, "Bugger off Satan". I was quite unaware of the bad language I had used, and a number of years later Barry Crown remembered that Cyril Bryan gently reproved me for my speech. I did not know that I had said any thing amiss so was unaware that I had even been reproved for using bad language. I don't think I knew what the words meant any way.

I Am Baptized

I knew from the scripture and believed I should be baptized and I expected Pastor Baker of the Assemblies of God Church to command me to be baptized. I knew this was the command of Jesus and it signified the new birth, which I had already experienced. It also symbolized my union with the Lord Jesus Christ in his death and resurrection. That through his death I was to reckon myself dead to sin and my former sinful ways and that by his resurrection I was to reckon myself risen with him to the newness of life, which is in him. No one spoke to me about being baptized.

At that time shortly after the Limes Avenue meetings I was taken to another group of Christians meeting at Fleet Street in a large shed. These were West Indians and the Pastor was Mr Bruce from

Luton. This group also was having a series of meetings leading up to a baptism. I heard they had permission to use the baptistery at Limes Avenue Baptist Church so I asked Pastor Bruce to baptize me. He said he would and asked me to attend baptism classes that week with other people being baptized.

Fleet Street Pentecostal. Pastor Bruce from Luton was the overseer did not know what this was all about but presumed it was to make sure the person being baptized knew what it was all about. I was not told that after the baptism I was expected to join the church meeting at Fleet Street.

Fleet Street Pentecostal

Fleet Street Pentecostal Meeting Hall

I was baptized (dipped or immersed) upon the confession of my faith in the Lord Jesus Christ early one Sunday morning at 7.00 a.m. at Lime Avenue Baptist Church. My friends turned up, Pat Jones, Paddy, Paul Brooks, Mrs. Knight and Mrs. Chapski. Pastor Bruce baptized me in the name of the Father, Son and Holy Ghost, according to the command of our Lord Jesus Christ. Matth. 28 19.

Where Pastor Bruce, of the Assemblies of God Church, meeting at Fleet Street, Aylesbury, baptized me. I say this because I had met some that were teaching baptism was only valid if it was administered in the name of Jesus only. The reason being that they say the name of the Father is Jesus and the name of the Son is Jesus and the name of the Holy Spirit is Jesus. Gordon Smith, of Albert Street, informed me that some considered it was necessary to be re baptized in the name of Jesus only and that all other baptisms were invalid. I was not impressed by their reasoning and stress upon the singular name of Jesus to the exclusion of the Father and Spirit for Jesus had commanded baptism to be performed in the name of all three persons.

Mormons and Baptism

It was about this time that two Mormons spoke to me, whilst I was on the drive of our home in Finmere Crescent, and they were insisting that my baptism was invalid, as it was not conducted by a person having the right authority. As I had read the scripture and understood what baptism was all about, I realized that these men were wrong. In later years I came across similar views by some Primitive Baptists in the Philippines, but there too were wrong. I had been baptized, according to the terms of the lord Jesus, and that by immersion. My baptism was as valid as if John the Baptist had baptized me himself.

I knew that as far as I could discern from scripture, a man could be dipped, ducked, dragged, drenched, soaked, sprinkled or dribbled with 10 thousand gallons of water it would make not a scrap of difference to his spiritual state. Baptism could not affect the new birth, remove sin or make a natural man a spiritual man for that was the sole prerogative of Him that proceeded from the Father and was sent by the Son. John 15 26. The new birth being the effect not of the will of the flesh, nor of the will of man, but of God alone. John 1 13. Therefore Baptism could not save a sinner.

Baptism In The Spirit

I soon realized there were few churches in Aylesbury that believed the Baptism in the Holy Spirit was a distinct experience to being born again. I had no reason to doubt this and took it as a truth revealed in the Scripture.

I had no problem with this, as that was how I had read the bible. I actually felt I was baptized in the Spirit when I first believed and Jesus spoke to me. The only thing I seemed to lack was speaking in tongues. This had not happened.

I remember speaking to Mr Sibthorpe, the pastor of the Strict Baptist Church at Limes Avenue, about these things and he gave me an article written by John Stott who denied the Baptism in the Spirit, as I knew it. I was amazed at the way these people twisted and wriggled out of what God had plainly spoken about.

At that time I read as much as I could because this experience was not recognized by any other group of Christians apart from the Elim Pentecostal Churches. The best book that I read, at that time, was by Derek Prince called, "From Jordan to Pentecost". This gave a very clear and biblical position about speaking in tongues and it being the evidence of the baptism in the sprit.

The Christian Life

Being converted unto Christ was by no means an outward imposed principle I was not under a set of rules. I was not under any kind of legal fear to serve God. A rule, which says do this and you will be OK. There was no rest in works that I could do. . It was in fact the rule of faith. It was to walk by faith, without which it is impossible to please God.

I was what the scripture describes a, "new man", with an inward desire to follow the Lord Jesus Christ. The scripture expressed these as God writing His laws upon the fleshly tablets of the heart Heb 8. 10- 13. I began to read the bible straight away and I read the Good New bible within two weeks of receiving it, which was good going for me who could barely read. I was able to understand most of what I read and thought I understood it all at first.

The Divine nature of Jesus Christ

Before this time I was ignorant of its contents and very soon the principal points of the gospel became very clear to me: The divine nature, or deity of Jesus Christ was essential to understand. Hell was real just as heaven was sure. The actual reality of Adam and Eve and the fall of our first parents. The need for the shed blood of Jesus Christ to remove sin. That salvation and the forgiveness of sins was by faith alone, without works done by us. We were not under the Law of Moses as the Jews were but under Christ Jesus' under his rule by His law the gospel of love and grace.

I remember trying to tell one of my friends about following Jesus saying that I didn't have to give up any thing to become a Christian. I simple found that I did not want to do certain things any more. It was not difficult. This lad came up to me sometime after this and I am sure he misunderstood me and in front of several other lads said, isn't it right you don't have to give up any thing to be a Christian. He was expecting my answer to be no you can carry on just as you are. However I said that's right you don't have to give up any thing except sin. This silence him and I think they all got the point

Preaching the gospel not musical entertainment

I learned that Gods way of saving people was through the preaching of Christ and him crucified. That the new birth was a must. What amazed me was the apparent lack of zeal and knowledge of them that had professed faith in Christ. Also how these persons tended to try and entertain people by means of music instead of preaching.

Giving My Testimony

On the 22nd May 1972 I was asked to give my testimony to a meeting of peopel in Luton to about 400 people. I was not sure what the meeting was all about so I simply spoke as I felt right to do. I spoke the gospel as best I could. I was not fully conversant with the doctrines of grace but I was soon to learn the word more perfectly. Providentially this meeting was recorded and may be viewed on:

(Click here) Converted on LSD Trip 1972 David Clarke

Every Day The Sabbath Day

Every day was the Lords day to me, as I awoke I was conscious of the presence of God and when I slept, yea even in my dreams. I knew of no distinctions of days such as holy days or the Sabbath day for I knew these to be abolished or fulfilled in Christ. Jesus Christ being the sum and substance of all the Mosaic Sabbath. He was the body that cast the shadow of Moses Law. Col. 2 16-17.

Authorized Version of the Bible

At the Assemblies of God Church, at Richford's hill, we had a representative from the Trinitarian Bible Society speak. Mr Cyril Bryan confirmed his belief how important it was to use a good translation of the Bible. It was pointed out to me that the modern versions often left out or changed the texts of scripture, which clearly taught the deity of Christ. From that time I began to be cautious of new versions and was happy to stick with the Authorized Version.

This was helpful because all the books that I had begun to read quoted from the Authorized Version and not modern translations.

Giving Money

On another occasion I was attending the evangelical meetings at Fleet Street Pentecostal church and there was an appeal for money to support the young musicians. The man making the appeal was so moving I felt I ought to give all I could. I reached to my pocket and put in the collection plate all that I had. I was giving as unto the Lord. I was given to believe it was for the Lords work and it was needed. I was happy to give. Shortly after this the same steward who had collected the money came back to me from the front of the meeting hall speaking and motioning to me with the roll of notes in his hand saying was I aware how much I had given. I said yes it was OK. It was probably about £200 as I was still use to carrying that sort of money around with me (1970).

Shortly after this at another meeting there was a visiting evangelist called C D Gilbert preaching and he too made similar moving appeals for money. I had also spoken to him about the tattoo on my arm. This was because I regretted having it. He had been saying if I believed God then it would go by a miracle. I asked him would he pray to have it removed. At the same meeting he appealed for money with a prophecy saying the Lord had told him that each one had to go to their bank tomorrow and draw 10 per cent of all their money and give it to his fund the next day. It followed by another vision of an accident that was going to take place if it was not done. At the same meeting he said there was some one in the meeting that doubted God and they must get of their seat and come forward that if they did not then another warning was issued. I knew because of our previous talk he had me in mind. I also knew his prophecy and visions were not of God but generated to control and maneuver people like witchcraft. I opposed this and would have nothing to do with it.

I even went to Mr Eric Connet and informed him that this type of talk and action was not genuine. Mr Connet was a preacher at the church and had some influence and could have helped to correct error.

I write this for the sake of any that may feel similar pressure from them who say that God sends them. Not all that is spoken in the name of Jesus is of God.

The Lord loves the cheerful giver. The Lord does not need our money. He wants our hearts. All that we have is His when this is the case. We are stewards of all that we own. I learned like the Sabbath there is no Sabbath day for every day is Sabbath, so with money there is no tithe of 10 percent but all our possessions are the Lords, not just 10 percent.

Doing The Work Of An Evangelist

I found it my natural desire to preach and speak about Jesus to who ever I could. I remember working on a car in Mount Street one Sunday morning and a crowd of street kids all who I knew were playing around doing nothing. I was dressed in my overalls and leather jacket and I suggested they come with me to church. I decided to take them to a former Brethren Assembly called Granville Street Evangelical. I knew all these lads and realized we were all untidily dressed and that we may not be readily accepted. I knew however the scripture, which taught when you are invited to a meal, then take the lowest seat or place in the room. I decided we should adopt this principle so when we went into the hall, part way through the meeting. We slipped in and I beckoned them all to sit down on the floor. This we did without any noise. These lads were Paul Mitchell, Clifford Atley (Tatty), Michael Clarke and one or two others.

Granville Street Evangelical Church. Aylesbury (former Brethren) where I took the lads from the street to the meeting one Sunday morning. All the eyes of the congregation seemed to be on me. The meeting was stopped and a man came up and sure enough according to the scripture we were invited to sit on chairs towards the front of the meeting room.

Granville Street former Brethren Church

Granville Street Evangelical

Later on in that meeting they had what was called the "breaking of bread". They were an open communion church and their custom was to allow any believer to partake of the bread and wine. As the bread and the cup passed by they could help them selves. This bread and wine spoke of the death of Jesus till he come again. On this occasion however when the plate and cup came to our row it was passed by. We were judged as ineligible. I felt upset at this, as the stewards had judged us by an outward appearance and not as God. The problem then I suppose," I did not dress as a Christian".

I meet Peter Howe minister of the gospel

It was at this time I met Mr Peter Howe, a former pastor at Hearne

Bay Evangelical Church, who also befriended my friends Paul and Sue Aston. Paul was a bible student studying at Watford and valued any help he could get. It was soon after this that Mr Peter Howe became the Pastor of the Ivanhoe Particular Baptist Church and Paul and his wife became members.

I was a Hyper-Calvinist

Mr Howe made it clear to me he was against what he called Hyper Calvinism which he stated was the position of the Gospel Standard Baptists. It was not possible to make head way with him, as he seemed insistent he was right. He was what is now called a Fullerite. He mocked the term "Dead Elect" a term that I understood to refer to the elect who were still dead in their trespasses and sins. I had no problem with this term and I had heard Mr Hill from Luton, use this from time to time.

Doctrinal Summery

By this time I had come to a fairly comprehensive knowledge if gospel truth. I had come to believe in the Sovereignty of God. The divinity of the Lord Jesus Christ and his eternal Sonship.The value and authority of the Authorized Version of the bible. The everlasting purposed of the trinity of persons in the Godhead Predestination. Election, Justification by imputed righteousness and the new birth. and a call to glorify God in declaring these things to others. And having knowledge of these things more than others abl'ed me to discern the many errors of many who too professed faith in Christ. I was shocked at the ignorance of so many.

I Hear Dr Martin Lloyd Jones Preach

I was encouraged by my friend to go to various Christian churches and on one occasion the church meeting at Long Crendon who had a visiting preached at their yearly anniversary service, he was Dr Martin Lloyd Jones.

Long Crendon Evangelical Church

Long Crendon Evangelical Church

This is where I heard Dr Martin Lloyd Jones preach This man had a real gift to preach and I could tell he understood doctrine, but he was never outspoken as to his belief in absolute predestination, although you could tell he would know these things and many more. I heard him also on another occasion as he preached also at the Ivanhoe Particular Baptist Church where Peter How had become the minister, and where Mr And Mrs Dix senior were members, along with Paul Aston and wife.

12 Getting a Job

This was a problem to me but I believed in God and I believed that I knew that through the grace of our Lord Jesus Christ I would be provided for.

I had been dismissed from Radio Rentals due to my confession of stealing one of their colour Televisions from the old peoples home in Winslow. All I knew was how to fix televisions and I was qualified to City and Guilds 111. I decided to take the first Job offered me through the labour exchange; this was with a firm called Electroloid in Aylesbury. I was being employed as a wireman and on the interview the foreman called Dennis asked why I had left my former job. I was determined to be honest so I explained I had been dismissed for theft. At this he asked no more questions and I was given the job. I was also able to negotiate for one day off a week, without pay so I could finish off my college course.

I soon acquired a good knowledge of the equipment, which I wired up and began to read the circuit diagrams. My knowledge was such that I was able to fault find and develop test equipment.

Electroloid were a company involved in making equipment for electro plating and the particular equipment I was involved in making was the controllers for the automatic dipping of parts that required plating. A microprocessor now would replace the whole control unit.

I was soon asked to go out on sight and trace faults on installed equipment. After six months I had been given the task of commissioning a controller in Southend. This involved doing what ever was necessary to get the new equipment operative. I spent a week away from home and successfully completed my task. I drew diagrams for the owner explaining how to fix things if things went wrong. The owner of the firm was so pleased he invited me to apply for a job as the maintenance engineer. However I declined the invitation, as I was not ready to leave Aylesbury as I had just found Christian friends. On reflection I perhaps should have gone after the job as I now realize Christians are all around not just in Aylesbury.

Acting Foolishly

I began to get bored and impatient when I wasn't trouble shooting, which lead me to act foolishly. I began to experiment with charging lead acid car batteries and notice how the gasses were emitted from the battery when charged at a high rate of charge.

During my tea break I decided I wanted to collect these Hydrogen Gasses in a very large plastic bag. The size of which, would cover and over coat. I then charged the battery at the rate of 50 A/H and soon the bag was filled with gas. I thought what would happen if this ignited so decided on a way to do it. I took two match heads and wrapped thin wire around them and then connected this to two long pieces of insulated wire. I hid behind a large metal cabinet and connected the wires to the car battery. This acted as the detonator. The "Bang" was so loud, the building shock and the whole factor stopped. The foreman came looking to see what had happened. I was so embarrassed I came out from behind the cabinet like a scolded dog with my tail between my legs. The manager whose name was Tom, asked what was happening. Before he spoke my conscience slew me. I felt a fool and had dishonour Jesus. I simple said the hydrogen from the car battery had ignites but all was well. I told my work college all about it when they returned from break. I laughed about it but inwardly felt ashamed and had let Jesus down because I had acted foolishly. Boredom, pride and self-seeking became a snare to me and I soon began to joke and mess about at work and I felt unclean.

Working For Self

I had worked for Electroloid for some time and I began to be dissatisfied with the repetitive work although the opportunities, which were opening up to me, were not identified by me. Or rather I did not welcome the fact this may involve me travelling away from home to work and missing my Christian friends.

At that time my brother was out of work and Jock Macallion who was replacing windows on a council estate in Richmondsworth had offered us work. So hastily I handed my notice in and my brother began to work together again. This work soon how ever came to an end but we soon found work in a building site as carpenters. We were paid £10 a day, which was good money and this lasted a few weeks. One day on the site the men laughed at me when I told them about the Lord Jesus Christ. It didn't bother me but my brother for the first time ever stuck up for me and told them what I was saying was true.

Delivered from fire Morgan Sports Car

After this we decided we would have to earn money at welding and spraying cars. I had the equipment and know how so we hired a barn in Little Horward and set up in business. It was cold at that time of the year in January and so we heated the workshop with an oil-burning stove called a "Salamander". We were supposed to use heating oil or paraffin but we used old engine oil.

This heater we called, "Sally the oil burning goose", because of the shape of the chimney. This was a dangerous heater as I shall now relate and I believed God delivered me from a catastrophe.

Sally The Oil Burning Goose

One day I had in the workshop a Morgan sports car, which was in for re spray. It was worth £1000 (1972). I was working alone preparing this car with old Sally burning away merrily but she began to bubble and spit. This meant water was in the oil. Normally when this happened we would shut her down and re-lite her but on this occasion she would not have it, She was so hot she erupted and oozed out gallons of hot engine oil, which flooded the floor. This went up in flames. The flames leapt up to the ceiling burning the polythene ceiling stretched across the rafters. The fumes and smoke and heat were so terrific I cannot describe the event and terror that I found my self in. What should I do? What could I do? All Alone in the middle of a field, in a wooden barn with a pool of leaping flames just about to burn down the Barn, and the Morgan car in side. My heart immediately motioned my soul to seek direct help from God. I had done all I could now I prayed aloud unto God for his intervention. I then left the barn with my back to it and my eye fell on an old damp tarpaulin big enough to unfold and use as a fire blanket. In I went using the opened damp tarpaulin as a blanket and threw it over the burning pool. The flames were put out and smoke filled the place. The flames reappeared a few time but I soon put them out. God had answered my prayer and the flames were put out. The barn was saved and our equipment. Here God gave me the wisdom and courage and initiative to apply a natural remedy to my dilemma. God had saved me yet again. Praise God.

About 15 minutes later Mike West and his wife arrived and the knights for a visit. They said I looked as white as a sheet. No wonder, so I explained all that had happened. From that time Mr. Knight inquired about getting insurance against such accidents but the insurance company refused it on the grounds it was too risky. Shortly after this I decided I would have to look for another kind of work.

I Find Work In Lowestoft

I found a job advertised in a national paper working as a faultfinder at the Pye TV factory at Fleet, Lowestoft. This was in the spring of 1972. I decided to take the job. I moved into a Y.M.C.A hostel leaving my home in Aylesbury and parents house. At the same time KK took a job at the same factory and both he and his wife moved to Lowestoft for a short while. They eventually decided not to stay.

The Elim Pentecostal Church

I felt very lonely but soon got involved in the Elim Pentecostal Church in the town. I visited the local Christian bookshop and ordered a book called, "The Sovereignty of God", by Arthur Pink. It was soon made known amongst the young people that I was a Calvinist because the mother of one of the girls served me in the shop. I found this out one evening when I was attending the young peoples meeting and on that occasion the girl (about 20) said she thought I was a Calvinist as I had bought this book from the bookshop. She then asked me directly saying was I a Calvinist.

I am a Calvinist I Speak To The Elders

I said yes I believed in the sovereignty of God. She was the daughter of one of the senior members of the Elim Church. Her response was YUK! And she turned around and walked away. I certainly felt hostility then. I decided I would speak to the elders of the church about some of the things that I had learned but the idea of God choosing some and leaving others was not received very well at that church. They also rejected the doctrine of Particular Redemption.

Whilst at the Y.M.C.A. I became very lonely and woke with a bad taste in my mouth. My mouth in fact tasted like the inside of a zoo keepers boot. This was a saying of Mike West. I decided to treat my self and ended up very ill. I began to take Andrews lived salts and at first this was very refreshing. It was so good I began to take it all the time, until one day at lunch I had stomach pains and when I tried to eat a salad then pain increased intensely. This set off a reaction, which lasted months and ended up me being treated for duodenal ulcers.

I Speak At The Factory

I remember speaking to one of the workers at the Lowestoft factory about Jesus Christ. I had told him all have sinned and come short of Gods standard. He did not accept he was a sinner as he had lived a good life and loved football. He asked me how going to a football match could possibly be wrong in the eyes of God and I gave a quick retort saying the scriptures say, "Go not with a crowd to do evil." I was thinking of the football hooligans but at that he said I was ridiculous.

In the summer holiday of that year I returned to Aylesbury and decide to apply for a Job as a television service engineer, in Tring. This was at Mr. C. J. Ward & Son. I got the job and so I left the Pye Lowestoft Factory.

13 Pentecostal Holiness Bierton

When I returned to Aylesbury, the summer of 1972, I attended the opening services of the newly opened Pentecostal Holiness Church, in Bierton, Buchinghamshire. A Rev. Gordon Hills, from High Wycombe, was the preacher and was the pastor at an Elim Pentecostal Church.

Pentecostal Holiness Church Bierton

Pentecostal Holiness Church Bierton

Five points of Calvinism

There was a series of meetings for one-week and I soon realized that he too was a Calvinist as each night his theme in preaching was one of the five points of Calvinism: Total depravity, Unconditional election, Limited atonement, Irresistible grace, and Perseverance of the saints. I certainly felt encouraged and assumed Mr Harrison the minister of the Bierton Pentecostal Holiness Church were in agreement with these truths. At last I felt here was a place where truth and the baptism in the spirit went hand in hand. I was so encouraged.

I began to attend as a regular and got involved in the young people's work and very soon we had far to many kids from of the street to deal with. I was hopeless at discipline and how to control them. There was a wonderful opportunity but I found I was out of my depth and did not cope. Not only that but no one else knew how to cope either so the youth work was closed.

Working for Mr C J Ward and Son

It was during the summer holidays when the Lowestoft Pye factory closed down that I looked for work nearer my home and I applied for an interview with C.J. Ward and Son, of Tring. When

I arrived for the interview it was said by Mr Ward, the owner, the reason why I had got the job was because I was on time exactly. I had not planned it that way I just arrived at that time. I started work on the 14th August 1972. With a salary of £2000 per year. I was very thankful to God for His mercy to me.

City and Guilds London Institute Award

During my time working for C.J Ward and Son I completed my college learning a Luton College of Technology and was awarded a final Certificate In Radio and Television Servicing, including a Colour Television Endorsement. This was course 48 and was the highest qualification in that subject that was later to prove very useful.

This was where I worked. However none of the staff at C.J. Ward had time for Christian things. In fact I felt I was considered as less than nothing. I was ridiculed when I said in the bible God mentioned there was a Synagogue of Satan. I was not the only one treated with contempt however as they also treated the apprentice as a servant, a and often humiliated him, which he did not like.

C J Ward and Son where I worked

C. J. Ward and Son. 72 Weston Road, Tring, Herts

Dr Gill's Practical and Theological Divinity

Whilst working for C. J Ward and Son the practice was to break for lunch between one and two o'clock and whilst all the staff returned to their homes for lunch, I was left alone for an hour each day during my break from work.

It was during this time I studied the scriptures and read various Christian books. You might say, "I esteemed Thy word more than my necessary food." I read "Mercies of a Covent God", By John Kershaw, the life of John Warburton, Martin Luther's "Bondage of the Will," William Huntington's "Kingdom of God taken by prayer". I also read Dr John Gill's Body of practical and Doctrinal Divinity. All of these books I had managed to obtain from America. It was my friend Peter Murray who recommended these theological books to me. I found this book very, very helpful and it was here that I learned the extent of the doctrines of grace. It was my school of learning, which was to last a number of years.

In my reading I studied John Calvin's Institutes of Christian Religion and in all I had to learn so many new words that my list covered several pages of full size paper. I had come a long way since reading comic and paperback books like James Bond, by Ian Fleming. All of these theological and spiritual books I now consider recommend reading. One excellent book was on by J.C. Philpot, The Eternal Son ship of Christ" along with an excellent sermon, "Winter Before Harvest".

I Leave The Pentecostal Holiness Church

At this time I had become unsettled at the Pentecostal Church over a few issues that I did not know how to deal with. When explaining to the minister, a Mr. Harrison, that I wanted to leave because they did not teach the doctrines of grace. He said I ought not to leave because of a little bit of doctrine being different. This I found rather strange and did not agree.

A Denial of Imputed Righteousness

I found the issue with Mr E.C. Connet serious because he did not believe or teach that the righteousness of the Lord Jesus Christ was imputed to us for our Justification. Although he had been a help to me he was one of the teachers in the church.

Mr Harrison said he believed in the total depravity of man (not that he used these words) he said that there must have been a little bit of good, though ever so small in us for God to love us and want to save us.

I knew that God set his love upon us and we had need of mercy and there was no good thing in us to recommend us to God. God did not love us because we are lovable. I relised God set his love upon us (the elect) before the foundation of the world. God did not love every body like this.

Scripture Should Guide Us Not Feelings

I also found the issue of being led by feelings rather that the Word of God very awkward.

I began at that time to question many things and realized how easy it would be to be deceived if we were lead by our feelings and not the Word of God.

An example of this was shown to me when the pastor Mr Harrison informed the church that the Lord had shown him the bungalow, which he wanted him to have. This was in Windermere Close in Aylesbury. He said he knew it was the Lords will because he had offered the people a cut price and it was immediately accepted. This was the means, which Mr Harrison knew it was the Lords will.

The next thing the church was informed was that there were 17 clauses in the deed of purchase, which were unacceptable, and therefore the Lord did not want Mr Harrison the buy the property. This was an example of what I mean, the Lord no more told Robert Harrison to buy the bungalow than he did to refrain from buying. I did not feel or believe that was being lead of the Holy Ghost.

Arminian Righteouness

Mr E.C. Connet was another man whom I respected and he attended the Pentecostal Church at Bierton. One day in conversation with him, about the things of God and what I was reading and learning, he turned on me and said it was doctrinally wrong to say the righteousness of Christ was imputed to us for our Justification. This was because each one of us had to have a righteousness of our own. Jesus had his own righteousness for himself and we to needed our own righteousness.

I was shocked and on every occasion I could I sought to reason with him, from scripture, that what I spoke about was true. I argued that as in Adam all Die so in Christ should all be made alive. So the imputation of sin (in Adam) also pointed to the imputation of righteousness (in Christ).

That as the sin and guilt of Adam (note: not the sin of Eve) brought about the imputation of sin to the whole of humanity so the righteousness of Jesus - his life and death brought about a righteousness that was imputed to all that believe. I stated that on this account only do we have right standing with God.

One Sunday morning he turned on me in anger and said all I did was talk about doctrine and never about the Lord.

I felt so wounded I just did not know what to do; I had always looked to this man for support and help. I groaned in spirit feeling so alone in this situation. I wondered how should I handle this.

These were the reasons for me leaving the Pentecostal Holiness Church at Bierton.

I Am Made Redundant

In 1973 during the economic crisis and the Governments imposition of a three-day week C. J Ward and Son fell upon hard times. And I received a letter dated 8th of Feb. 1974 informing me of my redundancy. This date became significant to me.

I was at home at the time of receiving this letter and when I realized I was unemployed I looked at the date of the letter. From this date I took courage, which helped me fight the haunting fears of not being able to get a job due to my past criminal record. The Judge Col. Tetley at the Aylesbury Magistrates Court had given me a conditional discharge from punishment from the crimes I had committed that lasted for three years. This was on 9th February 1971. In other words my three years (to the day) was up. I could now seek work knowing I was free from condemnation under the law and had no need to inform a future employer of my past criminal record (Unless they asked).

It was as though my God and Father were saying to me don't worry I will take care of you. I could now look for work knowing and feeling I was free with a clean sheet to start from.

Letter informing me of my redundancy

From: C.J. Ward & Son 8th February 1974

To: Mr. D Clarke 37 Finmere Crescents Aylesbury.

Dear David,

It is with deep distress the due to the present day economic position I greatly regret that we have to terminate your employment as from today week.

Rest assured this has no adverse reflection on your work or you present unfortunate illness, and will be more than pleased to give you any reference, which may be of help to you.

Should the economic position improve I would be pleased to consider any application you may wish to make at any time, and always pleased to see or help in any way possible.

Yours Sincerely,

C. J. Ward. Enclosed P.45 and N.I. Card.

Please note we have sent off your National Health certificate and have not deducted any money from this on next week's remuneration.

The following reference was enclosed

To whom it may concern.

Mr. David Clarke has been in our employ since August 1972 and has always proved himself to be industrious, courteous, efficient and reliable worked whom we have been pleased to have on our Staff. Since being with us he has taken advantage of Day College to obtain his City and Guilds endorsement to add to his previous knowledge and certificates. We can thoroughly recommend him for any similar position and wish him well in such. We regret that the present government and country unrest and economic position leaves us with great regret to dispense with his services.

C. J Ward.

14 Working for Granada TV Rentals

It was within two weeks of my redundancy that I had obtained a new job, working for Granada TV Rentals, as a service technician.

I started work for Granada TV Ltd. on 25/2/1974 being paid £37.27 per week. This car had a company logo printed on the side of the vehicle so one knew for whom I worked. I say this because this became a point of issue at a later date. I also was granted £3.72 per week as a vehicle allowance.

Granada TV Rentals Aylesbury

Michael Nicholson left, David. Phil Reason middle, Tony Burnham and Mrs Royce-Taylor

I Am Promoted To Service Manager

Within 6 months of working at Granada I was promoted to workshop manager and I found the work very challenging and rewarding. I found working for Granada a fresh breath of air and got on real well. The only problem was I worked too hard and was inefficient which led to a real case of depression, which I will relate later.

My visit to Northern Ireland

I was encouraged to have a break from work and in July 1974 I was invited by Owen McCrystal to visit his home in Northern Ireland. He lived in a town called Omagh in County Tyrone. Owen had a television business called, "Crystal T.V.". He started his business by bringing a van load of second hand T.V. sets from England to the town of Omagh and began to rent them out and repair washing machines and TV's. I was invited out to teach one of his employee's, called Ivan. I taught him how Colour T.V.'s work. Owen maintained he was a genius as he could fix TV sets without knowing how they worked. He maintained any one could repair a T.V. set if they knew how they worked so he must be a genius as he could repair them not knowing how they worked. Owen's wife was a Catholic and I think they viewed my religious beliefs with scepticism.

I was unaware of all the conflicts in Ireland and completely ignorant. I had heard people speak evil of Ian Paisley and all I knew was that the Rev. Ian Paisley had preached this sermon called, "Second Mile Religion" and I knew from that sermon he was a man of God and preached the truth about the Lord Jesus Christ. I decided on my way through Belfast I would stop the night and visit the Martyrs Memorial Church where Ian Paisley was the pastor the next day.

Martyrs Memorial Church building, Ravens hill Road Belfast

I Seek Ian Paisley

When I arrived in Belfast I was amazed to see all the soldiers with guns checking every body and watching out for trouble. It was the 12th of July 1974. When I arrived on the streets in Belfast I noticed all the shops and doorways were barred up and the streets very clear with soldiers on every corner. I was unaware of what the 12th of July was all about. It was the end of the day and a lot of parades and marches had gone on that day. It was a day of celebration to some people. I ended knocking on a guest house door to find two ladies running this guest house. I had arrived unannounced with a large suspicious suite case in my hand from England. I said would like to stay the night and asked if they knew where Martyrs Memorial Church building was. They looked at me "gone out" and asked me what was an English man was doing visiting Belfast during all these troubles. I said I wanted to hear Ian Paisley preach. I said I had heard him preach on a record and he preached the gospel. They said they were Catholics and they would be too afraid to go and hear him preach even though they would like to. They made me welcome and I had a pleasant stay learning a bit about the troubles in Northern Ireland

Suspicious Looking Suit Case

In the morning as I carried my suspicious looking suit case through the streets of Belfast I had occasion to ask a milkman the way to Martyrs Memorial Church and he replied I was in the wrong part of Belfast to be asking directions to that place and directed me along a certain road. I realized this must have been a Catholic area but I was really so naive I did not know what was going on at all.

The Wrong Part of Belfast

I ended up in a Newspaper shop asking directions and my eye caught the picture of a man called "Carson", on a post card. To make conversation I asked the shopkeeper who was this person Carson and she spoke scathingly to me say I ought not to ask such questions like that. I then realized I must have been in the wrong area.

I arrive at the Martyrs Memorial Church and Dr Paisley was preaching. It was a very large building with figureheads of the martyrs all around the building. Dr Paisley preached faithfully the truth about Jesus Christ and could not understand why people should oppose him like I had heard. In that meeting I heard no mention of Politics I only heard about Jesus Christ and what he had done for sinners. I concluded it must be his tone of voice or way of speaking I felt people must not be listening to his message but rather the tone of voice. I could imagine him speaking against the enemies of the truth using his tongue like a "Bastard file". After the meeting I asked Dr Paisley to direct me to some one who could help me get to Omagh, as I was a visitor. I finally got transport that day to Omar and ended up joining a group of Christians, from the Free Presbyterian Church in Omar. I was given an orange sash and joined their march along the streets and lanes of Omar. We then went to a meeting and the Preacher was Rev. William Macray.

I had a good time in Omar staying at my friend's home. Owen did not believe the gospel, he was a nominal Roman Catholic and we had long talks about the things of God. He employed a mancalled Ivan who confided in me that he was a Christian but he did not like to say too much to Owen as it might not go down too well for him and Owen could give him a hard time.

The pace of life seems so much slower than that in Aylesbury and every one I spoke to seemed to have a knowledge as to what it means to be, "born again" or to "be saved". Even Owen and his wife, who were Catholics, knew these terms and used them. It was not like this in England. I had a good time in Ireland and would like to go again.

We Employ Michael Nicholson

When I returned from my holiday we had a vacancy for a technician so in my capacity of workshop manage I contacted Michael Nicholson, of C J Ward, asking him if he wanted a job with Granada. He was the apprentice of C J Ward, and whilst working for them he told me he wanted to leave as soon as he could. He was fed up with being treated second rate. He hated having to stub out John Wards cigarette ends.

He came to Granada and past all the tests and was accepted. He joined Granada as a Technician in October 1974.

I am poached by C. J Ward and Son

It was in October 1974 that I received a call from Mr. C J Ward asking me if I wanted a job.

I went for the interview and asked all kinds of questions as this company had recently made me redundant. I explained my problem about being a Christian and having the three-year conditional discharge over Mr Ward and he seemed sympathetic saying he had not realized this at all. I told him about the Lord Jesus Christ and what he had done for me. He said had I told him these things before he may have been able to help.

I was offered £50 per week (I was only getting £ 40 a week at Granada) plus a company car - with a day off - I was really tempted. When he offered me £60 per week and would I start straight away and not work my week's notice I said yes, thinking this was the right thing to do. I had never had things so good. He wanted me to make a decision there and then, on the spot, without hesitation.

I thanked God for the promotion and this offer and Mr Ward seemed pleased as though he had won a prize. Here I was being offered £1000 per year more than I was getting at Granada.

After the interview I felt and asked the question was it the right thing to do and thought about my boss Tony Burnham - how would he cope? He had been good to me and got me the promotion at Granada. I then had second thoughts.

After thought and prayer I felt I should not take up the job so I rang Mr Ward saying I had decided against working for him.

The following is his letter, which shows I had obviously upset him. His letter certainly caused me concern so he got my reply.

Letter from Mr. Ward

Dear David,

I have to thank you for your letter dated 8th October, I have personally not written before as I have been trying to reconcile your actions with your religious beliefs, to this "God which spoke to you".

You spent all one Friday afternoon asking about four pages of questions, I began to think it was myself asking for a job, which apparently were answered to your satisfaction and you agreed to take the position at a wage well above your actual capabilities but I was willing to accept, capabilities which in part we paid for you to acquire, you shock hands with me to seal the bargain and when I asked if you required a contract you paid me the compliment of saying " No your word is good enough Mr Ward". What a pity that I cannot now pay the same compliment to you, as within 24 hours you had broken our agreement. One does not expect this from religious people of conviction; your religion is obviously different to mine. Just how it this compatible with seducing our apprentice away from us before he had completed his contract for which he so willingly, and at his own request signed for.

Yours Sincerely,

C J Ward.

My reply to Mr Ward

This reply from Mr Ward irritated me and I felt he was acting in spite so I wrote my reply 31/11/74

Dear Mr Ward,

I am sorry to hear you seem so bitter about my break of contract with you. I wrote firstly to apologize for inconveniencing you and wasting your time and money. My conscience had troubled me over saying I would start work for you and then turning your offer down.

What more can I say I know me saying sorry will not undo what has happened all I can do is apologize. Please accept my appology.

Surely you realized the reason why I asked you so many questions was because it was such a major decision I had to make. You wanted an immediate answer straight away so I had to weigh all the facts so to act in my own interest. Just as you acted in your own interest when you dismissed me before.

I am most grateful for your efforts in supplementing my training, which I realize, cost you money also. But Mr. Ward you did sack me I never intended to leave. And therefore I am under no obligation what so ever to you in that respect.

I did explain to you about Michael the last time we met. I hid nothing from you.

Whilst I worked with Michael he told me as soon as his apprenticeship was finished he was leaving you. It was under this impression I contacted him regarding working for Granada. I thought his contract finished this summer gone.

I never intended that he should break any contract. I explained to him that you had always treated me fairly and that he must make his own decisions. It was well within your own ability to freely agree to disannul the contract without aggravation to you or Michael. I am sure Michael would not have left unless you had agreed to dismiss him.

As to enticing and seducing him away and your religion being different from mine on this point it seems that is what you attempted to do with me when asked me to leave Granada without giving a weeks notice.

Your last point I admit my religion is different to yours.

The Lord God whom you speak against is my Lord and God. He is your creator and both you and me are accountable to him alone for our actions, words and thoughts. If He chooses to start a work of change in such a sinful person as my self and you speak against his work it is He you defy and not I. The Lord Jesus Christ came into the world to save his people from their sins. Not for the sake of the righteous. Only sick people need a doctor. I am the sinner and am in need of his forgiveness and mercy.

However I don't like upsetting people I hope you receive my answer to your letter and consider what I say. I don't wish to be on bad terms with you as I like you and admire your business ability.

Yours Sincerely,

David Clarke. Shortly after this Mr Ward was in serious difficulties, which those that know him will know all about.

Victor Prince the Crombie over coat

"In all thy ways acknowledge him and he shall direct thy paths"

The following extract is taken from my loose-leaf diary and relates to a remarkable experience, which demonstrates the wonder and way of the Spirit of God leading and teaching a believer.

On Friday, 30/8/74, it was my day off from work and during the day I was rebuilding our garage roof at 37 Finmere Crescent, Aylesbury. During the day I was thinking about the way God had dealt with me and led me thus far. I realized that each one that was child of God was special and God dealt with them personally. Each person had his own peculiar special work of God in his or her own life. This work was a personal work done in no other it was special to them. All were saved, being involved in a common salvation, but the work of God was peculiar and special to that individual. In this frame of mind I began to wonder about a particular trouble I had caused a certain Mr Victor Prince, many years earlier.

Mr Prince was a tailor and some years previously (about 5 years) I had employed him to make a Crombie over coat when I had just been released from Borstal. It was to cost £45 and I gave him £5 deposit to start the work. At that time I was living in London doing Government training course learning about Television servicing. My brother was due to be released from prison on home leave. He had a coat made by some one a year previously and on his home leave he came to see the coat before it was finished. After hearing how long it had been in the making he said it was taking far too long and he persuaded me to tell Mr Prince it was not good enough. He then picked holes in the coat in front of Mr Price and told him top stick the coat. Later on the telephone we were both nasty to Mr Prince. He thought I was saying I could not afford it and offered to keep it until I could. It was made especially for me and really would nod do any one else. I left it with Mr Price and thought no more of it until then when I was on the garage roof.

I felt bad about the way I had treated him and would have apologized to him if I could.

Contemplation On Divine Predestination

My mind was thinking upon the subject of predestination and reasoned that God had planned every thing in creation to bring about a display of his glory and Grace in Jesus Christ. I was a person created by God being responsible and accountable to God having a definite purpose for my existence. I was alive and active but God was working in and through me. I had been predestined to obtain salvation by Jesus Christ. This work of salvation being the means of displaying God's love, mercy and grace towards me. It was not my free will that saved me but Gods free grace that made me willing in the day of His power. Therefore glory was due to God the Father,

Son and Holy Spirit.

Feeling wretched over the way I treated Mr Prince I had resolved in my mind to pay the money I owed Mr Prince and apologized to him if ever I was to meet him again.

It was one week later on a Sunday the 8 /9/74 that I saw the amazing hand of God at work. Mrs Knight of Mount Street spoke to me on the way home from the Pentecostal Church at Bierton. She said her and Ken had met someone they had not seen for a long time. I stopped her speaking and told her it was Mr. Prince. She was amazed and wondered how I knew. They had met Mr. Prince in Aylesbury and he had though of asking Ken to repair his TV as it had gone wrong. They said perhaps they would ask me to do it and if he remembered me. He certainly did. Mrs Knight was able to inform him of me becoming a Christian and he left it to them to make arrangements to get his TV fixed.

I had not mentioned a thing to Mrs Knight and there was no way of this happening by chance. God had done it.

The first Sunday after this we all went to visit Mr Prince but he was out at a harvest thanks-giving service at a Methodist church. So we made arrangements to go on 18th of September. At first I did not know what to say as I was extremely embarrassed so I said very little. I soon repaired the TV and then spoke to Mr. prince about what had happened. I apologized and offer to pay the money I owed him quite forgetting about the coat.

It turned out he still had the coat even after several moves and the money owing was £38. All I was asked to pay was £34 so I paid this by cheque

(Cheque number 183901). I now had my coat; it is dark blue

Crombie over coat and still have it today.

15 Bierton Strict and Particular Baptists

I felt lead and right to leave the Pentecostal Church and attend the Bierton Strict and Particular Baptist Church. I felt I could no longer in conscience stay or continue at the church even though I had affection for all the people there when there was a company of people across the road at the Bierton Strict and Particular Baptist Church. They held to and professed the very gospel I had received. From that time I commenced to attend as a member of the congregation at this cause of truth.

Distinguishing Doctrines of Grace

A friend, who lived in Wendover, Mr Alan Benning, informed me that the Strict and Particular Baptist Church at Bierton, believed the doctrines of grace and that a Mr J Hill, a Gospel Standard minister (of Luton Ebenezer Church) was engaged to preach on an anniversary service in the near future. I was keen to hear him preach. So I began to attend their weeknight prayer meeting.

My hopes had been raised that I would hear the truth about Gods free sovereign grace for it was reported that Mr. Hill was a Gospel Standard minister. I was given to believe I would hear those truths preached by William Huntington, William Gadsby and John Kershaw. I had read their autobiographies and found their writings very helpful during my time at C. J. Ward and Son, and was encouraging by them as they gave all the praise and glory to Jesus Christ the Lord and not to man.

I started to go the Bierton church just before Mr Hill preached that anniversary year on the Wednesday night prayer meeting, and sat at the back of the chapel. At that time I had no idea of the manor of service or church government nor of any other ministers engaged to preach on a Lords Day or weeknight services.

Denham's Hymns

The folk at Bierton used Denham's collection of hymns called "The Saint's Melody" and the substances of these hymns were very pleasing to me. Even the singing pace was different to all the other churches I had attended being that much slower.

Miss Bertha Ellis would play the foot-peddled organ and the hymnbook used was Denham's Collection 19th century. The hymn singing was about half the speed of the hymns sung at other churches and the words of the hymns were wonderful and glorifying to God. The stile of meeting was generally Hymn, reading from the scripture (Authorized version King James), Hymn, Prayer, hymn, Sermon, finally hymn and then a closing prayer. A short while after I began to attend on a regular basis I was asked by Mr. King if I would engage in prayer when asked too. It was the custom for men to pray the women would keep silent.

I did engage in prayer and after the meeting Mr King asked me kindly to pray in future in reverent language and address God in terms of thee and thou rather then you and your because it could offend people. That was there custom.

I went away feeling offended thinking all kinds of thoughts. I was upset thinking what difference does the language make etc. but I bowed to their request and adopted their form of speech in order not to offend. I now find it difficult, to day, to break from that habit of using thee and thou. I.e. reverent language when addressing God.

Bierton Baptist Chapel

Bierton Strict and Particular Baptist Chapel. The Church was founded in 1831

The Doctrines of the Gospel

I was convinced the Word of God was infallible and the only rule of conduct and religious practice. I believed the scripture taught us of a sovereign true and living God. That though God be one God, the only self existent being, one in essence and nature, there subsists in the divine essence three divine persons; The Father, Son and Holy Ghost. I believed that person were truly and properly God by nature and that from all eternity. I believed that the divine nature was not divided but one in essence and each divine person possessing the whole of the divine essence.

I believed the scripture taught the Lord Jesus Christ is that only begotten son of the Father full of grace and truth, the only saviour of (Gods elect) lost sinners. He being one person yet having two natures. Being God from all eternity the divine Son of the Father and by nature truly God. Yet at the incarnation he took to himself that which he was not; our human nature and so was truly man.

Hence the glorious complex person of Jesus Christ is the Christ that should come into the world to save sinners. I believed that His glory was veiled during his time of humiliation.

This Jesus Had Called Me

I believed this same Jesus had called me by his grace directly and made him self-known to me, outside of the circles of any Christian church. It was he whom I sought and believed in when I went and heard Mr. Hill preach at the Bierton Anniversary Service he preached the distinguishing doctrines of grace very clearly. At that time I did not know many preachers who preached these things except, I had heard I heard Dr. Ian Paisley, on a record and that sermon was called "Second mile religion".

I had also heard Dr. Martin Lloyd Jones preach but he seamed not to emphasize the distinguishing doctrines of Grace, although it was evident that he believed in the sovereignty of God.

The churches I had attended, until this time, around Aylesbury and district appeared to only know of Arminian doctrine and held to a the false doctrine of universal love towards all mankind and a general atonement as distinct to particular redemption.

Not all preaching was good

Not all the preaching at Bierton was good as we had a range of visiting ministers. Some times I would groan and suffer 45 minute of difficult things to listen too. Very few were Gospel Standard ministers and some were opposed to the Gospel Standard position, they often liked to refer to the 1689 confession, a confession that I soon realized was in error. The Scottish Free Presbyterians Churches boasted of their 1646 confession as the best. Again I soon learned that this too was in error. Some of these preachers used notes

166

whilst others did not. Not that that helped, as some I felt would have benefited from notes to preach. Some preachers would not use notes and speak as they felt lead too. But I realized that too was no guarantee they could be listened too.

Miss Ruth Ellis

She was one of our members and she was a gem of a person and always ready to share a word or hymn. On several occasion mid week we would visit her and she would read from her books stories about choice Christian experience.

Unfortunately Ruth died and she ended her days at Bethesda Home in Harpendon.

Mr and Mrs Gurney were members and their son John attended our church as a member of the congregation. I noticed a plaque over the fireplace of their home and it read, "A Sabbath well spent brings a week of content but a Sabbath profaned, what err may be gained is a sure for runner of sorrow. I noticed this, as when I looked at the churches original trust deed there was no mention of Sabbath day keeping. It was only brought up in the spurious set of article presented to me when seeking membership of the Church.

Miss Bertha Ellis

She was a mother in Israel and looked after most of the visiting ministers and played the organ at our meetings, giving way to visiting people who were also able to ply such as John Snuggs and Mr Dix from Ivanhoe.

Miss Bertha Ellis informed me that the church was formed in 1831 and opened by the son of John Warburton. She had the minutes of that meeting which were signed in his own hand and the deed of trust upon which the church was formed. These articles of religion were very good and acceptable.

After my warm reception I was looking forward to hear Mr Hill of Luton preach at the anniversary service.

It was good to hear Mr Hill preached and he invited me and Alan Benning to his home in Luton and I spent time with him at his home.

Church Anniversary Services

During this time I was able to take time out of my work and attend the various Gospel Standard Baptist church anniversary services, which were held by other causes of truth. And it was because I was working for Granada TV rentals that I was a blessing because I was able to take time out of work to attend the various church anniversary services in our area. Had I been working for C.J. Ward and Son this would have proved impossible? I really looked forward to these meetings and seeing the various friends of our church and I often took with me some of the members of ours. These churches that we visited were, Linslaid, Prestwood, Barton Le clay, Waddesdon Hill, and Keeche's Chapel, in Winslow.

We also had our own anniversary services and visitors from the different churches in our area and from a far who came to our meetings.

It was at our anniversary meetings that I learned not every one was in favor of the Gospel Standard Articles of Religion. In particular Mr Dix senior expressed it and his wife (parents of Kenneth Dix the Pastor of Dunstable Baptist Church) that they opposed the articles and some, of the ways these Strict Baptists. I felt uneasy about hearing such things but kept them to my self.

Linslaid Strict and Particular Baptist Church

Linslaid Strict and Particular Baptist Chapel

This is where Mr Collier was the pastor. During this time Mr Alan Benning informed me of the Linslaid Strict and Particular Baptist, which was a listed Gospel Standard church, and from that time were we able to visit from time to time.

On one anniversary service we went to hear a Mr Andrew Randall's who apparently had been involved with the Brethren and I could tell from our conversations that he was aware of doctrinal issues of the day, and he had a very serious disposition.

Waddesdon Hill Strict and Particular Baptist Chapel

Another favourite anniversary was at Waddesdon Hill, where Mr James Hill was the preacher. This was a Gospel Standard cause and was founded as a Particular baptist church in 1752.

Waddesdon Hill Gospel Standard Chapel

Waddesdon Hill Gospel Standard Cause

Waddesdon Hill Strict and Particular Baptist Chapel where we heard Mr Hill, Pastor of Luton Ebenezer church, preached. and Mr Collier. I use to take Bertha and Ruth Ellis, Alan Benning and Grace knight to these meetings. I remember these meetings with fondness

Benjamin Keeche's chapel at Winslow

At this time, on one occasion each year, an anniversary meeting was held at Ketch's Chapel, the oldest place of non-conformist place of worship in England and Dr Ian Paisley was the preacher. I attended this meeting for a number of years afterward and was greatly blessed and heard Mr Collier from Linslaid and Mr Ramsbottom from Luton preached at those meetings.

Benjamin Keeche's Chapel at Winslow

Keeche's Chapel

Benjamin Keeche's Chapel Winslow where I heard Dr Ian Paisley, Mr Collier and Mr Ramsbottom preached.

Prestwood Strict and Particular Baptist Church

Prestwood Gospel Standard

Another one of the local churches that we attended on their anniversary services (that is Alan Benning, Bertha and Ruth Ellis and Mrs Grace Knight) was the Prestwood Strict and Particular Baptist Church. This church was a Gospel Standard listed Church.

Prestwood Strict and Particular Baptist Chapel. I was here that I first heard Mr Sparling-Tyler preach.

Barton Le Clay Hope Chapel Strict Baptist

It was at this chapel that I took both Bertha and Ruth Elis to hear Stanley Delves and on another occasion to hear Jessie Delves preach.

Meeting Other Christians and Friends

During this time I met John Snuggs from Eaton Bray who had come to work in Aylesbury. He came to our weeknight prayer meetings at Bierton and he introduced me to some of his friends who attended the young peoples meeting that were held once a month at Bethel Strict Baptist Church in Luton. Mr Ramsbottom would give a talk or lecture and afterward we were invited to the Bethesda Rest Home at Harpendon where we were given refreshments and able to meet and talk to other people from the various churches in the district. I found these meetings very helpful to meet other Christians.

Excessive work and depression

At this time I was working for Granada TV Rentals and within a few months had been promoted to Workshop manager. I thoroughly enjoyed the job but I found I spent more and more time thinking about work than any thing else. I was taken up with work.

The things of God paled. I went to the meetings but I could not shut off from work.

I soon realized I was not a good manager and found myself doing all the work. I worked long hours and my days off. Although I got the job done and we were the best branch in the district it was all at my expense.

After several months of this intense work I began to find I could not cope with the stress the job demanded and went though horrifying bouts of agony and fear of not being able to cope. I began to think

I was experiencing flash backs from the bad trip on LSD. This time how ever it was in the cold light of day with no LSD etc. I was so ill I wanted the ground to open up and swallow me thinking this would remove me from all the pain I was going through.

I Cried Out To God But Heavens as Brass.

My manager Tony Burnham, who was not a Christian had noticed a change in me as at one time, when I first began to work there, I continued my habit of reading during my lunch time break and he noticed me reading John Calvin's book on Daniel.

Due to my excessive workload I forsook my devotions and worked all the hours I could.

One afternoon on the garage roof at Mount Street I cracked up and realized I could not cope any more. I couldn't make decisions I could not think straight every problem was too much to face.

I ended up resigning from the manager's job and becoming a normal technician. This ended in me feeling a failure and depression set in that lasted about 3 years. It was during this time I learned that the Christian life could be very painful, which caused me to seek deliverance and rely totally on the God of all grace. I found my self-feeling very lonely and wondered if I would ever find a wife and marry.

I found the hymns and preaching at the Bierton Strict Baptist Church very helpful. In particular one hymn by John Newton I recall was most helpful.

John Newton's Hymn

I asked the Lord that I might grow

In faith, and love, and every grace;

Might more of His salvation know,

And seek more earnestly His face

'Twas He who taught me thus to pray,

And He, I trust, has answered prayer;

But it has been in such a way,

As almost drove me to despair.

I hoped that in some favored hour,

At once He'd answer my request;

And, by His love's constraining power,

Subdue my sins, and give me rest.

Instead of this, He made me feel

The hidden evils of my heart,

And let the angry powers of hell,

Assault my soul in every part.

Yea, more, with His own hand

He seemed Intent to aggravate my woe;

Crossed all the fair designs I schemed,

Blasted my gourds, and laid me low.

"Lord, why is this?" I trembled cried; "

Wilt Thou pursue Thy worm to death?"

"Tis in this way," the Lord replied,

"I answer prayer for grace and faith."

"These inward trials I employ,

From self and pride to set thee free;

And break thy schemes of earthly joy,

That thou mayst seek thy all in me."

----

16 I Join the Bierton Church

After a short while I wrote to the church expressing my wish to join the church at Bierton, as I believed that I had that responsibility having experience the new birth and being baptized. I reasoned that I ought to support the cause of Christ at Bierton.

I was received into church membership at the Bierton Strict and Particular Baptist Church on 8th January 1976.

A problem arose because in the articles of Religion that were given to me were not those listed in the trust deed of 1831 and I could not subscribe to them. There were two articles that I could not subscribe too.

Mr Hill of Luton Ebenezer helps the Church

I discussed my concerns and misgivings with Mr Hill, the Pastor of Luton Ebenezer church, who fully understood my concerns and after looking at the original articles of Religion , for the Bierton Church, it was realized that there was no record as to how these articles had come into existence. So the church was bound to be subject to their original articles of religion. These were listed in their trust deed of 1831 and these did not contain these items I could not in conscience subscribe too.

The church was please to allow me to join them upon my confession faith and my acceptance of the original Articles of Religion, and not the spurious ones. There was in fact no record of how these other articles of faith came to be in use.

Articles of Religion: The problem

Article 12. We believe that Christ has set apart a day of rest, to be kept holy, and for his honour and glory, which is the first day of the week, commonly called Sunday, Mark 2 27. Acts 16 13. Hebrew 4, 9.

I did not believe that was true or that these scripture taught that.

Article 16. We believe all infants who die in their infancy go to heaven by virtue of the death of Christ. Matth 19 13, 14&15.

Again I could not say I believed this. I grant if they do go to heaven then is must be by virtue of the death of Jesus. These scriptures quoted do not teach this view.

A Church Member Dies

Sadly, soon after I joined the church at Bierton, the husband of Mrs Evered died, who was a church member, and I was invited to the family funeral. I was later invited to the family home in Aylesbury and on that occasion I was asked to share my testimony, at the family meeting, after the funeral to which, I felt privileged to do. It was here that I met the Groom family, who were members of the Prestwood Strict Baptist church and had moved to Brighton.

I am introduced to Mr Sperling-Tyler

I had previously met Pastor Mr Sperling Tyler, at a meeting at the Prestwood Strict Baptist Chapel, in 1975, when Mrs Evered introduced me to Mr Sparling-Tyler, soon during my early days attending the Bierton Church. On that occasion Mr Tyler was very gracious and asked me had I found the lord Jesus Christ as my personal saviour to which I replied, " No but rather He had found me".

I am introduced to Pastor Frank L. Gosden

Mr Frank L Gosden Gilead Chapel Brighton

Mr Frank L. Gosden was the Pastor of the Church at Gilead where Mr and Mrs Groom were in attendance and they wanted me to meet their pastor. Frank L. Gosden also pastored churches at Heathfield (1939-1957) and Gilead, Brighton (1959-1980). Mr. Gosden once said that he believed a twofold test could be applied to every preacher: Will the things he speaks be things that will matter when we come to die? And will the things he speaks be a help to a poor, broken-hearted sinners?

Gilead Chapel Brighton

Gilead Chapel Brighton

Mr and Mrs Groom and Mrs Evered arranged for me to visit Mr Gosden, in order for me to share with him my experience of conversion and I was very honoured to do this. We spent the afternoon together, at his very modest home, and he gave me a gift when I was leaving. It was his very own personal copies of Dr. John Gill's commentaries of the whole bible, in 6 volumes, for which I felt very privileged to receive. And this became my source of instruction ever since. At that time I have obtained a very old copy of William Huntington's book entitled the Everlasting Love of God towards His Elect. On reading this it became very clear that the Arminians were in the dark and I felt if only I could talk to them then the opposition that I had experienced from those that I had met at Lowestoft would surely disappear and the news be received with gladness. Mr Groom commented on my reading the book expressing he felt it very deep reading. I can recommend this to any one to read.

Before Mr Frank L. Gosden was the pastor of Gilead church in Brighton Mr J K Popham (1847 to 1947) was their pastor who was the former editor of the Gospel Standard.

For 55 years pastor of Gilead Chapel Brighton. Editor of the Gospel Standard from 1905 -1937. Besides being a minister of the gospel he was a gifted writer and theologian. He was called upon to deal with many controversial issues of the times. His booklet Spiritual Counsel to the Young is still in print as are many of his sermons. A book on the life of letters of J.K. Popham was written by J.H. Gosden

Under the title 'Valiant For Truth'

James Kidwell Popham 1847-1937

A visitor from John Metcalfs group James from Scotland

On one of these occasions we had a visitor from the group meeting at the Bethlehem Meeting hall, at Penn, where John Metcalf, was their Pastor. I learned one or two things from our visitor, who was called James. He was a former Scotts Presbyterian and I think from the Free Presbyterian Church of Scotland whom I learned were renowned Calvinists. These I learned and opposed the Gospel Standard views of the none-offer of the Gospel and also the view that the Law of Moses was not the rule of life for the believer. They held to a view of a free offer of Christ to all men, a view I could not go along with, as Christ died for the elect only. Christ was to be preached to the entire world but He was not on offer.

The Law of Moses Not The Rule Of Life For The Believer

Also I knew that the Law could not be the rule of life for the believer because of their union to him in His death and resurrection whereby they are delivered form the Law of sin and death and had rule of life which was the whole gospel of Christ the perfect law of liberty.

James informed me that the Presbyterians were against John

Metcalf and his teaching because he too like William Huntington taught, like the Gospel Standard article convey that the Law was not the rule of life for the believer but rather the gospel was. This I agreed was the truth.

James came to our weeknight prayer meeting; his name was James and he later informed me that he wanted to hear Mr Sparling-Tyler preach, who was the Pastor of the church meeting at the Dicker. So I agreed to take him one Lord's Day. He had a problem though, because I worked for Granada TV Rentals and I had a company vehicle which, had the name of my company written on the side of the car. This was an embarrassment to him as he was acutely aware of the disapproval of many, who were opposed to any church member who had a television set. He wanted me to park the vehicle away from the chapel car park, so as not to show we were connected with the chapel. I felt slightly irritated with this mode of thinking but was sensitive enough to know how much he felt embarrassed, so we parked my company car out of the way. We then heard Mr Tyler speak in the Morning, afternoon and evening. Meetings of the church. It was here that I met the son of Mr Tyler and his wife who both attended the Linslaid Strict Baptist church.

Television A Concern For Many

In respect to the television I began to realize this had become an issue, not only amongst the Strict Baptists but also the Brethren. I had reason to consider the whole matter at a later date,

Zoar Strict Baptist Chapel

Zoar Strict Baptist Chapel, Lower Dicker

This was built in 1837 and enlarged in 1874. There is an extensive graveyard on three sides

Not All Preaching at Bierton Good

Our visiting preaches came from various local and far away places and only a few were from Gospel Standard causes, let alone gospel standard listed ministers. As I recall the names of some of those who visited us and preached, we shall see who were from Gospel Standard causes and who were listed ministers.

Our Ministers were:

Mr Hill, Luton, Pastor of Ebenezer Luton and one of our Trustee's GS

Mr Collier, Pastor Linslaid Bethel Strict and Particular Baptist GS

Mr Goode, Pastor, Dunstable Baptist

Mr Martin Hunt, Colnebrook Gospel Standard

Mr King, minister, Bierton Strict and Particular Baptist (Trustee)

Mr Martin White Colnebrook

Mr C. A Wood, Pastor Croydon, Strict and Particular Baptist GS

Mr Hope, Pastor Reading, Strict and Particular Baptist

Mr Howard Sayers, minister, Watford Strict and Particular Baptist GS

Mr Crane, minister, Lakenheath Strict and Particular

Mr Tim Martin, minister, Blunham Strict and Particular Baptist

Mr Levy, minister and Deacon, of Dunstable Baptist

Mr John Gosden, minister Southbourgh

Mr Lawrence, Evangelical from Harold

Mr Ramsbottom, Pastor Luton Bethel, and Gospel Standard editor GS

Mr Scott Pearson, Pastor, Baptist

Mr Baumber, minister Bedford Providence, Strict and Baptist (Trustee)

Mr Tim Martin, Blunham Strict Baptist (Trustee)

Mr Sayers, Pastor, Watford Strict and Particular Baptist

Mr Dawson Strict and Particular Baptist Kent

Mr Tanton, Tenterdon Strict Baptist

Mr Gould, minister, Limes Avenue Baptist

Mr Dix, pastor Dunstable Baptist and Trinitarian Bible Society representa

tive

Mr Terence Brown, minister and Secretary of the Trinitarian Bible Society

184

Mr Redhead, minister of Pottern End?

Mr Gerald Buss, minister Strict and Particular Baptist

Mr Buss (senior) Strict and Particular Baptist

Mr Howe Pastor of Ivanhoe Particular Baptist

Mr Paul Rowland (Presbyterian leanings)

Mr. G. Ashdown of the Protestant Alliance

A Range of doctrinal differences

It became apparent to me, through listening to the various visiting ministers and my conversations with them, that we had a range of ministers with differing degrees of understanding of scripture. Some had and held opposing views to each other. We had those who held to the 1689 confession of faith some the 1966 Strict Baptist confession, some who were convinced of the Presbyterian position. Some holding to "duty faith and repentance" and one who could not accept the Bierton Articles of Religion of 1831.

I Am Appointed Secretary and Correspondent

There came a time when we needed a correspondent and Secretary and I agree to take on this role and had the responsibility of engaging minister for the coming year. It was all-new to me and found it very difficult and a real sense of responsibility.

I had to deal with a request expressing in a letter from Colnebrook Strict and Particular Baptist Church who had informed the church (via me the secretary) that one of their members, Mr Martin Hunt was under censorship. Martin Hunt was one of our visiting ministers, who I found to be a very nice and polite man and had a good understanding of scripture. How ever Mr King and I were asked by the church to speak to Martin about this issue being raised and it was difficult to understand the problem. It was to do with particular redemption so in the end I asked Martin if he could subscribe to our Bierton Articles of Religion of 1831. His reply was no he could not. This resolved the matter and the Church decided not to invite Martin to preach again. This helped us not to judge this issue he had with his church but rather enabled us to respond to the concerns of the Colnebrook Church in the correct way.

I Read Former Church Minutes A Cause Of Concern

It was my responsibility as secretary to keep church minute and the church book and during this time I was able read the issues that had been spoken about and the decisions that were made before I became a member. I was shocked to find the Mr and Mrs Evered had put forward motions to prevent certain visiting ministers from preaching due to un-substantiated beliefs about their conduct. I knew that this would be contrary to the gospel and so I raised the matter with the church and stated the need to put the matter right. Unfortunately to one member who was implicated in this form of slander was so upset it was felt best to leave the matter as it was. I realized from that moment I had crossed Mrs Evered.

I continued being the secretary and correspondent until I married and moved briefly away to Leicester.

17 Caterham Strict Baptist Holiday

I meet my wife

It was during this time in 1976 I felt loneliness and fell into depression and friend's of Alan Benning, Paul and Susan Aston invited me to go with them on holiday with a Christian group, to Switzerland. Paul was a student at a Watford Evangelical Bible College and so I went. It was on that holiday that I was made more aware of a holiday being arranged by Caterham Strict Baptist being, held at the Elim Pentecostal Bible College,at Capel. It was here that I met my wife to be that year who is Irene Protheroe, from Shepsherd in Leicestershire where Paul Cook was the Pastor of the Evangelical Church.

I meet other Evangelicals

in Coventry doctrinal differences

My wife Irene had lived in Coventry and introduced me to her Christian friends including the Minister and Pastor of Holbrook's Evangelical Church. Here I meet good friends who had a desire to follow the Lord however in discussion they realized my views on predestination, particular redemption, the relationship of the Christian to the Law of Moses and the none offer of the gospel proved a divide between us. How ever we were able to discuss matters and agree to differ. These conversations enlightened me further to the differences between the Evangelicals and Strict and Particular Baptists and exclusive position of the views expressed in the Gospel Standard Articles of Religion. I was being cast into the mold of the Gospel Standard Baptists. I also learned that the minister of the London Evangelical Church called Westminster Chapel, where Dr Martin Lloyd Jones was a minister was now R.T. Kendal who taught a 4 point Calvinist position namely not particular Redemption. This raised the alarm bell in my mind.

Preparation For Marriage

We were engaged to be married in December 1977 and I had obtained a place on the Technical Teacher Training Course as Wolverhampton Teacher Training College. I resigned from my job at Granada TV Rentals and I moved into student lodgings at the college.

Mean while we purchased a house in Wigston at 64B Moat Street, which turned out as a good buy.

Regarding Marriage Counselling

During the time and lead up to my Marriage I was really concerned about the idea of birth control, as in conscience I was uncertain as its morality. In this connection I asked our only male married church member about the subject. I was very embarrassed but had to settle the matter for conscience sake. To my dismay the only response and reply to the question was, "moderation in all things". This was my answer to a very serious question. As I look back it is laughable and now realize how unhelpful ignorance was.

Our First Home

64B Moat Street Wigston

This is the first house we purchased and Irene lived here whilst I was living in student lodgings at Wolverhampton and me move in together the on our wedding day, 9th December 1976.

Marriage

I married my wife Irene Protheroe on the 9th December 1977 and the wedding took Place at Bethel Evangelical Church at Wigston.

Bethel Evangelical Church

Bethel Evangelical Church

Our move to Luton

My first teaching post was at Luton College of Higher Education and I commenced lecturing in Electronics in September 1978. And we were able to rent a council house at Lewsy Farm in Dunstable.

The funny thing was that we were obtained permission form the council to keep our two goats in the coal shed in the rear garden. building in Wigston were we were married on December 1976

Our move to Linslaid

My concern was that I wanted to be in a church with a Pastor particularly now that I had a wife who had been just introduced to the Strict Baptists, so I decided we should attend the Linslaid Strict and Particular Baptist church where Mr Collier was the pastor. We continued here for as short, while when we realized it would be more economical to purchase a house in Linslaid and I travel to Luton to work. In that case we would be near the local church. And so we were able to buy our house called "Fairhome"' for £14,000 with a mortgage in Linslaid.

Our Home In Linslaid

Our home in Linslaid "Fairholme", Queen Street

The Isle of Skye and the Presbyterian Churches

It was my desire to visit Scotland and some of the Presbyterian Churches we rented an old school house in Waternish on the Isle of Skye and we had to cross to the island on a ferry to Porter to get there. It turned out that the Old School house had belonged to Donavan who was a pop star during the 60's. It was a very quite place but very peaceful building at Staffing where I answered the question.. We were not aware at the time that the Presbyterian churches celebrate their communion twice a year and that particular "Sabbath" as they called it was the occasion of their "Mount of Ordinances". It was their communion to be held in the morning of that day. We attended the meeting in the morning and we were made very welcome and were asked where we were from.

Free Presbyterian Church

Free Presbyterian Church

Speak To The Question

During the meeting each male in attendance and whom the elders knew were asked to speak or answer a biblical question. And as their custom was, which I was totally unaware, I was addressed as Mr Clarke from the Strict Baptists would you please speak or answerer the question. This meant that I had to speak about a verse of scripture presented by the elder to the congregation. The verse of scripture was, Philippians 1 [1 v.] "For unto you it is given in the behalf of Christ, not only to believe on him, but also to suffer for his sake;" To which I gave my answer and exposition of the verse.

I believe my exposition was accepted for after the meeting

we were invited to renew our covenant vows and partake of the communion.

Not knowing what this meant I declined, as I knew nothing of renewing covenant vows from the scripture.

Called Before The Elders

After the communion meeting I was called by one of the men and told to put my jacket on and come before the Elders as they wish to ask my why I had not partaken of their communion. When I explained my reservation and ignorance of their practices they were pleased to be of further help. We were then invited to lunch at one of the Elders home.

Silence Woman These Are Guests

We had a delightful time and at the head of the table was a senior man in his 80's along with other visitors. One of the other guests enquired of us about the differences between Strict Baptists and Presbyterians. It came a shock to the lady, who had asked the question, that we do not baptize infants. She exclaimed, "What? You do not baptize infants?' At which point the senior man stepped in by saying, "Silence Woman these are guests". Which I found rather amusing but was not put out by the question and would have freely spoken about it.

Portree Rev Frazer MacDonald

That evening we went to the church in Porter where Rev. Frazer MacDonald was the minister.

Portree Free Presbyterian Church

Portree Free Presbyterian Church

This minister was a very good preacher and lifted up the Lord Jesus Christ and as their custom was they invited all men to come to Christ and he was very urgent in his exhortation.

I was questioned the "free offer"

We were later invited to another home, that evening, along with other guests and at one time I was challenged as to why I did not hold to the free offer of the gospel, as we had heard that night. It wasn't the time or place to go into detail but I realized then that there were real differences between the Free Presbyterian Churches of Scotland and the Strict Baptist (Gospel Standard) Churches in Great Britain and differences that were not to be ignored.

A Return To The Bierton Church

On our return from Sky we decided we could return to Bierton and give more support to the cause. This of course meant a move and the realization of finances, as property in Bierton was very expensive. This meant selling my property in Aylesbury to raise the money.

Angels Come To Help

(or so I thought)

I had bought a terraced house at Canal Side Aylesbury before I got married and I had renovated it. I had borrowed £3000 from Barclays' bank and was paying this back over a period of 3 years.

My House at Canal Side Terrace in Aylesbury

3 Canal Side Terrace, Aylesbury. My first House

In September 1977 I left Aylesbury and went to Wolverhampton Polytechnic (Formerly Wolverhampton Technical Teacher Training College) to train as a teacher. I rented out three rooms with shared amenities and had kept a room reserved for myself downstairs.

My mother looked after all the bills and collected rent. Whilst I was at Wolverhampton the boy friend of the lady who lived as a tenant asked if he too could rent a room. This seemed OK so I let a room to him. They soon got married and I saw no real problem. They then asked if they could have just the one double room. I explained that I needed to rent all the rooms but they could have the double room for an appropriate rent. I also said they could use my room down stairs when I wasn't there.

I thought things were OK but I had a problem three years later (October 1980) when I wanted to sell the house. I knew nothing about the law and the **Land Lord and Tenant Act.** I soon found a buyer for the house and made an offer to buy a house from Mr Groom at Great lane Bierton who was the son of Mr Groom Senior from Brighton.

The couple that rented rooms from me decided to claim they had right of occupation, which prevented me from selling the house. I went through all kinds of indignant feelings and was angry with them. They knew I had rented the rooms to them on condition if I wanted to return they would have to leave. They called in the **Rent Officer** and the officials coming in reducing the rent I was charging them. In the end I decided I would have to take them to court to get them to leave.

I had to say to Mr. Groom I could not proceed with the purchase and he was very upset as it messed all their plans up and cost him extra money because of the housing chain, which had been broken. He even asked me to meet the extra costs he had incurred. He felt I was morally obliged to pay towards the costs (£1000) due to us not being able to proceed with the purchase. I felt upset by this too.

I felt God was on the side of the righteous a believed it necessary to take my tenents to court to get them to leave. I flet if I were to present my case to the court I would get an order to get these people to leave.

I knew nothing about the law and did could not afford a Solicitor so I did it my self. I believed I could do all things through God who strengthened me.

The Judged asked me what the case was all about. I proceeded to read my script but he soon stopped me. He said you cannot do that and without explaining why asked the defendants solicitor to state the case.

Apparently you have to present things in a certain order and way and it must conform to a certain protocol. I knew nothing about protocol or the law all I knew was I had been wronged and I was looking for Justice.

The judge said I ought to seek legal help. My case was dismissed much to my dismay and my mother stopped up and protested in the courtroom. I got up and left saying no more. Needless to say I was dismayed and dumbfounded. Where was God where was justice. I realized then the law of out land has nothing to do with morality or right and wrong but was pedantic was according to strict rules. This was not justice. I looked to God for help. I had believed God would appear for my help.

What was All That About?

When I returned the next day to Canal Side to sort things out in the house the man, he was a big Irish man, said what was all that about last night? I did not know what he was talking about. I said what do you mean? He said, " Two men had been around with lumps of wood last night and said they wanted them out". I was amazed, as I knew nothing about it. I said I didn't know anything about it and he should go to the police.

I thought that these must be angels sent from God to warn them not to trifle with me. I felt comforted that this was the case. I began to believe it that things were going to be OK.

In the end I had to employ a Barrister to represent me and many months later the couple agreed to buy the house from me at a market rate. It cost me at least £800 in legal fees.

It was a number of years later that my brother confessed to me that he together with another friend of mine Pet Sinfiled had been those Angels.

Prevented From Buying A House

As I have already mentioned we had to pull out of buying his bungalow but he was upset by the fact we did not proceed with the purchase. This was his letter to me, which caused me concern.

17th November 1980

Dear David,

As you can see after you had withdrawn from the sale of Great Lane we were put in a very difficult position, because as you remember we had been given until the end of December to complete the purchase of this property. This proved to be quite impossible, and although the builders have been very helpful, they had to increase the price to us by £1500.

We had not bargained for this when we got our mortgage, and together with extra Solicitors fees that were involved, found us at the end of the sale needing to borrow the extra money. This of course must be paid back in the near future and we felt that, as this was not our fault really, that you might feel you could help us with a £1000 of it. We did give you the preference over the cash buyer we had because we wanted to help friends at Bierton Chapel.

If we could have managed in any other way without writing to you, believe me we would have done so.

Trusting that Irene and the children are well. May God bless you all?

Yours Sincerely,

John G

My Reply was as follows:

Dear Mr. G Re: Your letter dated 17th November 1980

I am pleased for you that at last you have moved to your new home but am sorry that the move proved more expensive than you anticipated.

Your request came as a surprise and has caused my conscience much exercise over the morality of the issue; since it would appear you feel Irene and I are obligated to repay some of your losses. However after careful reasoning we do not share the same view and do not accept the obligation. Not only so Irene and I are unable to do so as we are in financial difficulties our selves.

I would like to add that had we felt obliged then by the grace of God we would have offered payment for your loss. This did occur in my last transaction when trying to sell Canal Side. I presumed to give the intended purchaser vacant possession within a month of the exchange of contract but I was unable to do so since my tenants refused to leave. In this case I felt obliged to him and offered to pay the expenses of my intended purchaser because he had proceeded to purchase on that basis.

When we spoke to you we did not keep you in the dark over our circumstances and did keep you informed, and our arrangements were subject to contract, which at that time had not been drawn up nor signed at the time of our withdrawal.

I do apologize over the matter for it seems God in His providence intervened having His own reasons and although at the present time we cannot see why.

He may be pleased to show us one day.

Yours with Christian regards,

David Clarke.

Dealings like this always leave a bad taste in the mouth but I had to leave it in Gods hands. This shows that Christians are not immune from the normal trials of life and that this chain in buying and selling has a knock on effect. Mr. Groom felt I had let him down so I should compensate him. I too had been let down by the tenants.

Such is life and goes to show we are not immune from the normal difficulties men face in this world in business.

18 Bierton a Gospel Standard Cause 1981

During these times there were several moves, initiated by Mrs Evered for the church to join the Gospel Standard list of Churches, as she had been our secretary and was finding it difficult to obtain supply preachers. Her sister Mrs Groom and her brother in Law were members of Prestwood Strict and Particular Baptists and really wanted Bierton to become a listed church. I knew some members were quite happy with the ministers that were engaged to speak and did not see the need to become a Gospel Standard listed Church.

It was during the time we were trying to move back to Bierton, that on the 16th January 1981, our church decided to join the Gospel Standard list of Churches. Mr Hope, Pastor of Reading, Strict Baptist Church was the Chairman of the meeting and he agreed to do all the necessary documentation regarding this matter and we were duly listed as a Gospel Standard cause. Mr King had made the proposal and seconded by Mrs Evered and a unanimous decision by ballot was taken. It was agreed we became a Gospel Standard listed cause.

This was not how ever without opposition from without the Church. Mr Dix, the Pastor of Dunstable Baptist Church, stated to me personally that we were out of order and it was illegal for us to adopt the Gospel Standard Articles of religion and its Rules of Conduct. This I write about in "The Bierton Crisis 1984.

Ruth Ellis a Church Member Dies

At this time Ruth Ellis who had been a great encouragement to my wife and I before I married and I use to visit her regularly with a friend and have good fellowship in the lord. She eventfully need looking after and ended her days at the Bethesda Home in Harpendon. I believe it was noted that one could always have choice conversations with her on spiritual matters.

Mr Collier, Pastor of Linslaid, of Comes To Our Aid

In early April 1982 Mr Collier from Linslaid came to our Church midweek to our prayer meeting and he spoke on the subject of the Falkland war, this was because England was at war with Argentina in 1982. He informed the Church of the ancient conflict between the Roman Catholic system and the Reformation in Europe. Argantina being a Catholic country. Mr Collier was a friend of Dr Ian Paisley and through his connection we were able to here Ian Paisley preach in Mr Greens Church in London. It was always good to here him preach, as he was an excellent preacher even though he differed over certain points of doctrine.

In connection with Mr Collier it was remarked by his family that, "If he had been disturbed by events in the first twenty-five years of his pastorate he was even more profoundly disturbed by developments since. Blatantly heretical statements from so-called Church leaders, the fresh impetus given to the ecumenical drift by the charismatic movement, the historic visit of the Pope to this country in 1982 - all these things affected him deeply. His response, however, was not to project himself back into the past in a nostalgia for better days. It was to work for the present and for the future. It was to recognize that God is still working today in raising up a witness to the gospel. He found encouragement in his contact with other ministers both within his own denomination and outside; and it is a simple matter of fact that the extent of such contact increased in his latter days."

I Meet Dr Ian Paisley At Oxford

At this time there was a memorial rally held in Oxford to remember our Martyrs Cranmer, Latimer and Ridley. And I remember Ian Paisley echoing the words, Fear not we shall light a fire in England that will never be put out".

Shortly after the accession of Mary in 1553 a summons was sent to Latimer to appear before the council at Westminster. Though he might have escaped by flight, and though he knew, as he quaintly remarked, "Smithfield already groaned for him," he at once joyfully obeyed. The pursuant, he said, was "a welcome messenger." The hardships of his imprisonment, and the long disputations at Oxford, tolled severely on his health, but he endured all with unbroken cheerfulness.

On the 16th of October 1555 Hugh Latimer and Ridley were led to the stake at Oxford. Never was man more free than Latimer from the taint of fanaticism or less dominated by "vainglory," but the motives, which now inspired his courage, not only placed him beyond the influence of fear, but also enabled him to taste in dying an ineffable thrill of victorious achievement. Ridley he greeted with the words, "Be of good comfort, master Ridley, and play the man; we shall this day light such a candle by God's grace in England as (I trust) shall never be put out."

He "received the flame as it were embracing it. After he had stroked his face with his hands, and (as it were) bathed them a little in the fire, he soon died (as it appeared) with very little pain or none."

Archbishop Cranmer, on the day of his execution, he dramatically withdrew his recantations, to die a heretic to Roman Catholics and a martyr to others. His legacy lives on within the Church of England through the Book of Common Prayer and the Thirty-Nine Articles, an Anglican statement of faith derived from his work. He renounced the recantations that he had written or signed with his own hand since his degradation and as such he stated his hand would be punished by being burnt first.

He then said, "And as for the Pope, I refuse him, as Christ's enemy, and Antichrist with all his false doctrine". He was pulled from the pulpit and taken to where Latimer and Ridley had been burnt six months before. As the flames drew around him, he fulfilled his promise by placing his right hand into the heart of the fire and his dying words were, "Lord Jesus, receive my spirit... I see the heavens open and Jesus standing at the right hand of God."[97]

Rescuing Michael's Roles Royce

(About 1982)

Whilst these things were going on my brother got into serious difficulties. His business was failing and he became very depressed so much so he did not know how to sort some of his problems. He came to me one day explaining he had sold his Roles Royce to a person in Milton Keynes for £7000 and he was still owed £3,500. He was too ill to sort it out. The person kept giving one excuse after another as to why he could not pay the money.

I felt indignant and was not prepared to sit down and see some one-take advantage of my Michael because he was ill and could not sort his problems out.

I said to Michael come on I will go with him and get it sorted. I dressed in my Crombie over coat and suit and looked very official and we went to this person's house in Milton Keynes. I told Michael not to worry I would deal with any problems. When the person answered the door, early on morning, I said who I was and what we had come for and that I was a Christian and we intended to sort out the issue with the Roles Royce. The bloke looked at me gone out.

Michael decided he wanted the car back and so it was agreed that he would pay back the £3500 in cash and take the car. I found out that the previous deal had been done between another person as well as this man and the car was in his garage somewhere else. Also a problem with a finance company had arisen. This all seamed straight forward and we left with the intention (or so I thought) to return with the £3500 cash and collect the car that day.

My brother then explained that he understood that these men had raised money through a finance company to buy the car and he only got half the money. I then feared if he gave up the £3500 cash to them he would loose that as well, as the finance company would claim ownership of the car. He had already gone to the police but the police said it was not a problem they could deal with so my brother felt real down about the whole issue. He said he could not remember signing any forms with a finance company but I began to feel the case was not a straight forward, as it first seemed. Michael kept saying he could not remember what had happened.

I got the impression Michael had been party to some deal and was keeping some thing from me and these men had just tucked him up for £3500 and they now had no money to pay. Michael informed me years later that he did not know about this and that these men took him advantage of him, whilst he was ill.

Michael decided to get the car back so he paid a couple of his heavy friend's £250 to go and collect the car. Sure enough the next day the Roles Royce was in bed in my garage at Bierton, out of the way. I felt much better even though my brother didn't. This did not stop my brother worrying because apparently there was more to it than first met the eye there was some problem with the finance company.

I felt let down by Michael for not telling me all this. Had he told me all this in the beginning instead of being devious. (Michael now tells me I was wrong) I could have helped him. In the end the finance company contacted Michael and he by then realized the car belonged to the finance company. Michael, through not being able to cope with the worry, agreed to return the car as he realized the deal they had done was not straightforward.

This was all out of my hands and on reflection I think it would have been better to keep the car and give the finance company the £3500, but at the time I was not able to sort the issue out for Michael because he had kept things from me.

I felt upset for my brother because he had lost his car and all that money. We are always wise after an event.

19 A Call to Preach the Gospel

I believe that God puts the desire to preach and speak His Word into the hearts of them whom he calls. This desire was placed in my heart the day Jesus called me to hear him and believe in him. My desire to help others turn from the way that leads to hell and to Christ himself for salvation, was acknowledge by Jesus the night I got saved. His reply to me, when I asked what about the others, was all I could do was tell them. What better way than to preach the unsearchable riches of Christ to men.

I had spoken on a number of times at Bierton Church during the weeknight prayer meeting from the table not the pulpit. Gradually however I felt more and more uncomfortable when sitting in the pew just listening to sermons. Particularly when things were not very well expressed and some times serious errors were being spoken. It grieved me to listen to the ignorant talk off the religious whose eyes were blinded to the truth of God and who sought to bind burdens on peoples backs. This issue over the hat and lady visitor was an example. Not that I am against a head covering for a woman but what had happened to this lady visitor was wrong.

My wife Irene joins the Church at Bierton

At this time my wife Irene was received into membership of the church upon her confession of faith an acceptance of our Articles of religion as expressed in our trust deed of 1831,

As I have already mentioned not all our visiting ministers were good at preaching and we were not a Gospel Standard cause.

I had also been shocked by the reluctance of the Bierton church to use the chapel to conduct a meeting informing people of the error of the Papal system of Rome, and how we might act righteously in the present day since the Pope was to visit Britain that year.

I saw the Pope on the TV screen, when at Wembley Stadium, and the whole crowd, thousands of them, was singing praise to the Pope. They were singing, "He's got the whole world in his hands'. And the Pope received that praise. I saw it and heard it with my own eyes and ears. This man is an Anti Christ. I felt I must speak out other wise the stones would do.

I did not believe in Bible colleges

When I first became a Christian I did not believe in Bible Colleges. Thinking I do not want men to teach me, I wanted God to teach me. From what little I had seen of vicars and so called trained men I felt Bible Colleges were of no use because these people are not even born again.

Wolverhampton Polytechnic and Teacher Training

So I dismissed the idea of Bible college for me, never the less I wanted to learn all about God and speak his word in clarity and truth. This desire turned me to read about the lives of men of God. I went from reading the Beano and Dandy comics and James Bond books to the Bible and then on to the writings of John Bunyan, Dr. John Gill, John Owen and Calvin in a matter of two or three years. It was when I met my wife to be that she encourage train me to be a teacher and that is why I attended the Technical Training College in Wolverhampton, to learn how to teach technical subjects.

An Ulterior Motive

My ulterior motive was to learn how to teach so that I could then teach the gospel. I took one year out from work and studied at

Wolverhampton Polytechnic and finally graduated with a teaching Certificate in Education. This was awarded by Birmingham University in 1978.

Wolverhampton Teacher Training Group

David (bottom centre right) at Wolverhampton Polytechnic

I believed that I could learn from secular professional teachers how to teach and then would then be able to take the substance of what God was showing me and then present it to men in a way they could understand. This was my desire.

I took my first teaching post at Luton College of Higher Education commencing teaching in 1978.

I inform the Church at Bierton of my felt call to preach

It was during this time at Luton College and at Bierton Church that I felt it right to make known my desire to the church as I believe I was being called by God to preach the word of Jesus Christ.

A meeting with Mr Hill and Mr Hope ministers of the Gospel

Mr. Hill of Luton and minister of the Gospel and Mr. Hope of Reading, both Gospel Standard ministers invited me to share with them my calling.

Questioned about the Law of Moses

Mr Hill questioned my belief regarding the Law of Moses and both he and Mr Hope listened. I expressed my understing of the bleivers relationship to the Law of Moses and concluded that that Law of Moses did not make the Lord Jesus righteous as he was always righteous.. He had an essensial righteouness indipendant of the Law. He did not have to fulfill the Law to become righteous. He always was righteous. Had he been judged according to the law he would have been declared righteous and so he was.

That imputed righteousness is the righteousness of God, given to all who believe, that Christ's Righteousness imputed justifies us, without our works according to the Law.

Mr Hill's Conclusion

Mr Hill concluded that my leadings were right and Mr Hope agreed. It was then put to the church that I should preach and exercise any gift I had. This was duly done and a few people came from Albert Street Oxford and Eaton Bray church, to hear me preach the word of God that weeknight meeting at Bierton.

Sent by the Church to Preach

It was agreed without question that I should preach, as the Lord opened up the way, and from that day letters came from different churches asking me to preach at various Strict Baptist Chapels throughout the country. This was my being sent out to preach the gospel as the Lord open up the door for me to speak. This came with the blessing of the church believing that the gifts and callings of God are without repentance.

The Papal visit 1982

This year Pope John Paul 11 was due to visit Britain. This was to be the first time in 400 years.

Very few people saw the significance of this and I felt the need to inform people about such an event.

I wrote to the Bierton Church, which meet on the 16th January 1982 (This was 14 years to the day of my conversion) asking if we could invite a member of The British Council of Protestant Christian Churches, Using the Bierton Chapel to meet and to teach clear biblical principles as to how we could act responsibly and maintain a Godly witness in the present time. I suggested it would be helpful to many churches in the area.

Mrs. E. expressed the Bierton Chapel was not the place to hold such a meeting but some other place like the village hall. Mr. King said they had Roman Catholic friends and would not wish to offend them!

From this time I began to wonder about the church at Bierton and believed I would see the hand of God out against her.

I remembered, "They that honour me I will honour".

I held the meeting in my house and invited several people from different churches and Rev Gordon Ferguson came and preached for us.

We eventually was able to by a property in Bierton it was a detached bungalow just down the road from the Bierton Strict Baptist Chapel. I felt really blessed by God to own it and being so near to our chapel.

Our Home at Bierton

187 Aylesbury Road

Our Home At Bierton

Just a few minutes walk from our Bierton Chapel 187 Aylesbury Road

Hats Or Head Coverings For Ladies

Trouble was on its way in the form of religious oppression. On Sunday morning in 1983 I took to church a friend of mine's daughter. This was the daughter of Dick Holmes who I use to work with as an aerial rigger. She had been through a divorce and was having a difficult time. I suggested she came with me to church, as she needed help from God.

She was dressed in tight black slacks and a short top, which showed all her figure. She had long peroxide blond hair and her face was made up. This mode of dress was a striking contrast to the elderly ladies who dressed very modestly with very little make up on and all ware hats to cover their heads in church.

Unfortunately this was too much for Mrs. Evered who came up to me after the service (I call it a meeting because the meetings of the New Testament churches were not called services) and she said to me the next time I bring a female to chapel I should tell her to wear a hat.

Mrs. Evered said that all Gospel Standard Churches insisted women cover their heads and so should we.

I responded that by saying, " what ever others do that was their concern they were wrong if they enforced the covering of the head upon a none church member and women visitor having no profession of the Christian faith."

I said she must raise this issue at our church meeting.

This spirit of legalism naturally took me back. Here was a young woman in sever distress needing the mercy and love of God as revealed in Jesus Christ and all Mrs. Evered seemed to be concerned with was the wearing of a Hat.

I knew the principle of a believing women dressing modestly and being in subjection to her own husband and covering her head in worship. I also knew the principle of the woman not exercising authority over the man or teaching a man but this action of Mrs Evered to use the phrase, "took the biscuit".

I was a man and was being instructed by a woman, Mrs Evered, to order or insist a visiting unbelieving female wear a hat In order to uphold the principle that it was a shame for a woman to worship God without a head covering.

This covering according to the scripture was to show the angels she was in subjection to the man and not usurping authority over him.

Mrs. Evered missed the whole point of the gospel and in her religious zeal to maintaining an outward form of religion transgressed the rule she sought to maintain.

This religious spirit was not of God and I believed the gospel needed to be preached to set men free from such darkness. But who would do this?

A Spanking From the Pulpit

I was very conscious of the instruction that I was responsible to God for the discipline of my children and knew the scriptures, which speak of spoiling children through lack of discipline. And the exhortation that if I spare the rod of correction I would spoil the child (Prov. 13. 24). The other scripture, which spoke to me, was that of how a good father ought to " Rule his house well, his children being obedient and subject to him ". That if I did not know how to rule my own house how should I be able to take care of the church of God (1 Tim 3. 5 - 12. I believed the scripture spoke clearly about corporal punishment and it was a must. (Prov 29. 15 and Prov 23. 13).

The first occasion I felt the need to exercise corporal punishment was on Isaac when he was very small. As I write this now I smile and I am sure he would do too. I think he needs corporal punishment now at the age of 20 years old.

Isaac had done some thing, which warranted correction, and I felt this occasion I would use the rod of correction. I was a small thin garden cane, a green one. I made him stand away from me and I said it hurt me more than it would hurt him, to have to correct him like this. He was about 4 years old. I smacked his bottom with the cane and he jumped and couldn't say a word for a few moments. Then he burst into tears saying, " daddy that stings". From that day forward that cane was called the "stinging stick". That was not the last time the stinging stick was used.

On another occasion I was preaching in Bierton Chapel and

Isaac and Esther were sitting with there mum on the back row of the chapel. During the sermon Isaac was playing his mum up and he would not sit still and kept messing about. His behaviour was unacceptable. I was gradually becoming cross with him until I felt I must do some thing about it.

I stopped speaking and said to the congregation " excuse me" and climbed down the pulpit steps and went to the back of the chapel. I picked Isaac up and took him out side the chapel and informed him I was displeased with his behaviour and gave his three smacks on the bottom. With this he burst into tears and when he stopped I took him back in the chapel and placed him besides his mum. I then went back into the pulpit and apologized for the interruption and proceeded with the sermon as though nothing had happened.

I heard afterwards the spanking was heard through out the chapel and a couple of the ladies were horrified at what I had done but they said nothing to me. I felt I had done the right thing using the rod of correction to drive foolishness from the child (prove. 22. 15).

Is Corporal punishment what Jesus wants?

Hatred stirs up strife's but love covereth all sins. (Prov. 10. 12)

Prov 10 13. A rod is for the back of him that is void of understanding.

Prov 13 24. He that spareth the rod hateth his son: he that loveth him chasteneth him betimes.

Prov 19 18. Chasten thy son whilst there is hope spare not for his crying.

Prov 19 29. Judgments are prepared for scorns and stripes for the back of fools.

Prov 19 30. The blueness of a wound cleanseth away evil: so do stripes the inward parts of the belly.

Prov 22. 15 Foolishness is bound up in the heart of the child but the rod of correction will drive it far from him.

Prov 23. With hold not correction from the child: for If 13 - 14 thou beatest him with the rod he shall not die.

Prov 29 15. The rod and reproof give wisdom: but a child left to himself bringeth his mother to shame.

Answer: Yes.

I Preach at various Churches

In a very short period of time I was engaged to preach at the following Strict Baptist Chapels throughout the country:

Reading "Hope Chapel" Strict and Particular Baptist GS	Oxford "Hope" Chapel Strict and Particular Baptists GS
Wantage Strict and Particular Baptists GS	Stamford Strict and Particular Baptists GS
Oakington Strict and Particular Baptists	Horsham Strict and Particular
Fenstanton Strict and Particular Baptists GS	Romford Room Strict and Particular Baptists
Matfield Strict and Particular Baptists GS	Eaton Bray Strict and Particular Baptists GS
Walgrave Strict and Particular Baptists	Bradford Strict and Particular Baptists
Beeches Road Strict and Particular Baptists	Evington Strict and Particular Baptists GS
Leicester "Zion" Strict and Particular Baptists	Nottinghamshire Strict and Particular Baptists
New Mill Baptists	Winslow Baptists

Reading "Hope Chapel" Strict and Particular Baptist GS	Oxford "Hope" Chapel Strict and Particular Baptists GS
Black Heath Strict and Particular Baptists	Attleborough Strict and Particular Baptists

The Bierton Pulpit

David preaching at Bierton Strict and Particular Baptist Church, 5th June 1983 I Preach At Various Churches

In fact I was so overwhelmed with being asked to preach at so many places, I could have been preaching three times on a Sunday every week of the year and during the week on weeknight services. This was on top of my full timework, which involved teaching two nights a week at Luton College as well as continuing my studies with the Open University.

Eaton Bray Strict and Particular Baptist Church

Eaton Bray Strict and Particular Baptist Chapel
(Gospel Standard)

This church was situated not too far from our home in Bierton and Mr Jane's senior was one of our trustees. It was here that questions were raised regarding the added articles and duty faith and repentance. This cause some concern and I felt lead to speak on the subject of **particular redemption** and God commanding all men every where to repent, in doing so pointing out that this repentance was legal and not evangelical. The matters of **'duty faith' and ' duty repentance'.** Some of the members had actually opposed my doctrinal stand over this issue. At this church I preached from the text in Acts 17 and defended article 26 of the Gospel Standard articles. I was judged as being wrong, both in the substance and my method of preaching and at a later date gently reproved by Mr Godly, who was a minister in membership of the cause at Eaton Bray. The church at Eaton Bray was a Gospel Standard listed church.

Albert Street Strict Baptist Chapel Oxford

Hope Strict Baptist Church in Albert Street Oxford

The friends from Hope Strict Baptist Church, along with Mr Philip Hope from Reading and David Cook a university student, and folk from Eaton Bray came to the meeting when my preaching gift was exercised and I was accepted as minister sent by the church to preach.

The Strict Baptist Church at Uffington

Uffinton Strict Baptist

One of the churches I was engaged to preach at was the Strict Baptist Chapel in Uffington. Where I learned later that this was the chapel that Sir John Betjeman, the British, poet laureate attended in the 1930's and who wrote his children's book entitled "Archie and the Strict Baptists". He also wrote a poem called "Undenominational".

I am not certain but I met a young lady from the Peppler family and on one of these occasions and she invited my wife and I to a Christian holiday organized by Mr Peter Fry. It was on this holiday I was introduced to Errol Hulse who was the guest speaker.

New Mill Baptist

New Mill Baptist, near Tring, Hertfordshire

Winslow Baptist Tabernacle, Buchinghamshire

Opposition to the Gospel Standard Position

Errol Hulse had written a book about the Baptists and he divided them into three groups. The High Calvinist (Gospel Standard Baptists) who he was against, the middle Calvinist (of which he was), those following the 1689 London confession and the General Baptists who denied particular Baptists.

Grove Chapel

Grove Chapel Wantage

Grove Strict and Particular Baptists

It became apparent that these men were opposed to the high Calvinist position and were always suggesting that I was wrong to hold such views. This was because we were members of the Bierton Church who had become a Gospel Standard cause and I felt it right to give an apologetic reply to them all. So I would seek to defend my position with them. They were in favour of the Free Presbyterian position with respect to the Free Offer of the gospel but I am not sure of their view of the Presbyterian view of Sabbath keeping as Miss Anne Peppler told me a Joke about the Free Presbyterian beliefs in this respect.

A certain minister Macdonald was engaged to preach but the ferry the night before was stopped due to Ice. So he travelled to preach across the lake on his ice skates.

The elders came to MacDonald, as he was now under censor for an apparent breach of the Sabbath; he had skated on the Sabbath. MacDonald in his defence felt he was doing the right thing in his zeal and desire to honour his preaching engagement.

How ever the elders stated they accept that and is commendable for that action but their examination revealed they were concerned over a deeper matter they said skating was acceptable but they wanted to know if he had enjoyed it". Had he enjoyed it he was guilty of a Sabbath breach.

The Strict Baptist Church at Evington

Evington Chapel, Leicester

This is where David Oldham was the pastor and also the Pastor of Peterborough Salem Strict Baptist where J.C. Philpot was once its pastor.

David Came to my help when I experienced difficulties later on at the Bierton Church.

Zion Leicester

Zion Leicester New Building

Mr. Grey Hazelrigg who was pastor from 1873 to 1912 founded the Strict Baptist Church at Leicester in 1873. Who was the former pastor of Trinity Chapel, Leicester?

The old chapel was a very large building, in the centre of Leicester, with a small congregation. It was at the old Chapel that I preached in 1982 and 1983 and I recall that they still had the old amplifying system with wonderful carbon granule microphones

The Strict Baptist Church at Luton

Ebenezer Strict Baptist Chapel

This is where Pastor James Hill was the pastor and invited me to preach in 1983.

Pastor James Hill, who was a great help to me wrote and asked me to preach at the church he was pastor of in Luton. This is Ebenezer and it is now a listed grade 2 building in Hasting Street.

Reading Strict Baptist

Zoar Strict Baptist Reading

Mr P Hope was the minister and our helper at our Bierton Church

Fenstanton Particular Baptist Chapel

Fenstanton, Particular Baptist Chapel

I was so concerned to put God first and to fulfil my calling that when my twins, David and Eleanor were born on 29th October 1983 and were due to come home. I postponed bringing my wife and them home from hospital in order not to cancel a preaching engagement I had made in the fear of God.

Various people this day tell me I was wrong I should have put my wife first. What do you think?

Attleborough Strict and Particular Baptist Church

The Cave of Adulam

Jireh Strict Baptist Chapel

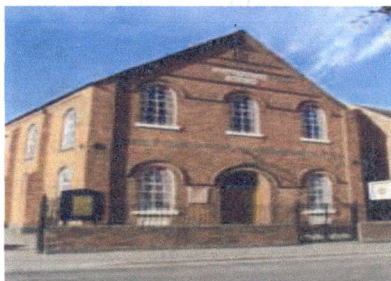

Attleborough

It was here I meet David Crowther and had reason to discuss some controversial issues, which I mention in "The Bierton Crisis".

Beeches Road Strict and Particular Baptist Church

The Beeches Road Strict Baptist Chapel began over one hundred fifty years ago at its current location. Known then as Cave Adulam Strict Baptist Chapel, it was a well-known and well-attended Strict Baptist church in the Black Country. The main chapel was officially opened in 1897 and is capable of seating around five hundred adults.

Zoar Particular Baptist Chapel Bradford

Darfield Street

Hope Strict Baptist Church Nottingham

The New Building

I preached here on one occasion. It was large building and had its own library and I was kindly give some books which included another set of Dr John Gill's commentary of the bible. A set of 6 books in red. And as a result I was able to help the father of Stephen Royce, who was a member of the Watford Strict Baptist. He was having difficulties with the Added Articles of the Gospel Standard so I felt he really could use these books. I kept the set **given me by Hope Chapel and still have them today** and I gave the set of commentaries', given to me, by Frank L. Gosden to him. I believed this would help, as they had been a great help to me and in due course his son Stephen Royce from Luton.

Matfield Strict and Particular Baptist Church

Matfield Strict Baptist Chapel

I preached at the Matfield Strict and Particular Baptist and it was here the matters relating to the use of a television was first raised and brought to my attention in a serious context.

20 The Papal Visit

I write to D.B. an Anglican Vicar

Since the recent visit of the Pope to Britain, in 1982, I was compelled to examine the claims of the papacy and the Roman Catholic Church. During August 1983.

After that time I was very much alert to the activity of the Church of Rome and the trend for the Anglican Church to move closer to Rome. About one year after this time I read an article in a magazine called "Contact", by Rev D.B. an Anglican Vicar at Walton Street Church of England. I was move to write to him.

Here is the letter:

187 Aylesbury Road Bierton Buckinghamshire

Dear Mr. Brewin,   17th August 198

Having read your article, which appeared in Mays issue of "Contact" (1982), titled Roman Catholicism, I am constrained to write to you as a preliminary step. For you express views concerning Roman Catholicism and Pope John Paul II which are not shared by many Christians. You indicate your views concerning the Pope by stating the John Paul the II are a man of deep spirituality and courage and so worthy of our respect. You say he is a Christian, and a Christian Leader, although you differ on the authority he and his church lays claim too. Never the less there are common grounds between Anglicans and Roman Catholic as fellow Christians and belonging to a Christian Church.

You list four basic areas of common ground for this recognition:

A You are (Anglican and Roman Catholic) are both people

of Christ.

B Are both people of the bible

C Have Sacraments of Baptism and Holy Communion

D Are both people of the Holy Spirit.

You then express the real differences, which you believe ought to be remembered.

Now as a minister of the Gospel of the Lord Jesus Christ I write to you believing your article and beliefs do endanger the flock of Christ, over which you are and over seer and I would be failing in my responsibility should I remain silent and not approach you.

May I then go through some of the points you mention?

A You are both people of Christ

The justification for saying this is that both churches call upon the name of Christ and worship Him as saviour and Lord. My question to you is where is the evidence of this? To own him as saviour and Lord is to call upon no other name than his. This being demonstrated by rejecting all others whether lords of lordesses. Is this true of both churches?

My evidence is the present Pope John Paul II calls upon Mary the Queen of Heaven in prayer. (Quotation from "Return to Poland" Collins)

Before the Black Madonna of Jasn Gora (where he had many times in the past whispered "totus tuus" i.e.. completely yours) there he re consecrated Poland to the immaculate heart of Mary as the Queen of the popish kingdom.

He further told the image " I consecrate to you the whole

Church- every where and to the ends of the earth. I consecrate to you all humanity; all men and women. All the peoples and nations. I consecrate to you Europe and all the continents, I consecrate to you Rome and Poland (who are) now united through your servant. Mother accept us all! Mother do not abandon us! Mother be our Guide!

This shows a plain contradiction to you first statement that the Church of Rome calls upon Christ's name as Lord. How can is be said of him he is a man of God of deep spirituality worthy of our respect and a Christian. A man stooped in idolatry and spiritual darkness.

B You are both people of the bible

The evidence for this statement is that since the Vatican Council, 20 years ago, the Roman Catholic Church has put great emphasis on bible study for individuals and groups. With a profound effect.

But which bible do they advance to be the word of God is my question. My evidence is that:

a) The tradition of the Roman Catholic Church is of equal authority with the bible and the Apocryphal books must be considered as scripture. (Council of Trent 1545). Hence the bible which the Catholics are lead to read contains the Apocrypha and the reason being they require 11 Maccabees 12 verse 40 - 45 to teach and maintain their heretical doctrines of prayers for the dead. (The Apocrypha must be accepted as scripture under the penalty of a mortal sin).

b) The bible is subject to the churches interpretation of the Douay or Confraternity i.e. those versions, which are tailored to teach Catholic Doctrine, and notes are the version put forward as scripture. Again it is still a mortal sin for a Catholic to read a Protestant version except the R.S.V. (Catholic Edition). Hence the Catholic is not free to read the scripture and interpret it for himself. The Roman Catholic Church under the infallible Pope when reading the bible must rule him. For there can be no other interpretation than what the Church dictates.

C Both have the Sacraments of Baptism and Holy Communion

This however is without qualification. My evidence is that the Roman Catholic Church have the Mass and Sacrificing priest, both of which are heretical and opposed to the Holy Communion or Lords Supper.

As for baptism the Roman Catholic Church maintains the doctrine of baptismal regeneration by which means all past sins are forgiven. Hence baptism is essential to salvation. (See Trent catechism) quote Infants, unless regenerated unto God by the grace of baptism, whether their parents be Christian of infidels are born to eternal misery and perdition). Hence we see the Church of Rome has no Christian Ordinances but the reverse.

D Your are both people of the Holy Spirit

Your evidence for this is that the renewal movement has made a good impression upon the Roman Catholic Church with the effect of bringing many Christians together even within the Church of England. Here you place undoubted reliance upon renewal and gathering together imputing this work to the Holy Spirit. Hence concluding the Spirit of God makes no distinction so who are we to put up doctrinal barriers hindering our gathering together with which we please?

Here I would ask the following: If both communions have the

same Spirit of truth, light and love for Jesus Christ why are they not lead in the same way. If the Holy Spirit say, " Come out of her my people that ye be not partakers of her sins (Rev. 18 verse 4) what spirit is it that keeps them in the Church of Rome or moves the Anglican Community to seek such unity with her. Rome is an Apostate Church.

If the spirit which is in the Roman Catholic Church which leads them to blaspheme the Son of God in the sacrifice of the mass and bow do,wn to idols and seeks the aid of departed saints then what spirit moved Luther and the reformers to obey the truth and leave Rome, and the Papal Pontiff, and establish true Christian Churches?

What biblical evidence do we have that the Roman Catholic Church is possessed and moved by the Spirit of God.

You also express your personal belief in respect of the Pope being no Anti- Christ. However the Church of England and her founders held opposite views. Remember Cranmer, Latimer and Ridley. We should surely keep as close to the bible as these fathers in the faith and defend the little ones of Christ's fold against all error and preserve them as a chaste virgin unto Him (2 Cor 11 verse 2)

Now my prayer to God is that Christian men of Aylesbury be united in Christ's cause and truth having love for the brethren and his dear children in the bonds of true Gospel unity and peace.

May the Grace of our Lord Jesus Christ be the cause and the communion of the Holy Spirit the means and life of His Church now and forever more?

Yours in Christian concern,

David Clarke. In membership of Bierton Strict and Particular Baptist Church

21 I Go Fishing For Men

In May 1983 I was engaged to preach at the church in Bierton on Sunday 5th June 1983. I have always had that desire to catch men for Jesus Christ but how do you do it. I was now living in Aylesbury and a lot of my former friends were still in and around Aylesbury, having no hope and without God in the world.

The Bucks Herald

THURSDAY 19th May 1983 price 8d

Former thief says: Come and be helped

David fishes for men - Bierton Meeting 5th June 1983

I felt compelled to do some thing to get the message of the love of God in Jesus Christ, to them some how. Jesus had done for me and that I was preaching at Bierton Church I decided I should go and ask the Bucks Herald,a local news paper to give me some free advertising. I simply went to the Bucks Herald office and told them my story. I said I wanted to reach all my old friends to tell them what the Lord on, 5th of June that they were all welcome.

I was prepared to advertise but I know I was being cheeky in asking for it free. Little did I realize it but I was giving them their front-page news for the week. Before I knew it the photographer was out to see me and a reporter taking notes for a story. It all happened so quickly

The story appeared as follows on the front page of the Bucks Herald on Thursday, May 19th 1983. **Providentially this meeting was televised and can be viewed on Youtube**

(Click here to view) David Preaches at Bierton Chapel 5th June 1983

A News Paper Report

I was landed with a problem as I did not expect any of this to happen and I hadn't informed the church and so I felt the need to explain what had happened in case it offended any one. I felt relieved when no one was upset.

I felt the need to be very careful because in October 1982 I had already found some opposition from one part of the church and I was not out cause trouble. They were against a certain good minister and visiting preacher because he had used the term Evangelical Repentance and that he read the Evangelical Times. I had defended this man in every way I knew how but for the sake of peace the church decided not to asked this man to preach again. I was very sad and disturbed by this and I believed from that time Satan was provoked by my actions. And there was more to come. So for this reason I felt the need to be extra careful.

Meeting Televised

The Bierton Pulpit

The following week I went fishing, looking in the pubs, and visiting people's homes looking for my former friends in crime, in order to bring them along to hear what Jesus had done for me and could do for them.

It wasn't long before the national news network were on to me and wanted the story which I believe appeared in one of the national news papers. I was disappointed in the write up because I felt it was trivializing the reality of what was going on. This is the official transcript:

Dear David Here's what we put out on the national Telex service. Looking forward to seeing you at the service June 5th Yours Peter Game

From Peter Game, OX and Bucks NA Catch: Service Reformed crook David Clarke is hot on the trail of his mates in crime. He's turned detective to trace thieves, drug pushers, burglars, bandits and drunks in a massive one man round-up aimed at changing their lives.

And it could result in the most bizarre meeting of shady characters a town has eve known.

David, 33 wants to pack them all into a tiny church at Bierton, bucks, and tell them how God saved him from spending a life behind bars.

And if the Local C.I.D. force at nearby Aylesbury, bucks wants to turn up and join in the hymn singing too they are welcome. David a married man with two children from Aylesbury Road, Bierton, is a lay preacher in the Baptist church.

He said, "God helped me and can help all my old buddies too".

David an Electronics lecturer at a Polytechnic explained:

" I 've already persuaded some old villainous pals to come along. I want to pack the church with criminals, but it's going to be a tough job".

The former thief and drug user left Borstal aged 18 and decided to lead a life of luxury based on crime.

"I was in a car ringing business, thieving vehicles and knocking them out again," he confessed.

" I've broken into an old peoples home to steal a colour telly, taken garage equipment, nicked from tills, walked of with speed boat engines, and taken drugs. I've even sold drugs and got involved in permissive sex.

"There were times when I used to keep an axe and a mallet in my car just in case. Now it has all changed.

His life took a drastic change when he "met Jesus Christ" during LSD trip and joined the Baptist Church.

And when detectives questioned him about an offence he did not commit he confessed to 24 he did carry out.

He Added " I've had a clean sheet for 13 years. I'm not going to preach the bible at the bad boys --- Just show them how God helped me and let them make up their minds".

Ends.

Memo to news desk: Service on June 5th. We believe this man is absolutely genuine in his actions.

Memo End.

Out Come Of The Meeting

The meeting went ahead as planned but not many people turned up. I heard that some did not come because they did not wish to be associated with each other. Pat Jones and Malcolm Kirkham were now enemies. Pat Jones had not long ago been around Malcolm's house to blast him with a shotgun. Malcolm had been in evolved in drug pushing and other things.

Mike West said he wasn't prepared to sit or be associated with drug pushers and criminal's etc.

I had spoken as faithfully as I could at that meeting of the Lord Jesus Christ and I remember saying from the pulpit how good God had been to me in blessing me with a good Job, a wife, a nice house, children being in church and many friends what more could a natural man want. I had comments made by several people that God had really blessed me providentially and I knew it.

On reflection it seems from this time I was battered from every way. First my church membership was lost, then my health, which affected my call to preach. Then my children were attacked, then my home was lost, and then my Job was lost. Then my faith in God was lost, which led to me giving up on my marriage. I write about all these thing in my latter book, **Converted on LSD Trip 2nd Edition.** Published 16th January 2012.

My troubles appear to begin after this meeting

As I write this it reminds me of the story of Job who was truly blessed by God in his own soul and in material things, then Satan came seeking to destroy his faith in God. God gave Satan leave to do it but the end of Job best better than his beginning. Thanks be to God. I hope my story will reflect the same faithfulness of God to me.

Stephen Royce and family at Eaton Bray

Shortly after this time I met Stephen Royce and his family including his father and mother who were members of Watford Strict Baptist Church. Stephen had become a believer and was seeking to resolve difficulties that he had in receiving the wording of the added articles of the Gospel Standard.

He had been brought up at the Watford Strict Baptist Church, where Mr Hill was the pastor but he had moved to Luton Ebenezer and Mr Sayers's senior was the new pastor and his son Howard Sayers was a minister sent from the Watford church. At that time Howard made it clear he did not accept the added articles o f the Gospel Standard that of course was no help to Stephen Royce or his father.

Stephen writes to me about the Added Articles

Stephen Royce was had become a Christian and believed he should be baptized but Mr Ramsbottom, the pastor of Luton, would not put forward his request to be baptized to the church as he in conscience could not subscribe in totality to these added articles.

This became a real problem to him and he wondered why he could not be baptized, as a believer and simply not join the Church meeting at Bethel chapel. As he could not in conscience agree with the wording of the Added Article because they appeared to deny scripture.

I fully understood his problem and felt for him so I put pen to paper (or type face) and sought to answer his questions, since I was a member of a Gospel Standard listed Church and sent minister from that Church.

My reply to Stephen Royce is published in,"The Bierton Crisis" and I believe was a scriptural answer and support to the non-offer of the gospel that we had declared to be the case in the Gospel Standard Articles.

22 Waddesdon Hill Strict Baptist Chapel

In 1984 a Mr. Rose of Luton, a former trustee of the Waddesdon Hill Strict Baptist Chapel wrote to me whilst I was living at Bierton. Asking if we at Bierton Strict and Particular Baptist Church would wish to hold evangelistic meetings at the Waddesdon Strict Baptist Chapel during the time when Billy Graham was preaching in England and Mission England was going on. He suggested I wrote to the new Trustees who were now the Metropolitan Association of Strict Baptist Churches.

The Waddesdon Hill chapel was a very quaint chapel out on its own along the village road in Waddesdon. It had closed down due to too few people attending. Each year since 1976 I had attended an anniversary service there conducted by a Mr. Collier, minister of Linslaid Strict Baptist church then Mr. Hill of the Luton Strict Baptist church.

Waddesdon Hill Gospel Standard Chapel

Waddesdon Hill Strict Baptist Chapel

Our church at Bierton would not be interested in Billy Graham or want anything to do with Mission England because of their Arminian ways, so I wrote to the Trustees explaining what had happened and asked if few others and I could use the chapel during this period to preach the gospel. I explained this was Mr. Roses request and I was very willing to be involved. I explained we had a few Christian friends who would wish to be involved including the church at Eaton Bray.

Association of Metropolitan of Strict Baptists

A letter to the chairman of the trust

Dear Mr. Knight   27/4/1984

With reference to our telephone conversation of Tuesday I write on behalf of a number of people with a request to hold public meetings for the purpose of preaching the Word of God and worship at the chapel situated at Waddesdon Hill.

This initial proposal is to hold three of four meetings during the summer months, say the 1st Saturday of each month, June, July, August and September, in the PM.

I am a Particular Baptist (and minister of the Gospel) in membership of Bierton Strict and Particular Baptist Church. Whilst our church does not wish to be responsible for such meetings they have no objection to my personal involvement and organization of any such meetings.

Enclosed is a subscriber list of names offering mutual help and support.

I understand you are to meet shortly and we would be grateful if permission could be granted to our request. If this is possible may we have a copy of the "Articles of Faith" and clauses in the trust deed with your reply?

Yours Sincerely,

David Clarke.

My request turned down

My request was turned down, as they wanted a properly formed church to take over the chapel such as the Limes Avenue Strict Baptist Church. I found this way of doing things very chilling and help formed my view of such organized associations. I would not commend them.

We Try To Buy the Waddesdon Hill Chapel

Shortly after this after I had succeeded from the Bierton chapel and a few of us were meeting in our home at Bierton I was informed the Waddesdon Hill Chapel was up for sale. I thought perhaps this was a way forward and we could use the chapel to meet in and we may be in the position to form a church.

I wrote to the trustee's explaining my situation. I asked them to forward me a copy of the trust deed as I felt since I had attended the meetings held by the former trustee's it was quite probable that we would qualify to use the chapel if we fitted the characters of those set out in the trust deed.

I was invited to meet with the committee and put forward my case and during meeting one of the trustees said they wanted some one dynamic to go into Waddesdon village and make an impact. I thought this was not how I saw things. God was well able to do it his way. I replied it sounded as though he wanted the Lord Jesus to go there.

I am offered the chapel on unsatisfactory terms

I was offered the chapel on the basis that I form a church using their confession of faith, which was the 1966 Strict Baptist Confession. I said I could not do that because I believed them to be wrong but would be able to do so if they were, as the Gospel Standard Articles, without those added ones. My request and offer was turned down.

I offer to buy the chapel for 1 penny more than the highest bidder

Not being prepared to let it go, I offered to buy the chapel and since they were going to sell it I would offer one penny more that the highest bidder. They were not prepared to do this. So I left it.

23 The Holy Table

About this time, I took my children to church and I had my brother's daughter with me and she would have been about 5 years old. After the Sunday school before the morning meeting began I happened to place her cardigan on the table at the front of the chapel. This was the table used when conducting church affairs and for the communion. The pulpit was behind this were the preacher stood and preached. The table was where the hymns were announced and given out.

Mrs. Evered, in her lovely manor, came up to me and said that I was to take the cardigan off, "The Holy Table". I was shocked by this remark. What was this all about we now had a Holy Table? We were not Roman Catholic or High Anglicans. I was dismayed at such heresy and after the morning meeting I asked the church members to stay behind whilst I established what was going on. I began to realize I was unearthing more religious errors, which would have to be dealt with sooner than later.

I asked the few members of the church, in front of Mrs. Evered about the "Holy table". I said there was no such thing as a holy table in the New Testament this was religious error and just like the Roman Catholics and their superstitions. I said I would not stand by and let this error go unchecked. To my surprise and disappointment Miss G Ellis became angry and walked out saying she was feed up with it all. She said she would not want a pair of shoe put on the kitchen table and she walked out in anger. I thought to my self we are in two different worlds what was going on in the minds of the church and congregation at Bierton. I felt so taken up with zeal for the cause of God and truth I could have taken a large axe and cut the table up in front of every one. I decided to do it another way. I would use the "sword of the spirit".

The Television Radio and Cassette Recorder

I was all too well aware of the issues regarding the television set as it was the general consensus of opinion it was wrong to own or view a television. This matter had arisen not only in our church but also anther churches that I had visited.

I had no problem with the television because I did not watch it and after all it could be switch off if one had one. I had been a television engineer working for Granada TV Rentals and had visited the Dicker, taking with me, in the company car, my Scotts Presbyterian friend James. This was with the company advertising on the side of the vehicle, which had caused him embarrassment. I had also taken Mrs Evered, in that very vehicle, all the way to Brighten, to visit her relatives, including Mr Frank Gosden.

Also I had on many occasions taken our church members to the various anniversary meetings in my company car. All of these churches were Gospel Standard churches. So I was aware of the issues involved. I had discussed the matter with Mr Joseph Rutt, a minister from Bethel Church Luton, who had been very expressive of his opinions against the use and ownership, by church members, of a television set and had made his views known to all.

I am informed it is wrong for me to teach electronics

Mrs Evered had express it was wrong for me to teach the subject of electronics at Luton College because it helped students repair television sets. It was therefore a matter I could not ignore but deal with in due season. I had discovered far more serious issues that needed to be treated first. I could well imagine the same kind of problems occurring over the Radio, Newspapers and the cassette
248

recorder and future electronic means of communication.

Escorted out of St. Albans Abbey after a protest

In October 1983 I was informed that officials of St. Albans Abbey, a Church of England establishment, were for the first time in 400 years giving official recognition to the practice of the Roman Catholic Mass. This was probably as a direct result of the Papal visit to Britain in 1982.

They had invited a Roman Catholic Father Plourde to serve in the Anglican Church and he was to offer Mass on a regular basis at the St. Albans Abbey. This was in fact illegal and against the principles of the Act of Settlement.

No one seemed to care or could see what was happening I had studied the teaching of the Roman Catholic Church and found it in very serious error.

I felt constrained to support any kind of protest just to let people know what was going on throughout the world. The Mass had no place in the Christian faith.

I decided to take my two children Isaac John (5) and Esther Jane (4) with me to protest against this evil

I attended the meeting on a Saturday afternoon and before very long a Mr. Scott Person of the British Council of Protestant Churches stood up and made a formal protest. He was escorted out.

I waited a while and just before the meeting resumed I stood up and made my protest. I too was escorted out of the meeting with Isaac and Esther in my hands.

This event hit the headline news again in Aylesbury and also in the local news in Luton these articles appear as follows:

AN unholy uproar involving a Bierton man and others broke out at St. Albans Abbey on Saturday because of the involvement of a Roman Catholic priest in the service.

The protest by Mr. David Clarke, of 187 Aylesbury Road, concerned Father Robert Plourde who, along with Methodist minister the Rev. Donald Lee, was being welcomed to the Abbey.

An initial protest was made by a representative from Malden, in Bedfordshire, of the British Council of Protestant Christian Churches, who then left the Abbey.

Before the service resumed however Mr. Clarke stood up and said he protested about a Catholic priest being appointed as an assistant in the Church of England.

Mr. Clarke told the clergy and congregation that to invite what he described as a Popish person to conduct masses, was contrary to Christian principles and the Gospel of Christ.

The authorities of the Abbey were betraying the people into the hands of the Papal Anti-Christ, he stated. At this point he was escorted from the Abbey.

David Clarke

accompanied by his four-year-old son and three-year-old daughter.

Mr. Clarke, a 34-year-old lecturer of electronics at Luton College of Higher Education, is a member of the Baptist Church in Bierton, and himself preaches in various churches.

This was the first official service in the Church of England, as far as he knew, to give recognition in that way, he said.

A representative of the Abbey said the two part-time ecumenical chaplains had already been appointed and were being welcomed on Saturday at the inter-denominational service.

Father Plourde would now be able to celebrate Mass in the Abbey for people who wanted to take it, she said, pointing out that all were welcome at the Abbey.

"There is a long tradition of welcoming all Christians, and of supporting Christian unity at the Abbey," she commented.

Teacher's protest in Abbey

The Bucks Herald front page

A Luton college lecturer was ejected from St. Albans Abbey after a stand up argument in the middle of a special service.

David Clarke was escorted from the building after protesting about involvement of a Roman Catholic priest in the proceedings.

This week 34- year old Mr Clarke, who lecturers in electronics at Luton College of Higher Education, Park Square, told why he challenged the welcoming of Father Robert Plourde to the service.

He said: To have a Roman Catholic priest appointed as an assistant in an Anglican Church is contrary to the Church of England articles of religion.

The service had been stopped by a protest from Rev. Scott Pearson, the Baptist minister of Maulden, representing the British Council of Protestant Christian Churches.

He left the Abbey, but before the ceremony could resume father-of- two Mr Clarke stood up to voice his opinions.

"I told the congregation the involvement of a Popish person was against Christian principles and offensive". He was escorted out of the Abbey with his two children.

He said the welcoming of Father Plourde and Methodist minister the Rev Donald Lee on Saturday last week was part of a move to bring the churches together.

Mr Clarke of Aylesbury Road, Bierton Buckinghamshire, who sometimes preaches in the Luton Area, said he was saved from a life of crime and drug taking through Jesus Christ spoke to him when experiencing a bad LSD Trip.

I had some opposition and response via The Bucks Herald, our local paper and these are: Thursday 20th October 1983

An evil wind is blowing

Sir, - It was a feeling of sick despair, all to often felt in these times, that I read in this weeks issue of your paper the account of David Clarke's conduct in St Albans Abbey.

In his position as a preacher at his local church he has maybe raised doubt in the minds of many and laid his own church open to criticism and most unfairly There is and evil wind blowing through the world and the despairing cries of victims caught in the midst of sectarian wars. Above their cries are heard louder voices declaiming "We do this for God" and each names God in different tongues.

Men and women of good faith striving for peace and brotherhood brought about the delicate and vulnerable progress towards unification of the various denominations slowly and arduously. Such a balance could be disturbed and for what purpose? Search the bible that you are so prominently featured holding, Mr. Clarke and there you find that Jesus preached love, compassion and tolerance. Not the condemning of hatred against those of us, of every faith and creed, who are still striving towards further enlightenment.

Christ's teachings are simple and clear cut. Are you certain you are following the true leader?

Mrs. Cecilia Brooks 30 York Place, Aylesbury.

NEWS/GAZETTE, October 20, 1983 Teachers Protest

Another upset person also wrote the following in the same paper:

Playing "Fantastic tricks"

Sir, - Like myself, many of your readers must have been filled with dismay to see your recent headlines **"Anti - Pope rumpus in Abbey"**.

They must also have regretted that, when the two great Christian leaders, thePope and the Archbishop of Canterbury, are striving to promote peace and understanding between religious denominations, well- meaning but fanatics should seek to destroy their endeavours.

Half the cold-blooded murders in Ireland wear the cloke of religion as else where in the world, whilst the Russians persecute Baptists and the Mujahedeen. And in Iran the unfortunate Baha'is -

men, women and children - are martyred for their faith.

Do we want the days of the Tudors to come back and flames rekindled at Amersham or Oxford?

No- one should suppose that tolerance and indifference are one and the same.

The tolerance, in which I believe, means respect to others and for all God's creation- man and beast and plant.

It also means love for one's neighbour but, as Shakespeare wrote; Man proud man, dressed in a little brief authority, plays such fantastic tricks before high heaven as makes the angels weep".

K.M.D. Dunbar Firethorn London Road Aston Clinton Buckinghamshire.

The Lord, through Malcolm Kirkham, encouraged me. I was move to write my reply to the newspaper and it appeared on the 27th October 1983, which was as follows:

Cannot Remain Silent

Sir, - I did not wish to provoke hatred, violence or anger when making my protest over a popish person now conducting the mass at the Anglican Church at St. Albans.

Can it not be seen my actions were of those of a loving and faithful Christian? All Christians believe, "faithful are the wounds of a friend ".

My protest was based on the fact that the Roman Catholic Mass has no place in the Christian Church since it is a blasphemy against the Lord Jesus Christ. (Article 31 Church of England).

The Roman Catholic Church proclaims a person cannot be saved unless he partakes of the sacrifice of the mass, nor experience the salvation of the Lord Jesus Christ.

My concern was for those newly seeking the Lord Jesus Christ and to indicate to them the devices of those who should know better.

I have a wife and family and twins on the way. I have a responsible lecturing post and teach people of all ages. I am experienced in danger and believe I should point out such dangers to the innocent.

I am currently teaching the gospel to a now reformed drug pusher, criminal and convict. Directing him and his wife unto the Lord Jesus Christ the saviour and not the Mass or any other device of men.

To Cecilia Brooks and K.M. Dunbar, who believe many were horrified and dismayed, may I say I think not but be consoled with the words of a wise man (Acts 5.38) "Refrain from these fears and anxieties for if my actions be merely of myself it will come to naught: but if it be of God, ye cannot over throw it, lest happily, ye be found even to speak evil of the evil wind, that is said to be blowing, when in fact it is the Spirit of God.

As a preacher of Christ's love to men, I cannot remain silent but must oppose those kisses, though ever so sweet are deceitful.

My home is open to all that are genuinely seeking the truth as in the Lord Jesus Christ.

You may come to see the church at Bierton as well to hear the Word of God spoken.

DAVID CLARKE (Minister of the Gospel)
27/10/8

24 Truth Causes A Division

Luke 2. 51

This section deals with those issues that I would not normally publish. However as a result of the very serious doctrinal errors and practice that I encountered I am fully persuaded that it is right to publish them as a warning for others. The following is an account of an issue that resulted in me withdrawing from the communion, over matters of conscience, due to the unresolved churches issues and departure from the truth and misconduct of the church.

The following sermon notes were made before and after I preached at the weeknight meeting, at the Bierton Strict and Particular Baptist Chapel, on Wednesday the 20th of April 1983. I believe that sermon was the instrument laid at the root of the error, which caused the division, and parting of the ways between the Bierton Church and I. This led to my secession on the 26th of June 1984.

Particular Redemption

I had clearly spoken on the subject of particular redemption and providentially one sermon was recorderded and can be heard on YouTube:

A sermon preached a defence of Particular Redemption 1983 (Click here)

On Wednesday, the 20th of April, I preached a sermon, during our week evening meeting. The text being, this is a faithful saying and these things I will that thou affirm constantly. That they, which have believed in God, might be careful to maintain good works' (Titus 3 8).

In my attempt to apply the truth of this text, bearing in mind the current needs and position of our church at Bierton, I gave examples, by way of direct application.

I stated how we might be found to take heed to this exhortation if we restored a suitable children's hymn book which did not contain hymns expressing general redemption & universal redeeming love to all children. Some how a blue children's hymnbook, published by the Metropolitan Association of Strict Baptists Sunday schools, had been introduced to the Sunday school. I stated also it would be a good work to set our church in order even though some would not credit this to be a good work. That in this pursuit there may be a thing not acceptable to our natural carnal desires and us as individuals.

School Hymn Book

The National Association of Strict Baptist Sunday

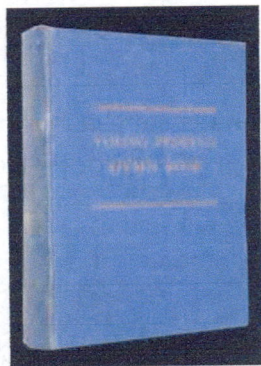

The Childrens Hymn Book

The examples given in order

We had no ruling authority and needed a pastor or minister for teaching and ruling well.

We should teach truth in our Sunday school and not error as was being taught by Mr King, such as "universal redeeming love" for all children. I asserted it was wrong to teach the children or led them to believe in general redemption and that a step to avoid this would be to restore a suitable hymnbook, which was in accordance with our own Confession of Faith..

Effects of this address During this address I observed the countenance of Mr. King who shook his head from Side to side. This was at the point that I said it was heresy to teach the children Jesus died for them each one. He said, at another time, he knew not by what spirit I spoke that evening. Mr King was the only other male member of the church and had been sent by the church as a minister to preach. I do not know how long he had been a minister or when he was sent to preach but as such he was responsible for the things he taught.

A Church Meeting To Resolve The Issue

Mrs. Gurney after the meeting asked when we could have a church meeting to discuss these matters. Our quarterly meeting was due to be held that April so we booked the 27th day of April at 2:30 pm. At this meeting Mr. King red from the 23rd Psalm and was our appointed chairman. Mr King was a sent minister of our church and had been then one to propose that we become a Gospel Standard cause. He was a responsible adult and church member.

The chairman (Mr King) made introductory comments regarding his position as chairman and that by the next church meeting he would have fulfilled that office for one year and that he wished the church to seek a chairman to succeed him. This was because he could not conduct church affairs whilst there were disagreements amongst the members.

Chairman refuses to allow discussion causing Concern.

The chairman expressed his disapproval of the matter to be discussed since he said this matter could not be raised since, as it was contrary to the rule 15 of the Gospel Standard rule book of which we were governed. He stated Mr. D Clarke was out of order and must have the permission of the church to discuss this matter.

Mr. D Clarke expressed his view, that since it was a case of serious disorder and the Cause of truth would suffer prejudice if left for one month, rule 15 allowed for his action. Also that it would be wrong to leave the church for a whole month with such a charge being unanswered. (P.S. I believed, at the time, this delay was a tactic of Satan and so I then Devil was resisted, in the same way as Cromwell resisted and deposed the ruling king of England, who maintained "the divine right of a king to rule in unrighteousness".

Mr King asks for an honourable dismissal

to leave the church

Mr King asked for an honourable dismissal from membership. How ever I informed him, at the church meeting, he could not be given leave with honour unless he move to other church of the same faith and order, simply because he would not be subject to a lawful enquiry of the church as to the doctrines he was advancing. **See our Gospel Standard rules of conduct Rule 15.**

Chairman comments upon the sermon

The chairman stated that I had made serious charges against the Bierton church and that he wished the ' chair ' to be respected and honoured by this ruling authority .

Chair opposed

After general matters had been discussed and church business had finished Mr. D. Clarke opposed the Chairman regarding the sermon preached explaining he wished the church to give their opinion as to their belief in respect of teaching the children and their unconverted Parents, at the Sunday school Good Friday meetings. This was because general redemption in opposition to particular redemption was being taught. I said my charge of them teaching heresy was justifiable for Mr. King had said himself, at the Good Friday service both last year and this year, Jesus had died for each one of the children. Also they were teaching the children to sing Jesus had died for them and he loves them all.

The matter was not resolved at that meeting so I gave the chair back to Mr King to conclude the meeting.

The Holy Table (No idolatry Here)

After the issue of the hymn book and my defence of particular redemption that matter regarding the Holy Table arose again. I also wrote to Mrs. Evered, in order to discuss and explore the matter further. This was because this matter was so serious it needed to be put right. Mrs Evered should have known better, after all it was here declared her intention to return the Bierton Church to true Christian practice and preserve the traditions that she had held from a girl now we were amongst Gospel Standard Baptists. She returned the letter to me unread. She informed me she knew the truth and nothing would change her mind. She inferred that I was young and did not know these things as she had been brought up with the truth.

This was blatant idolatry that could not be ignored. This whole matter and my attempts to resolve these serious issues are recorded in detail, along with all the correspondence to all concerned, in my publication, **'The Bierton Crisis', published in 1984"**.

I Preach A Moving Sermon in 1983

On the 26th October 1983 I had the responsibility to lead the prayer meeting on the Wednesday evening and speak from the scriptures as I felt lead. On this occasion four of the congregation got up and left, my sermon was obviously was a moving sermon.

Essence of the sermon: The Chapel not the House of God.

I explained I had been called by grace 14 years ago and had testified to them of the goodness of God to me. That was in saving me from a life of crime, drug taking etc. I had learned about Jesus through reading the bible. I recalled the facts that I had come to the Bierton church because they too had knowledge of the truth of Jesus Christ, his dying for our sins. His justifying righteousness, and the Sovereignty of God in all his work towards us.

I said I believed God had called me to preach the Gospel of Jesus Christ and I had responsibilities to them all to make known what God had shown me.

I said the building was not the "House of God". There were no such things as holy tables etc. and we must not reverence these things as was common amongst Roman Catholics.

At this point a member of the church shouted out. "Well is not this the house of God" pointing to the roof of the building. Then another rose to their feet saying this is just like a church meeting and walked out. Then two other persons, Mr. King and his wife and John Snuggs got up and left.

I was staggered and alarmed for I had not risen my voice, not spoke severely or in a hard way. Never the less the truth as revealed in Jesus Christ had provoked this reaction.

From that time Mr King withdrew from fellowship and no longer attended our meetings.

I then recalled a dream that I had had previously and it had now come to pass.

I had previously spoken to Mr Collier about the problems that had arisen at Bierton regarding Mr King teaching general redemption and I had requested our church to invite him to help resolve those issues at our church. However Mr King did not wish him to be involved and the matter never was resolved. Mr Collier stated that we must change the hymnbook, as what we had was wrong.

Mr Collier Dies

It was a sad loss for us at Bierton in 1982 when Mr Collier died he had been a great help to me and the church at Bierton. Many people attended his funeral and Paul Watts his grand son and Dr Ian Paisley the minister of the Free Presbyterian Church of Northern Ireland conducted this. Mr Collier had been a good friend and helper to the church at Bierton and he was surely to be missed.

Mr Crane of Lakenheath Appointed Our Overseer

During this very difficult period Mr Crane responded to our request for help to resolve our difficulties and he did a very good job, and the best he could. However matters were never resolved during the time I remained in membership. We went to several church meetings in order to resolve issues that had arisen but unfortunately they were never resolved. Mean while other issues began to arise that needed to be dealt with.

Mr Steven Royce of Luton requested help Article 26

It was during my first year of preaching that I met Stephen Royce at the Eaton Bray Chapel at Eddelesbourgh. His parents were members of the Watford Strict and Particular Baptist Church and he was very keen to hear the things of God. At that time he and his wife was attending the Bethel Strict and Particular Baptist Chapel along with his wife and children. It soon became apparent he had believed and trusted in the Lord Jesus for salvation and I encourage him to join the church he was attending. Unfortunately for him he was presented with a problem because he found the wording of the Gospel Standard Added Articles in accurate, at best, and wished to come to terms with their meaning. He reason that because I was a sent minister from a Gospel Standard Church then I would be the ideal person to assist in resolving his dilemma. The particular article was number 26. He was informed that unless he could subscribe to them without hesitation or question then the minister of the Church would not put he forward as a candidate for church membership.

I really understood his difficulties, as I too had to deal with the same issues when our church at Bierton became a Gospel Standard listed Church. It is a very serious thing to adopt articles of religion that affect our conduct and practice in connection with other people. The way I dealt with the problem has been recorded in The Bierton Crisis under the chapter The Gospel Standard Article of Religion. My experience with the many and varied religious groups and opinions of the day served to ensure that I had an informed mind and conscience regarding Articles of Religion and practical conduct.

Mr Stephen Royce had a valid point and his questioning and

concerns were valid. He deserved a good answer, so I did the best I could. See the Bierton Crisis for my answer.

I Am Asked To Help

It was because of Stephens's difficulty of just accepting these articles, without question he wrote to me and we discussed the whole matter. I in turn wrote my reply and suggestions as to how he could deal with the matter, I understood his problem completely and it was a real matter that needed to be resolved and not brushed away as though it did not matter. It did. My response and answer to Stephen is recorded in my book, The Bierton Crisis.

Stephen found this hindrance, preventing him form being baptized, a real Burdon which had been placed upon his shoulders. In order to obey the Lord he requested just baptism rather than full church membership but this was refused without any scriptural reason why not. His response to a question that really was being asked by him was, what doth hinder me from being baptized.

What Doth Hinder Me From Being Baptized

The answer he received was his inability to agree to something the he, in conscience, could not agreed with out adequate clarification, and a definitive clear statement of truth regarding the matter, prevented him from being baptised. I trusted that my answer to him was sufficient. You will have to ask him. In the end another minister baptized him and he was not required to become a member of a church.

Paul Rowland a visiting minister singing of Psalms

One of our visiting ministers was Mr Paul Rowland who expressed his objection to the singing of hymns rather than the psalms. Mr Rowland also worked as a buyer for the Trinitarian Bible Society. I had no problem in the singing of psalms and was very interested in his objections, which were a matter of conscience. He also expressed his objections to the added articles of the Gospel Standard to which by now I was no stranger. As the secretary of the church I was responsible fro engaging our ministers. In order to accommodate Mr Rowland problems regarding the singing of psalms I agreed for him to provide us with psalm books and we sang psalms rather that songs from our Denham's Collection called the "Saint's Melodies".

It was interesting to talk to Paul as he also expressed his belief that the Presbyterian System was more scriptural and of course I had meet some Presbyterians when visiting the Isle of Skye but believed them to be wrong on several issues.

Linslaid and Children's Hymns

Soon after Mr Collier died we joined their members on their Lords Day afternoon meetings. It was good to meet other believes and I had been invited to join them by Peter Janes. However I was surprised to realize that one of the ladies had chosen a children's hymn just like Bierton which taught general redemption and I began to realize things were not as it appeared and began to think was this replicated in other strict Baptist churches and was this just the tip of the ice burg ?

Meeting Richard Bolt

At this time I met an old acquaintance, a Christian man called Dr. John Verna who too had met Mr John Metcalfe. I had first met him when I first became a Christian, at the age of 20. He was a

Doctor working at Stoke Mandeville Hospital working in particular with paraplegic patients. He used to help with the Hospital outreach meetings, which were held every month at the hospital. Several Christians from various churches had joined a group of Christian from the Assemblies of God Church in Aylesbury, to reach patients detained in Hospital. Each month patients were individually invited to the Saturday night gospel meeting held specifically for patients and staff in the Archery unit of the paraplegics department. They would be collected from the various wards in their beds and a different speaker, each month, would give a gospel address and we would pray for them.

Dr. John Verna and his wife helped and encouraged and worked with this group of Christians.

I talked with John about my position at Bierton Church and he seemed keen to help and support me. He introduced me to a dear friend of his a Mr. Richard Bolt from a place in Kent near Matfield. John Verna believed Richard Bolt to have an apostolic ministry.

He and Richard Bolt came to my home and we spent quite some time together and I was encouraged by them both to continue to seek God for direction. Richard Bolt was a very straightforward man, direct encouraging and thoughtful. A man of conviction And I believed had the fear of the Lord. I respected him for his honesty and sincerity. It was good to meet him.

I expressed my misgivings about my dealings in the Pentecostal Churches and my new position in the Strict and Particlar Baptist church.

Both groups it had occurred to me went to extremes. One held to the belief in the gifts of the supernatural gifts and Baptism in the Holy Ghost (Spirit) and looked for and expected manifestations of spiritual gifts in believers including the working of miracles (Pentecostal). They were very subjective and looked inward to them selves for the evidence of God working in and through them. Whilst the other group (Strict Baptists) denied the operation of supernatural operation of spiritual gift such as speaking in tongues and gifts of healing etc. but rather looked inwardly to the evidence of Gods dealing with them by how unworthy they might feel to receive any thing from God. That doubts of salvation were a good sign and an evidence of faith rather than presumption. Both group depended on God the Holy Ghost to work and save. I had concluded both groups could go to extremes.

Both Richard Bolt and John were convinced of the supernatural baptism in the Holy Ghost (spirit) and looked for and expected God to operate the nine gifts of the Spirit including the working of miracles according to Mark 16 verse 17. They believed in the fullness of New Testament Christianity and I was keen to learn and hear even though I was cautious and careful.

One thing I observed was that Richard had lost many of his teeth and I assumed this was because he had believed God for healing and looked to God for divine health. I thought to my self that if Christian were to expect and experience divine healing in this day and age then how come Richard had so few teeth. I did not ask him about his teeth, as I did not know him sufficiently to ask such a direct and personal question.

I meet John Metcalfe of Tyler's Green Chapel

Whilst speaking to Dr. John Verna he informed me he and his wife had met with John Metcalf of Penn, near High Wycombe, Buckinghamshire and that some of the people there often had a stall on the Market Square in Aylesbury selling Christian literature and the bibles they sold were only the Authorized King James version.

I was interested and because I had recently picked up a small tract written by John Metcalf called "The Gospel of God", which was about the claims of the Papacy and John Paul the second. I wished to meet John Metcalf because I recalled our visitor to the Bierton Church James who had attended Mr Metcalf's ministry and I understood and agreed with his writings in the tract. This had been most helpful and encouraging to me.

John Verna and Richard Bolt left and I felt encouraged by our meeting and I decided to go and visit the Church at Penn so as to meet Mr. John Metcalfe.

One Sunday evening I decided to go and I took my daughter Esther, she must have been about 3 or 4 years old and we drove to Penn and found the old chapel called Tyler's Green Chapel, Bethlehem Meeting Hall. Old-fashioned metal railings enclosed it and the gate was locked with no way in to the front door. It felt strange because the people were inside and a meeting was being held. I thought to my self had this door been locked deliberately to give a psychological shock to late comers and the feeling of being locked out as would be the case of the 5 foolish virgins mentioned by Jesus in Matth 25 verse 2).

It was damp outside and getting dark but I was determined to meet Mr. Metcalf so Esther and I waited outside, in the road, until the meeting had finished. Eventually the meeting ended and the people filled out sedately and quietly. I took courage and walked up to the man I believed to be John Metcalfe. Not too tall, well dressed, with a cream or white raincoat and white or grey hair. He was very courteous and when I introduced my self and explained my intent. I asked him about the chapel gates being locked gates he smiled when I explained my thoughts about the 5 foolish virgins. He then explained they locked the gates to prevent vandalism during the meetings, as they had had trouble in the past.

He informed his daughter and noted my persistence in waiting and that I had read his tract on John Paul the II, which seemed to encourage him. He then invited me back to his home for supper.

Esther and I were received graciously and we exchanged much conversation. Mr. Metcalfe's daughters made a fuss of Esther and gave her chocolate biscuits. I was invited to share my testimony of how I became a Christian and I deliberately decided to tell all that took place the night of my conversion holding nothing back.

(See full account of my conversion). All was very quite and nothing was said that I remember. I explained my present situation at Bierton Strict Baptist Church and the issues I had encountered regarding Particular Redemption, Law and Gospel, Added articles and finally Holy Tables. I was asked about my work and family and I explained I was a Lecturer at Luton College and a minister of the gospel in membership of a Strict Baptist church.

I felt greatly encouraged and noticed how nicely the house was kept. All in a lovely garden, spacious and it was beautiful. It was old and charming just as a Royal house and John Metcalfe kept an Alsatian as a guard dog.

John Metcalfe was a charming person a man of conviction, decisive and uncompromising. He seemed determined to follow God. I liked him and admired these qualities. I felt I could learn many things from this man. He had dealings with the Rev Ian Paisley but opposed him for unknown reasons. He despised the title Dr. and Dr. John Gill for accepting such titles. Also he had known Dr. Martin Lloyd Jones and eminent Christian ministers but opposed many things.

After that evening I returned another time with my wife and we were invited to attend the meeting at Tyler's Green Chapel one Sunday morning when Mr. Metcalfe would be preaching. It was arranged that one of the members of the church would look after our four children whist we attended that morning meeting. This we did. This was a remarkable sermon and I had never heard such powerful preaching. I was greatly encouraged and I realized later to substance of his sermon was that contained in his publication " Messiah". The sermon was eloquent, powerful and I believed very faithful to the word of God. I was greatly encouraged and admired the man and wanted to support his work.

After the meeting I was asked by Mr. Metcalfe how I had got on and he seemed to be looking for feedback. I had become unaccustomed to give any kind of feedback, which could give rise to puff the old man up (rightly or wrongly), so I found this situation awkward. I kept quiet even though I was moved with excitement and wanted to express how well I had got on with the message spoken. It was so encouraging that I wanted to tell all my friends in excitement come and here a man speak the things of God.

Paul Rowland And I Visit John Metcalf

It was shortly after this that Paul Rowland's, a minister in the Strict Baptist Church, who also worked for the Trinitarian Bible Society, came to preach at Bierton Church. He was a great advocate of the Free Scottish Presbyterian Church system and by conviction would only sing Psalms in Christian meetings. I spoke to Paul about John Metcalfe and invited him to meet him. Mr. Metcalfe seemed interested to meet Paul and I together, so we were invited across to his home at Penn one evening together.

The Shot Gun And Our Pockets Searched

Paul and I went one evening to John Metcalfe's home and we were received well and our coats taken to be hung up. We were invited to sit in a large lounge rather like a large study and library. It was beautiful decorated and very eloquent. John Metcalfe was dressed in a smart suit and tie.

John Metcalfe spoke about his work and recent publications the Psalms, Spiritual Songs, and Hymns of the New Testament. Paul Rowland got involved in talk regarding the Presbyterian Church and the Scottish Psalm Book. They soon spoke on doctrinal issues regarding the Law of Moses and legal Righteousness.

Christ Righteousness not imputed for our Justification

John Metcalfe maintained that he opposed the views put forward by the Calvinistic Presbyterians who maintained the righteousness of Christ (that which he wrought out by obedience to The Law) was our justifying righteousness before God. He said he had had a lot of opposition from the Scottish Churches because he maintained the righteousness of Christ is not mentioned once in the New Testament only the Righteousness of God. This righteousness being distinct from Law.

I was not full well aware at the time of the significance to this distinction and at first did not understand the issue. How ever the evening went well and was very stimulating and not without surprise. John Metcalfe posed us with a question as though it was a riddle asking was the fruit that Adam ate good or bad. It was as though he did not expect us to answer because he reminded us God had said his work was very good. I knew the answer straight away I did not need to think but thinking there must be some reason behind the question I awaited and Paul answered. This answer was not satisfactory to Mr. Metcalfe and the issue was discussed. I did not answer because shortly after this John Metcalfe reached behind a curtain and brought out a shotgun in a dramatic gesture and preceded to take out the cartridges. John Metcalfe was not amused when I laughed in amusement he said he was suspicious of our visit that the IRA had threatened him and had to be very careful. He also had just been informed that our pockets had been searched to check up on us and that tobacco had been found in one of the pockets. Mr. John Metcalfe later used this against the person in derogatory comments.

Our visit to Mr. Metcalfe was one not to be forgotten and was quite Remarkable.

This cause me to consider many things and I tried to understand and unfathomed the discussion regarding Justification. I had at that time been considering the view of eternal justification of Gods elect. I knew of the controversy of Antinomian and the legalists. I had shared with John Metcalfe a love of the writings of William Huntington and about Martin Luther's issue of Justification by faith.

It was the misunderstanding of the conversation that he had with Paul Rowland regarding Justification that made me consider the issues that I thought they raised and understood the truth to be. These were:

Justification

1 Gods act of Justification, when viewed from the point before the world existed, was from all eternity. In one sense the elect were justified in Christ from all eternity (in the mind of God). However the

work and merits of a justifying righteousness was to be performed in time by none other than our Lord Jesus Christ.

2 He was righteous by virtue of his person and spotless humanity. He did not become righteous by any works of the Law to Moses. He fulfilled the law and walked according to it.

The gentiles were never under the Law of Moses but rather by it excluded from the benefits that the Jews were promised to those who kept it. The Law never promised spiritual blessings only natural ones. All spiritual blessings, such as regeneration, adoption and the gift of faith, came only through the Lord Jesus Christ.

Also the Law of Moses was not, like the Presbyterians Calvinist's say given to Adam as a rule to be kept and that eternal life promised to those who kept it. It was not.

I understood that in the Lord Jesus's righteousness sinners are clothed and accepted as righteous before God. This being the righteousness of God imputed to all that believe. This being the source and merits of a believer's justification.

3 In actual experience however, in time, the sentence of Justification takes place upon the person believing God, as Abraham believed God. It is received by faith and takes place in the conscience, when first we believe and receive the Lord Jesus Christ as our saviour. This is justification by faith. (Rom. 5 verse 1). From this springs the joy of salvation, which of course involves the senses of the soul. This experience is justification by faith.

Justification by Blood

It could only be brought about by blood and made effectual by blood. Jesus himself being made a vicarious sacrifice. That being by the death of Jesus in the cross. By His death our sins are removed and we be made clean from all our sins. (Rom 5 verse 9). Justification being the declaration by God that we, being clothed in the righteousness of Christ, we are counted righteous for Jesus sake.

This was not the issue

I learned later how after this was not the issue with Paul Roland and John Metcalfe.

The follow Saturday morning I had a telephone call from John Metcalfe, I did not realize it was him at first thinking it was Dr. John Verna and I addressed him as John. This did not go down well he said I was being too familiar and I must address him as Mr. Metcalfe. Needless to say I felt awkward and that this man was being unnecessarily rude. We got on to speak about the feedback he wanted and I said I had things to say but would rather wait until I saw him face to face rather than on the telephone. He became very impatient and demanded I say there and then on the telephone what I had to say. I felt threatened and awkward and was not at ease at all. So I decided I would say about the things I found awkward and unacceptable first explaining that the tract he had written was in fact in error.

His reply was, "look mate I have more theology than I would ever have in 1000 years. That my testimony of what Jesus had done for me was disgusting and that I was in the same danger as the Pharisees, which blasphemed the Holy Ghost during the ministry of Jesus. There the conversation ended.

During all this time my wife had been concerned about me becoming involved with the man as she had notice how much and effect he had had on me.

That following week I was away on a week's study at Durham University as I was a student with the Open University. Here I wrote to Mr. John Metcalfe.

My response to John Metcalfe

Dear Mr. Metcalfe   26th July 1984

Further to our telephone conversation I have decided against meeting with you when I return from Durham for the following reasons:

You allow not the children of God to do as the apostle exhorts: " despise not prophesying. Prove all things; hold fast that which is good. Abstain from all appearance of evil" 1 Thes 5 verse 20 - 22.

My words to you on the telephone were that on the one hand I could rejoice with you thanking God for " here was a man I respected and trust in the things of God (for various reasons) whilst on the other hand I got cross with you and could take extreme dislike to you for what appeared to be a sinister way, This I took exception too.

Now you did not inquire as to what I meant but rather justified all your ways, methods and actions by stating your beliefs, saying that for the first time I had come under the preaching of the word of God in the unction of the Holy Ghost. That as the opponents of Christ questioned the spirit by which the Lord Jesus performed his mighty works, so too I come very close to their fearful condition.

You then stated your beliefs in respect of my own testimony; either you rejected what I said as true or was in doubt as to its reality and substance (correct me if I am wrong).

I am sorry if I offended you and your family when I gave my

testimony, please forgive me. How ever I am not the only believer to speak of vile things. Deut 28 verses 53. Lam 2 verse 26 and Hos 1 verse 2 and many more. Do you impute guilt to these also as you do me? Never the less what I spoke was true and an actual account and not as you seem to imply an opportunity to speak of self. For that true account I offer no apology.

If you reject what I said as truth I protest I am no liar. And if you are in doubts as to the reality well I cannot add to or diminish what the Lord Jesus works or works not. You are entitled to your opinion but pray give me the same liberty to judge you, your preaching, writings and assertions.

I still do not understand your impatience with me questioning you regarding the statement in the tract, "The Gospel of God".

You say the issue at the Reformation was: Given the merits of Christ person, how are they imputed and his person imparted. Page 33. I said to you. I could understand the statement of " the merits of Christ's person being imputed but not his person imparted.

I gave you room to explain, owned an ignorance and awaited further light and even said I would reconsider the statement. Here however you said you knew more theology in your little finger than I ever would ever know in a 1000 years, given it were possible I should be granted such time; called me mate and kept me at a formal distance.

Well be that as it may I still await a theological precise statement, whether it be in realms of high and heavenly things or in terrestrial ones.

I say persons are communed with and not, with natures, imparted. Neither persons nor natures imputed. I would suggest your tract should read: Given the merits of Christ's person, how are these imputed and His nature imparted. I say I was not seeking to find faults; it stuck out like a sore thumb, just as my incorrect spelling may do.

Here again I beg your pardon and apologize for any seeming impertinence. I say to you this behaviour of yours displays no humility, of which you say is lacking in me. Also according to your judgment I am not low enough yet before God. You judge by appearances; so do I but are you right? Only God knows the agonies, the heart searching and tears shed since our conversation and that is no pretense.

On these points I have mentioned I beg your reply and answers. For how can two walk together if these differences divide? I certainly have no intention of being your enemy.

You said at one stage you wondered if I be teachable. Well I am allowing my feelings and reason to act in judgment over these issues. This I do as you set the example and encourage, or have I got this wrong as well?

I get excited for you, over the production of the Psalms and hymnbook and would like to have seen them in use. I hope my letter to you now will not cause that breach to prevent it.

I have read your tract 2 and have found both 1 and 2 very relevant, pertinent and well written. They search me. Particularly tract 2 and I find I have walked the path of your tract. May they be blessed of God for the furtherance of the Gospel and the purpose for which they were written?

I could comment on the tract 3 about Taylor Brethren but not unless you wish

Yours very Sincerely. David Clarke.

Following this letter in hot pursuit I wrote the next letter this would have arrived the next day.

Dear Mr. Metcalfe,

I also think it wrong to speak of the merits of the person of Christ.

The merits of Christ yes! But not the merits of his person. The reason for this is:

As the Son of God he is a divine person. By nature He is God. Essentially God by nature but personally the Son of the Father. To speak then of the merits of a divine person is abhorrent to the delicate and gracious soul for one cannot admit any imperfections in God nor demerit as to perfection's, councils, actions or purposes. God is by definition essentially righteous. Perfectly just and right in all and in everything. Whether this glory be revealed or veiled always was and ever shall be.

The scripture speaks of the Lord Jesus Christ being the express image of the Fathers person.

I admit a complexity; in that the Lord Jesus Christ is bi natural, that is to say he has two natures. Yet he is but one person, co.-equal with the Father and Holy Ghost. By nature eternally God taking unto into union with himself, at the incarnation, our humanity, that which he was not, becoming truly man. There is now then a union of divine and human natures (never to be dissolved) in the person of the SOn of God, hence Christ Jesus the Lord is a glorious complex person.

We may speak of the merits of Christ Jesus for he is truly a human being, having a real soul created when made man; this man may accrue merit by virtue of living in this world being not only made under the Law of Moses but under every divine rule, him being subject unto his God and Father. The divine servant.

The expression then, "how can the merits of Christ's person be imputed?" I say is too loose and really the whole quotation should read: given the merits of the Lord Jesus Christ how are they imputed and His nature imparted? This being the question at the Reformation.

If you think I am being nit picking then what kind of 1000-year theological course do you advocate as being worthwhile.

I write this way because I trust it will be of help to you. You certainly have helped me in causing me to consider many things. I also add I stand to be corrected and ask you to do so.

I expect I have touched on your doctrine of justification and perhaps you have deliberately phrased your statement in the tract the way you have because they reflect your views of justification. Am I right?

Please excuse this hurried note but I must write, as I am able. Yours Sincerely

David Clarke

Durham. 25th   July 1984.

My two letters were returned with no comments. I took it that that was meant to express he rejected my observations or council, against himself.

25 I leave the Bierton Church

The events, which had taken place in our Bierton Church, had convinced me Satan's kingdom was being plundered. I had been instrumental in causing no small stir in the church. By October 1983 of that year the church was dysfunctional.

I had been engaged to preach and to conduct the communion service but felt unable to do so because in conscience it wrong for me to do so. This was because the communion represented the common fellowship we all had in Christ but our fellowship due to these severe difficulties divided our church. I believed until the issues were sorted out and the church was in order and of one mind in the Lord, it would be wrong for me to conduct the communion service.

Mrs. Evered, the person who had objected to the term's evangelical repentance, of course had pointed the finger at me. The incident regarding evangelical repentance was another serious issue, which I deal with in **"The Bierton Crisis"**. It was said I caused these difficulties since April 1983 as I had written to Mr. King, a member of our church, and a sent preacher from the church. Mr. King had been advancing views of general redemption, which I objected too and opposed him.

Our articles of Faith clearly stated a belief in particular redemption and also Mr king and Mrs Evered had been the ones to propose and second we join the Gospel Standard. So they had no excuse due to ignorance. I had attempted to correct these errors by speaking to Mr. King personally and finally ended up writing to him and also to Mrs Evered so as to make it quite clear what I was saying and found unacceptable. This letter was said by Mr. King to be, "Full of condemnation" and Mr. King had read parts of that letter to the church before he resigned. This letter is recorded in "The Bierton Crisis" and Mrs Evered had returned my letter that I had given her unread.

Not only this but the issue of Ladies wearing hats- I say head covering- had surfaced (not that I was against women wearing a head covering as the scripture taught this) but rather against this insistence of ensuring visiting unbelievers wearing them. Then there was the issue of "The Holy Table" all of which were heretical views and introduce by Mrs Evered, the church member who had insisted she knew best, and had known the truth since a girl.

Jesus The Sum and Substance Of The Sabbath

Then finally the issue of Law and Gospel surfaced again. It was now being maintained by Mrs Evered that the Sabbath Day (the Mosaic Sabbath) was to be kept by every one. Where the scripture teaches that the Lord Jesus Christ is the sum and substance of the Sabbath. He is the rest for the people of God and we must enter into this rest (the true Sabbath) not the Sabbath day according to the Law. I asserted every day was the Sabbath. The Sabbath under the Law pointed to the true Sabboth rest we enjoy in Christs. Matters at Bierton seemed to get worse See the following articles and sermons:

1 J C Philpot's sermon on the Law and The Gospel

2 Also an article By Philip Mauro

The Gentile Believer and The Law of Moses

3 Gilbert Beebe's article on the Christian Sabbath.

to be found In the appendix.

I actually felt the old serpent there and I was about to stamp on the Old Serpent. Looking back I realize I had been contending not against flesh and blood but against those principalities and powers, which had kept many believers in bondage and chains.

I felt in the end it was me that was causing the trouble at the church and I should leave things alone. I now believe, on reflection that was a satanic suggestion. I had been standing for the truths of the Lord Jesus Christ but had met with all kinds of false religious spirits all of which, I was naming and opposing.

I Secede from the Bierton Church

From that meeting at the Bierton Church in April 27th 1983 until the 26th June 1984 when I seceded from the Bierton Strict and Particular Baptist Church.

I contended for the truth of the gospel of Christ our with our church members, in particular with Mr King and Mrs Evered, regarding these very serious errors in belief and practice.

The whole of the matter I wrote about and published my article to all our Trustees and all persons connected with the controversy. This Publication was privately published in 1984 and circulated personally by me to all concerned and entitled "The Bierton Crisis".

This ended in me seceding from the Bierton Strict and Particular Baptist Church on 26th June 1984. I did this because I saw no hope if people wished to remain in darkness. I could not act in faith by staying in a situation I believe I should withdraw from. According to our rule the church could have dishonourably dismissed me and my wife for the none attendance of the church communion, from membership but as no doubt advised by Mr Paul Crane our elected over seer, they had no real grounds. Neither my wife, Mr king, or me were dishonourably dismissed from membership of the church.

I inform all our trustees of my actions

I felt is my responsibility to inform our trustees of the whole matter and this record, and report, is contained in **"The Bierton Crisis"**.

I Preach at Home

Having left the Bierton church I found it very difficult to adjust to our new situation. I considered going to another church but where was the question. In the mean while we met at home and I preached to my family and friends on Sunday mornings. I felt I had been under siege and my home was now my refuge. I was now preaching in the same room that Gordon Ferguson had preached during 1982 when we considered the times and imminent visit to the uK of the Pope of Rome.

I did however believe we should be in a local church but where could we join. I was very aware of the failing in the Gospel Standard way of things as they were at Bierton. Bierton church had in fact fallen from the way of grace of God. Even though their words were full of the language. Their Articles of Faith were clear that the Gospel is the rule of life for the believer but in practice the Law of Moses and their own tradition had become law. Also the position of their added articles was very shaky and I found them inappropriate to adopt as a confession of faith. We found ourselves unchurched and I believed we should do something about it.

I have written about this in my article "The Bierton Crisis". See appendix.

I sought God in prayer and felt we should be prepared to move house and job in order to be in a church where God wanted us to be.

I Experience Anxiety

After the conflict at Bierton and my seeking to know the mind of God and seeking His direction I began to feel very weak and fearful. I began to fear going out to preach. I soon was unable to face going out to fulfill those preaching engagements. I did not feel it right to go preaching and get other churches unnecessarily involved in judging the issues that I had with the church at Bierton. There appeared to be just too much to deal with. I became fearful and it crippled or disabled. I felt like I was having a breakdown of some kind. I just did not know how to cope. I was not managing and I needed help. The conflict with John Metcalfe made me very cautious.

A very serious issue occurs

At this time a very serious matter occurred, which affected my whole family and others and required the involvement of the police. I now realize that had we been in a functioning church the matter could have been dealt with. A Strict Communion church order would have been a safeguard and a help to resolves such an issue. I am prepared to share this matter with any one on a private basis if it will help as it is very serious and such matters cannot be ignored.

I Learn The Sense of Strict Communion

It was this event that led me to see the sense of strict communion, as the church had the power to deal with such an issue when the law of the land failed.

I Seek a City whose builder and maker is God

I felt compelled to write, The Bierton Crisis" and circulated it to all who were effected as I believed not only had I been called to preach but was also set for a defence and confirmation of the

Gospel. I was to learn again that those things that had happened to me were to turn our for the furtherance of the Gospel. Phil 1 verse 12. But I would ye should understand, brethren, that the things which happened unto me have fallen out rather unto the furtherance of the gospel;

David Oldham Pastor of Evington offers help

After the publication of, 'The Bierton Crisis", Mr David Oldham, pastor of Stamford and Evington Strict and Particular Baptist Churches invited me to spent the day with him at Leicester and we were able to talk through some of the issues that I had written about. I was very thankful for this help, as I felt at that time so alone.

26 I Seek a City

Whose builder and maker is God (Heb. 11 v 10)

Leprosy Discovered

(An extract form The Bierton Crisis).

In chapter 13 of the Bierton Crisis I relate how the communion of the church was restored but this led onto another more serious problem, which needed to be resolved. That being the distinction between the Law of Moses being a rule of life for the believer and the gospel. Sadly to say the truth of this matter lies under much debris at the Bierton Church today, but I believe will surely shine when God fulfils His word as spoken in Act 15:16.

Restoration Of The Communion at Bierton

After our church meeting in February my conscience gave me leave to conduct the communion service with the Bierton church that following March. I preached from the text Acts 15:16 during that day: **'After this will I return and build again the tabernacle of David which is fallen down**; and I will build again the ruins thereof, and I will set it up:'

Mrs Evered was not present at those meetings but we partook of the communion that evening with myself presiding.

Leprosy Cannot Be Cured

At the next church meeting it was evident to me that the deeper one probed to discover the nature of a disorder the worse things became. I say the disease became apparent to all who have eyes to see, and I will say unto them that give a glib answer to the question as to whether the law of Moses be our rule of life or the gospel: I say remain silent and only speak of those things you know from experience and according to the oracles of God. For this I say is the root of the matter; Mrs Evered has Moses as her rule while I had the rule of the Lord Jesus. That is to say His gospel. The church meeting of 21st April revealed the disease. Let the reader read the following quotation from The Bierton Crisis.

Church meeting 12th June 1984

The following is a full account of the address given the evening of my secession and was delivered on Wednesday the 12th of June 1984 at 8: 15pm

Commencing prayer

Our Dear Lord God thou hast promised to hear when thy people call upon thee; and we do call in Jesus' name. Please come to our aid for His sake we ask.

Amen.

An Address To The Problem

What I have to say tonight is very important, since the reaction, which must take place, will have far reaching effects. It is so important to you all that I am constrained to record (cassette) what lays heavily upon my mind, for the benefit of all concerned and may afterwards be used and freely available by any who are concerned to maintain the cause of truth here at Bierton or elsewhere.

You may find what I say will move you to say, we have had enough. We do not understand the bible the way you do. We believe you are wrong and cannot walk with you any longer and it would be best if you depart and trouble us no more. If that were your hearts response I charge you before God and the elect angels to accept my resignation as already given to you for me leave to do what I must.

Whatever other response we get my prayer and hope is that it will turn out for the good of all concerned and the cause of the Lord Jesus Christ. I am certain of this that where God is at work the enemies of truth will speak evil of all the good which I hope will come as a result of these proceedings.

I apologize for the unorthodox way, or none traditional or in etiquette manner I may have, but realize this: the Lord God is not bound or tied to work by the rules and traditions or etiquette of man. I act as I do for we are at a crisis point. Satan has wrought provoke trouble and made the people of God ill at ease. It cannot go on. We must not let it go on. Enough is enough.

Dire straits require dire measures for correction. Epidemic sickness, epidemic measures for rectification. Times of war are not as times of peace. Cheeseparing manors have no place in the battlefield, so I beg the pardon of any who judge me out of order.

I have spoken to Mr Crane and informed him of my recent announcement of Wednesday last, to resign from both the office of secretary and membership. He made a special visit to discuss with me my points of discord and reasons for my actions but we were unable to conclude or settle the matters that I raised. Mr. Crane left with a note of caution to not act in haste, to maintain sound doctrine.

Now since my announcement to you and in much prayer, I am persuaded I must put forward to you all the actions we must take, as a people professing godliness, given the constraints we all have and are faced with. By constrains I mean the following:

Our relative ages and abilities. Our current membership and

geographic locations; of us all including Mr. Crane. Our constitution set out in the trust deed and relationship with the Gospel Standard group of Strict Baptists.

Now I show a way forward and actions for things cannot remain as they are.

A remedy must be sought and that remedy which will do us good must come from the Lord, whom I trust we seek. Therefore we must appeal to the God of heaven, seek directions from the word of the Lord and put in action the principles taught us in the word. This must be the way and is only way.

Let me remind you of my announcement and reasons for action in May/June of this year. I said then, I have two immediate matters of importance that effect the church at Bierton which must be dealt with:

My resignation from office as secretary

My resignation from membership

Resignation from office of Secretary and membership

This being important and must be dealt with immediately for this month must be spent in engaging ministers for 1985. It being common practice for ministers to give their dates for preaching after the end of this month for the period January to December 1985. This is of prime importance for the remaining members.

Resignation from office This being a mere formality but having repercussions must be treated as soon as possible.

Resignation from membership

It has been necessary for me to examine my reasons for faith and religious practice and find my ever-increasing compromise inconsistent with those possessed of a true faith in the Lord Jesus Christ and the fear of God. This rendering my activities of preaching and teaching in the church at Bierton and elsewhere ineffectual having not the approbation of God though I have spoken truth in the fear of God in and amongst you, by me remaining silent and holding my peace for the sake of peace and unity, afterwards this has removed any base and ground for my faith towards God in this matter and hence I can no longer exercise faith expecting God to appear by the way of building again that which is fallen down, here at Bierton.

Areas of Compromise (Secretaries responsibilities)

As secretary I have to engage only those ministers which church wish to engage. The church consisting effectively only of women. In this matter then the women exercise authority and power over the man, which the scripture forbids.

The rejection of some ministers by the women on un-scriptural grounds Ministers have on several occasions, by the will, wish and desire of the women: and in my view to the detriment, harm and hurt of the cause of truth. The rejection of these men being based upon the maxim that peace must be kept at all cost, even at the expense of truth and righteousness. In this practice I will no longer continue. For example, Mr. C Lawrence, minister at Harold. Mr. S. Scott – Pearson, minister at Maulden. Mr. Redhead, Mr. Payne and a Mr. Butler (of Chelmsford), were all rejected by the women voting.

A Women Pastor At Winslow

This matter came to a head after my visit to the chapel at Winslow where I was engaged to preach. I was shocked and surprise to find they had a women pastor and I was led to believe they were to hold a united service that evening with the Anglican and Roman Catholic churches.

After preaching in the morning the need to earnestly contend for the faith and for the scripture to be our only rule of faith and practice I felt constrained to write to the Deacon, Mr. Paul Duffet, and express my shock in respect of a women having such authority and the so called united service with the Roman Catholic church, thus making no distinction between the false church of Rome and the church of Christ. At this my conscience accused me in this way: but look at you at Bierton, the women are they that rule. How can you write to a man and justly point out the error and unbiblical practice of the Winslow Baptist church when you at Bierton are equally guilty of the same charges. Hence I was powerless to act, as I should do. Example 2:

Contention over the Children's Hymns

Contention for truth: My recent contention with the church regarding the singing Hymns by the children, is judged by the women as not an important point of concern. Yea rather, we know better. I maintain children must not be taught that Jesus died for them each one. (Hymn 169). In this matter the church or women disagree and so the women have their say.

Example 3:

The Reverence Of The Building, Table and the Fear of Man

I have plainly taught and openly rejected the notion that the chapel is a Holy Place, to be reverenced and that the table is not in any way to be reverenced. Both matters caused contention. My belief being that unless these heresies are stamped out the Lord will not appear to repair the ruins at Bierton. Hence I cannot exercise faith nor hope in God to bless is as a people in church while such notions go unchecked. On a number of occasions I have listened and heard our ministers refer to the House of God etc., terms very loosely used. In each case I believe the ministers aught to be acquainted with the views of Mrs. Evered for they would then be very careful not to use such loose expressions and rightly refer to the church of Christ as the house of God and not the building. Act 7 verses 49. Hence I cannot expect nor exercise faith in God to appear for us unless these affairs are set in order.

Call of Abraham

I must obey God rather than man. I do not know what lies ahead for my family, and me but I must teach my friends and family the ways of the Lord Jesus Christ. To do so I must not remain in a compromised stifled position, for every man must give an account unto God and we must each act and walk according to the measure of faith given. I have a family to bring up and I must do free from false religion.

Whilst I am bound and tied by my membership here and the church pulls one way and that being the opposite way to the way I must walk, I am not free to walk by faith nor am I true to the " Faith ". Hence truth would cease to be a governing principle in my life.

My experience having lead me to the belief that the structure and government of the Bierton Church (like many churches) inhibits truth: that truth is not able to flourish once the primary purpose of our activity is to protect our own authority, power and the Status Quo. Truth becomes subservient to this end and so ceases to be truth and exist in its own right and so cease to be true. Truth cannot then be said to have set us free in this case.

Recommendation

At this point in the meeting. I went on to give my recommendation, but I would like to stop here and explain my last concluding statement relating to truth. This I did mention to Mr. Crane but not to you at that meeting.

Cessation of truth

By this I mean truth is not a prime concern only in so far that it keeps or preserves the traditions and order, which you have become used to. Whether that order or way of life be according to the word of God or not.

For example:

A False View Of A Gospel Church

If I speak of a Strict Baptist or the denomination in general say the Gospel Standard churches, I think a picture that may present itself to many like you may be as follows:

A A particular stile of chapel building. The forms of worship were an opening hymn is sung followed by a reading from the scripture and prayer (20 minutes) then notices. A second hymn followed by preaching. A final hymn closing with a benediction (1 hours)

B All ladies being expected to cover their heads in worship.

C The preacher engaged to preach often having come a long distance and in membership of a similar Strict Baptist cause. His ministry being acceptable provided: He is suitably dressed (generally a dark suit and tie). His speech is that familiar to the people, i.e.

Uses phrases like free grace and denies free will and has a standard range of terms for speech. This being whether he be intelligible or nor provided what is said does not disturb the people and gives assurance that all is well, if not God will appear for them if they continue just as they are. If this were the case he will generally be asked to preach again the next year, and so the cause goes on.

D The general picture one may gather is that to read the Gospel Standard and to support the other chapels at their anniversaries and follow the general trend of the majority of the chapel people, and then this is being faithful to the cause of Christ.

E Because this is the common and hence normal conduct of the majority of people one might be lead and expected to think that this is the way spoken of in the scripture. That such order in the church is the way of life we should preserve and contend for. That any deviation from this is to fall away and become wide of the mark and so fallen from truth. Hence the people gear themselves up to serve this way of life. To promote it. It becomes the habitual norm, a way we expect our children to follow. That the grace of God tempers us to serve this way for after all it is the way, the truth and the life.

Now when this happens I say the people, like Samson have had their eyes gouged out, and are made to tread the mill. This is the tradition of men.

The evidence to support my charge is as follows:

The evidence I have to support my assertions that truth ceases to be truth for such a people is as follows:

When I charged the church at Bierton, which is a Strict and Particular Baptist, Gospel Standard cause with teaching general redemption or suffering it to be taught by means of the hymns or otherwise, the church were offended and not at all repentant. It appears to me the general consensus of opinion is what can be wrong in using the phrases, when speaking to the children, the Lord Jesus has died for them each one and the Lord Jesus loves them all.

It is also argued because the scripture uses the phrases all the world etc. then we cannot be wrong in this matter of using hymns expressing redemption for all, even though we know it cannot mean all.

I say here truth does not govern the people but rather an unguarded sentiment for the children and a pattern, which has been adopted over a period of years. If the people cannot see the error here then they have no eyes to see in this matter.

The same may be said over the affair of the Holy Table and the chapel building. I maintain truth has not been the guiding principle in the minds of the people but rather a carnal view and long-term acceptance of untrue sentiments relating to a place of worship and the church of Christ. That some of our ministers are responsible for using loose phrases of speech in this matter and Satan has used this to seduce people. My question is this: Do the people love the chapel more than the truth? I know it brings back memories etc. But will we forsake it for truth? If not seduction has taken place and so truth ceases to be a prime mover in our lives. Just as the church of Rome relies upon its historic background also tradition and structure and has come to view the primary purposes for its existence is to extend its territory, preserve its identity and use all means to maintain its cause believing it peruses a God honouring and God blessed end. Seeks to resolve difficulties by compromising truth for peace sake, such a church has left the foundation upon which the church of Christ is built. The end thereof is death.

How then can I be at peace or rest where this takes place? I seek a city whose builder and maker is God, not a chapel or people that will not forsake all for Christ yea even the chapel, family and life long friends. I think in the whole affair we are learning the truth, by experience, of what the Lord Jesus said he came not to bring peace to the earth but a sword, that they that shall be our enemies shall be they of our own households

Conclusion

I concluded by giving a recommendation that Gwen should act as secretary and by no means Mrs Evered. I commended you to God and the word of his grace, which is able to build you up and give you an inheritance among them that are sanctified.

I further explained, that I would write to the churches where I was engaged to preach to avoid them embarrassment for they could not have me preach being out of membership with you or any one.

Having left the Bierton Strict and Particular Baptist Church I was full well aware of the New Testament order of Christian life. Scripture taught we should not forsake the assembling of ourselves together (Heb. 10 verse 25). But rather be in fellowship with other believers. I sought therefore God in prayer and looked out for direction from the Lord as to where and what I should do.

I had concluded that my withdrawal from the communion of the Bierton Church was the honourable thing to do. It became clear the church was not infallible. And neither was I. However we have to walk by faith with a good conscience before God. It was wrong to go through the motions of partaking in the Lords Supper, which symbolized the unity of the church by the one bread and one cup and all being of one mind, when in fact we were not in spiritual union or fellowship together.

I had stood for the truths and tenets of our Bierton Strict and Particular Baptist Articles of Religion and our stand as a Gospel Standard listed cause and just confirmed our position but amongst our members was the practice of heresy and religious adultery with no insight as to how to put right or deal with matters which were out of order.

The case was very clear the Lord Jesus Christ had died for the elect only. This is Particular Redemption. On that basis there was no room to teach general redemption or teach any mixed groups of people, let alone children, that God loved them all. The scripture is clear Jacob have I loved Esau have I hated. All the problems associated with the Added Articles of the Gospel Standard articles could be resolved with right understanding of Particular Redemption- why make it complicated as it appeared to have happened in the case of Stephen Royce.

Mrs Evered had displayed her allegiance to the Law of Moses and her reverence for the holy table and chapel building demonstrated she rejected the truth that the Gospel was the rule of life for the believer. She sought to bring men into the bondage that she was in

The Church's responsibility

It was now the responsibility of the Bierton church to terminate my/our membership, according to the Gospel Standard rules adopted in 1981, as any member does not have the authority to terminate their own membership. The Church must do this its self. So long as the church members existed we were still members. The Bierton Church did not, or ever did, terminate the membership of myself, Mrs Irene Clarke or Mr King. This means that should the remaining members die then the remaining member are legitimate inheritors of

296

the churches assets and Trusts. The church members alone can elect new trustee or one become a sole trustees. See Gospel Standard Articles and rules.

Every one informed including our trustees

Trustees and all churches and people concerned were notified of my actions by me sending a copy of "The Bierton Crisis" which has now been published along with this book.

The matter was therefore left and the Lord Him self would b the judge between us.

Our church order and rules are very clear regarding cessation of membership Rule 22 reads.

Severance Of Membership Rules

The severance of any member from this church may be only effected by the church itself acting under its duly appointed officers (pastor and deacons), at a properly convened church meeting (see rules 12-15), in the following instances: -

(a) In respect of an orderly member for transfer to another church of the same faith and order, in which event an honourable dismissal should be granted; or,

(b) By disciplinary action of withdrawal AS A LAST RESORT in the case of any disorderly member neglecting to hear either;

(1) An offended member's private remonstrance; or, after that,

(2) The additional exhortations of two or three other brethren; or still further,

(3) The admonition of the whole church, according to Matt. 18. 15-17.

The Church did not terminate the membership of Mr King, Irene Clarke or Myself. We remain members to this day and I continued my calling as a preacher and teacher of the gospel not only in the UK but also the Philippines as will be unfolded as my story continues.

27 The Bierton Society of Strict

and Particular Baptists

Our Articles of Religion

Founded in 1831 (Indenture)

And whereas certain persons meet together, and with the blessing of God, will continue to meet together, for the purpose of divine worship, at a chapel or place of worship adjoining the said hereditament and called the Bierton Baptist Chapel and the said persons call them selves "The Society of Particular Baptists" and such persons are herein after meant and referred to by the expression of "The Church" and the said persons believe and pledge themselves to the promulgation and support of the tenets or articles of faith herein after set forth, that is to say,

1 They believe that the scriptures of the Old and New Testaments are given by inspiration of God and are the only rule of faith and practice and that these scriptures reveal the one true and only God who is self-existent, infinite and eternal. That there are three self existent co-eternal persons in the Godhead namely the Father the Son and the Holy Ghost and these three are one God and that the Lord Jesus Christ is very God and very man in one glorious complex person.

2 That Before the world began God did elect a certain number of the human race unto everlasting life and salvation whom He did predestine to the adoption of Children by Jesus Christ of his own free grace and according to the good pleasure of His will.

3 That God created Adam upright and all his posterity fell in him, he being the federal head and representative of all mankind.

4 That the Lord Jesus Christ in the fullness of time became incarnate and that he really suffered and died as the substitute for the elect of God only and in their stead whereby he made all the satisfaction for their sins which the law and justice of God could require as well as made a way for the bestowments of all those blessings which are needful for them for time and eternity.

5 That the eternal redemption which Christ hath obtained by the shedding of his blood is special and particular that it is only and intentionally designed for the elect of God who only can share its spiritual blessings.

6 That the justification of Gods elect is only by the righteousness of Christ imputed to them and received by faith without consideration of any works of righteousness done by them and that the full and free pardon of all there sins and transgressions is only through the full free pardon of all their sins and transgressions is only through the blood of Christ according to the riches of Gods grace.

7 That regeneration, conversion, sanctification and faith are the work of the Almighty efficacious and invincible grace of God the Holy Ghost.

8 That all those chosen by the Father, redeemed by the Son and sanctified by the Spirit shall certainly and finally persevere unto eternal life.

9 That there is a resurrection of the dead both of the just and the unjust and that Christ will come a second time to judge the quick and the dead when he will consign the wicked to everlasting punishment and introduce His own people into his kingdom and Glory where they shall be for ever with Him.

Custom and Practice

That baptism of believers by immersion and the Lords Supper are ordinances of Christ to be continued until His coming again and that the former is absolutely requisite to the latter, that is to say that only those are to be admitted as members of the church and participate in its privileges including the ordinance of the Lords supper who upon profession of their faith have been baptized namely immersed in water in the name of the Father, Son and Holy Ghost. And that no person who has not been baptized as afore said shall on any account be permitted to sit down or commune at the "Lords table" within the said school room and whereas for the purpose of giving effect to the objects and intentions of the parties hereto and of the said church it has been agreed that the said hereditaments shall be conveyed to the trustees upon the trust and for the purpose hereinafter contained and these present have been approved by the members of the said Church meeting called for that purpose and held at the said chapel on or before the date hereof.

The indenture further witnesses

1 That in further pursuance and consideration of the premises they the Trustees do hereby severally covenant and agree amongst themselves and with each other and with the church that they the trustees their successors and assigns shall and henceforth stand and be possessed of the hereditament And premises hereinbefore conveyed unto them un trust to dedicate and devote and preserve the same for the purpose of holy and divine according to the tenets or articles of faith herein set forth.

2 That the election of any future pastor of the said church and the removal of any pastor shall be decided by the vote of two thirds of the church assembled at a regularly convened church meeting together with the object for which it is convened having been publicly

announce for four successive Lords days. No member eligible to vote has to have been four times to the Lords table in six months unless prevented by illness etc.

3 No minister shall be elected to the pastoral office or continue therein but such as holds to the doctrines and communion aforesaid nor shall it be lawful for the said church to receive into fellowship any such persons as members but such as have been baptized that is by immersed in water upon confession of their faith in Christ and are able to give some satisfactory account of a work of grace having passed upon their souls in being called out of darkness into Gods marvellous light, nor shall it be lawful for the said church to admit to her communion (in which term is include the ordinance of the Lords supper) any person who has not been baptized by immersion in water on a profession of faith in the name of Jesus.

28 A Call from the Philippines

I had left the Bierton church with my eyes towards heaven looking for that Heavenly City whose builder and maker was God and between the period of June 1984 to the present I experienced the help and testimonies of the provision and deliverances of my gracious God and Father through our Lord Jesus Christ and live to tell the tale. This is despite my failing and falls. These dealings of God with my life since June 1984 are fully recorded in my various books. Please read in the Appendix at the end of this book.

A period of many years past until December, 2002 when Mr King closed the Bierton Chapel for worship as the last of our senior member had died.

This occurred whilst I was on mission work in the Philippines preaching and teaching the gospel in the Jails. And this is the next part of the story to be told.

You will recall that Mr king seceded from our church in 1983, as he was not prepared to give an account of the reasons for teaching general redemption. Never the less he remained a member of the church, as the Church never terminated his membership. He was a trustee along with Mr Janes from Eaton Bray, Mr Martin of Northamtonshire and Mr Baumber from Bedford.

I later learned that all our trustees changed their doctrinal views and did not support our church being a Gospel Standard cause and it was for this reason a serious issue occurred that I will relate I due course.

News from the Philippines

It was April 1995 during my lunch period whilst teaching at

Fareham College my technician was watching the news on the television and the headlines were about a certain Michael John Clarke, a travel agent from Eastbourne. It was my brother he had been arrested in the Philippines on a serious charge and I was shocked at what I heard.

I want the reader to be aware that Michael had attended the meeting at Bierton chapel on 5th June 1983 when I related my testimony as to the Lords dealing with me and I recall him making light of the matters after that meeting with all my family there. Now here in the United Kingdom news of his arrest in the Philippines had become international news and as a result of his crimes he was to be sentenced to a term of 16 years, to be served in Asia's largest Prison in the Far East, New Bilibid Prison, Muntinlupa City, Philippines.

Mission of Help

I pray I can save my criminal brother

by Lizzy Miller and
Darren Beck
The News

ON THE left is Dave Clarke – college lecturer and committed Christian.

On the right is his brother Michael – currently languishing in a prison cell in the Philippines.

Dave spends much of his spare time trying to help young people turn away from a life of crime.

Now he is on his most important mission yet – trying to save his brother's soul.

Dave converted to Christianity almost 20 years ago after sharing a life of crime with his brother in their youth. But his brother Michael went further off the rails and is now in a jail in the Philippines.

Dave, 42, of Hayling Close, said regular letters from his brother showed he was sick of his lifelong criminal past and was thinking of becoming a Christian.

He said: Michael wrote to me saying his was despairing and suicidal and asked me about my faith.

"I've been praying hard for him and believe he has now come to know the Lord as his personal saviour. I think he is listening to what I write.

Both brothers were notorious criminals in Buckinghamshire where they lived in the

1960s. They were jailed for maliciously wounding after shooting a woman in the face with an air weapon at Marston.

Dave said: "When I came out I knew everything there was to know about crime. It was a good school.

"I was determined to have the best of everything and went about it with determination.

"I was riding on my brother's reputation as a lout. I set up a garage business for stolen cars."

Dave went to borstal for 12 months while his brother, who denied the charge, went to Maidstone prison for two years.

Father-of-five Dave went straight after converting to Christianity in 1977. He moved to Fareham where he

began teaching electronics at the town's college and became involved with the Christian Gospel Church.

His brother went on the run after being given home leave from prison but was recaptured and served his full sentence.

Michael is now four years into a 16-year jail sentence in a prison in the Philippines for promoting sex tourism.

Dave Clarke, left, and his brother Michael – they grew up to share a life of crime

Dave Clarke, left, now prays for his brother Michael

Islands' seedy sex business

MICHAEL Clarke discovered the Philippines and its cheap sex in 1996 when he set himself up as a tour operator.

He placed an advertisement under the name Paradise Express in Exchange and Mart and produced crude brochures describing a 12-night holiday as "the dirty dozen" and with photos of bikini-clad woman as well as giving details on how to find a Filipino wife.

Clarke, who is divorced with a daughter, had been arrested for agreeing that underage prostitutes should be procured after he had been captured on a hidden camera. He is appealing against conviction.

Dave said he hoped his

A picture from one of the brochures

brother would now find God and give up crime.

He added: "I regret all the hurt and pain I caused but I realise I had to go through what I have because what I saw to kids to keep them out of trouble I have credibility.

Michael's Story

Michaels story is fully told in our book Trojan Warriors, Michael began to write home before our parents died and at first he seemed hopeful that he would be acquitted after a retrial but this takes time in the Philippines. At this time he sent an audio recording to my parents

This can be listened to on YouTube (Click Here Michael Clarke Olongapo).

He had no money at the time and so he had to do all the legal work him self. During which time I noticed a change I his letters. From being totally cast down and in ill health with his teeth falling out he began to sound hopeful and he informed me he had read C.S. Lewes book, "Mere Christianity" and he was convinced that Jesus was the Christ the Son of the living God.

Suny Wilson Released

In December 1999 Sumy Wilson who had been sentenced to death fro an alleged crime of rape was acquitted after a long and lengthy appeal. His story is told in, "Condemned to Death", By E Wilkerson and Alan C. Atkins, and through Alan C. Atkin's diligent study he was able to present the information to his brief to present his case for retrial. Suny was acquitted by the Supreme Court and suddenly personally escorted back to England with his wife to be by the British Ambassador. This was because the media had moved the masses to cry for his blood so to speak. They wanted to se the British Pig executed by Lethal Injection,

His story is told in "Sentenced to Death" a YouTube Video (Click Here to view)

Suny Wilson acquitted was on the 19th December and arrived safely back in the UK and on the 25th December he called me with news of Michael. He had with him the National Bureau of Investigation (NBI) Report, from the Philippines, that had investigated his case and it was clear the Michael's case was one of entrapment. A foundation called PREDA whose Director was one Shay Cullen, along with an ITN News crew consisting of Adam Holloway and Martin Cottingham, a so called Christian Aid worker had worked together to find evidence to convict him of a crime. It was a classical case of entrapment. The story is told in out book 'Trojan Warriors". (See appendix for further details) in this book we tell of Michael's arrest, his crime, sentence and his conversion from crime to Christ, along with an account of him being baptized as a believer in an old oil drum, in New Bilibid Prison, on the 16th September 2000.

Inmates at the Baptism of Michael

Michael on the lower Right

Michael being Baptised by Lucas Dangatan

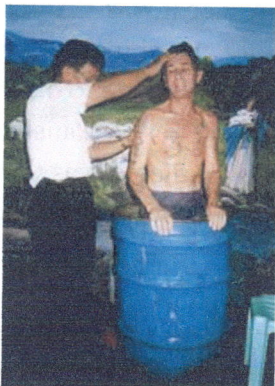

Michael's Baptism in an old US Army Oil Drum

It was a direct result the news of Michael conversion from crime to Christ that I felt compelled to finish my story. I had always since my conversion felt compelled to tell the world of what the lord had done for me and I had kept diary notes since the 16th January 1970 to do so. After its publication its title was, "Converted on LSD Trip", which when published the Bucks Herald newspaper told the story yet again. As a result of that Gordon Smith contacted me after 30 years of not seeing him and we there and then over the telephone decided to go and bring help and assistance to my brother in the Philippines.

We took 8 copies of my book to the Philippines on our first mission be circulated in the Prison and to be given certain persons including the Director of the Prison and the President herself Gloria Macapagal Arroyo.

Cast Your Net The Other Side Of The Ship.

I had a strong conviction that my story could be of great help to others and although I had tried to tell it in England a scriptural verse pressed hard on my conscience it was, "And he said unto them, Cast the net on the right side of the ship, and ye shall find. They cast therefore, and now they were not able to draw it for the multitude of fishes. John 21 v 6. And they were astonished at the draft of fishes they had taken. The sense I gathered was that for years I had toiled to fish in my home country now I was to cast the net on the other side of the world- Philippines was where we were headed.

A Successful Mission to the Philippines 2001

As a result of that very successful mission in August 2001 through to October 2001, Gordon and I not only preached the gospel to many inmate of New Bilibid Prison but also in Angeles City Jail, Barretto District Jail and various churches.

Writing Trojan Warriors

In August 2001, at one particular meeting within New Bilibid Prison, Michael and I had an idea (vision), which came to us simultaneously, we believed it would help and assist those inmates. There were many who had been converted from crime to Christ and so we requested 100 men to write an account of their conversions. We promised to return the next year with their life stories printed in a book. We named that book there and then, "Trojan Warriors". It was purposed that each man would be able to take a copy of their book with the accounts of the 100 men's conversion from Crime to Christ as a tool for evangelism. So upon their release they could go back to their own cities, towns or villages and tell of all what the lord had done for them and others.

TransWorld Radio

On my return from this first mission I was asked to relay an account of the mission work we was doing and again providentially this too was recorded. Here it is on Youtube

Converted on LSD Trip Trans World Radio (Click here)

A Joint Effort We Worked Together

It was during the next year Michael, Lucas Dangatan and I, worked closely together and the book was written, published and printed and in fact 66 men eventually submitted their testimonies. The book, by chance was written with 365 pages. A copy of the book was given to each of the inmates on our return visit in October 2002. The Articles of Religion of our Trojan Horse mission were clearly stated and were a transcript of the Bierton Strict and Particular Baptist Articles of Religion of which I remained a member by default.

Sending William Poloc to Baguio

William C. Poloc was one of our Trojan Warriors and his testimony is number 63 in our book Trojan Warriors. He was due for release in August 2002 and Michael and I commissioned him to return to his own City in Baguio and preach in the City Jail and Benguet Provincial Jail. He did this very successfully. We funded him with a monthly allowance of Php 6600 per month, plus expenses from August to January 2003, and he did a very good job.

Again the doctrinal basis of William's work were those of the Bierton Strict and Particular Baptist, 1831. As printed in our book Trojan Warriors.

Our second Mission to the Philippines

Our second mission had taken one year to prepare and we took a team of 5 from England who were: Gordon Smith, Alastair Sutherland, Andy MacDonnell, Catherine Farr and Dr Richard Kent.

Funding of the mission

I don't' wish to really talk about money, as the Lord provided funds for his work in His own way. How ever because evil men and people who pry into other peoples business, and also to silence the gainsayers, for the record both Michael and I provided all the funds from our personal resources. And between September 2000 and May 2005 we provided all the funds for the mission work, to the tune of £50,000.00. English pounds and on Michael's death he left £10,000.00 to his daughter.

We received no funds from anywhere else except a gift from the Christian Gospel Church, of £400, in July 2001. Our Trojan Horse funds supplied all the return airfares for all our 4-team members, all their accommodation expenses and travel arrangements for the 2002 mission. The mission was paid for bby my Michael and I the directors of Trojan Horse. We had no funds from anywhere else and we did not seek sponsorship. The accounts for our Trojan Horse are available upon request.

A Decision to stay in the Philippines

It was during this second mission to the Philippines that we had some serious difficulties and I received some serious news from England. The first blow was I got news of my wife's divorce petition and as a result I felt it right to remain in the Philippines, rather that return to the UK and deal with all the evil hurtful side of a divorce. I decided that it would be better to bring further assistance to Michael and complete the work that we had begun. This matter is told in my book Converted on LSD Trip 2nd Edition.

Opposition to our work

Without going into two much detail we encountered remarkable opposition on this mission and a lot of obstacles were presented to us, in the form of serious life issues. Issues that would affect any one involve in the ministry who were seeking to preach the gospel and issues that effect to all classes of men.

It was almost as though some one was deliberately seeking to put a stop to all the good work we were doing. On every hand we it difficulties and hurt and opposition. Issues that I felt compelled to record and write about, This I have done in my book, Before the Cock Crows.

1. The first serious issue we faced was a the messy separation of our hosts. Our host was a Christian Mission, a man and wife team, who had sadly separated 6 months before we arrived. One had levelled a charge of adultery against their partner. When we did the best we could to help I was faced with a serious threat of deportation from the offended partner when our team had returned to the UK. The problem deteriorated and none scriptural actions were employed to sort things out that lead to serious injustice.

2. One Filipino member of the team was being challenge and condemned for working with the Trojan Horse and it was rumoured we were a fake organization. This particular Religious Volunteer (RVO) also felt it wrong to drink wine or sing secular pop songs and he took offence when he heard I not only drank wine but also mixed with sinners land sang songs with them late at night in the Prison. He felt threatened and said it was a serious problem. It was no problem to me as that was the ministry that I had received from the lord but as a result my actions spread by rumours all around the prison. This RVO felt threatened by my actions and he did not wish

to associate with a mission whose Director drinks wine, mixed with sinners late at night within the Prison. So that was his problem but it posed a real problem to him. My view was that we were Christian mission work, where by we sought to reach men in whatever state they were to inform them that The Lord Jesus Christ came into the world to save sinners. We were not there in the Philippines or its jail to support false religion or bow down to idols set up in the minds of the religious.

3. The were difference of opinion as how we should conduct preaching or ministry and with hindsight this was due to the various differences in doctrinal beliefs and practices. Michael and I believed in the Sovereignty of God and that through sharing, speaking communication and preaching the gospel men would be saved. This could be done in various was. Some team member felt we should take every opportunity, when we had crowds listening to launch into making Billy Graham appeals for me to come forward and be saved. It was because Michael did not go along that route that some team members murmured say we had missed a great opportunity.

4. Our Trojan Horse International (CM) ministry had not been registered by Lucas Dangatan, with the Securitas Exchange in SEC Building, EDSA, Greenhill's, Mandaluyong City, which proved awkward once we had enemies as they sough to use this against us seeking to deny our existence

5. The RVO who took exception to me drinking wine had also been responsible to register our incorporation once I discovered Lucas Dangatan had not done so with the Security Exchange Commission. The leader of SonLight Ministries then warned this RVO that Trojan Horse did not exist and we were a bogus organization and a warning was issued to his all to stay clear of us.

6. The next rumours that were spread were that the Catholic Church in the Philippines had banned our book Trojan Warriors and so we should be avoided. 7 It was then rumored that Michael and I had received money by way of sponsorship to the tune of $4,000,000 from America.

7. The next wind of half-truths came with a gale and they were straightforward lies. It was spread around the prison that I had left my wife and daughter in the UK, was selling our family home and had a Filipino girl friend. And that I was a drunkard having drinking sprees in the prison.

8. Then came a more sinister blow, which really hurt me personally. When I learned that Lucas had not registered our Trojan Horse ministry with the Securities Exchange and that the RVO that I have mentioned had not completed the task, even though Lucas had been given the money to get the job done in January 2002, I insisted it be done immediately. It them turned out that this particular RVO had removed, Gordon, Alastair and our names from being directors of the Incorporation, which meant only those remaining Filipino's had the legal right in the affairs of the ministry. It was being placed into the hands of Lucas and his Filipino men. To add to this listen to the next incriminating thing.

9. To resolve the problem I insisted that Lucas P. Dangatan return from his bank account, the remainder of the Trojan Horse funds that had personally given himwhich was Php 1.500,000.00 at the beginning of the mission in September 2002. He had had already had Php 600,000 for the registration of the ministry. When I asked for the remainder of the money once I realized our ministry had not been registered, Lucas returned Php 1.1000,000 on 6th December 2002. That meant we had spent Php 400,000.00 on our mission since

September 2002 and December 10th 2002.

10. It was four days after this that Lucas P. Dangatan ordered his men in New Bilibid Prison Theological Institute to write a petition against Michael and I and the Trojan Horse seeking to deny our existence and have us banned from the prison. The whole matter is recorder in our book, "Before the Cock Crows".

11. The sad thing was that the news of these affairs was reported back to England, via Lucas and Gani using e-mail along with miss -correspondence from my estranged wife in the UK, to certain people in the UK and the Philippines. As a result Gordon, Alastair and the church elders of the Christian Gospel Church in Portsmouth withdrew from me and it was stated that in their opinion I should withdraw from the work we were engaged in and return to the UK.

To cut it short those things that militated against us were all the result of so called religious men who were governed by those natural fallen mans actions. Which were: Gossip, lies, slander, jealousy, rumours, greed money, a denial of truth, opposition to truth, Arminian righteousness, ignorance, blindness.

Recollection of the Bierton Crisis

It came with surprising clarity that the show of religious zeal, which was apparent everywhere in the Philippines was deceptive, as underneath it all there was found every evil work. In a similar way to my observations and experience that I had seen and experienced in the Bierton Church, those many years ago. It was just another face. In the Bierton situation the evils were more sophisticated but in the Philippines they were more blatant.

Conclusion

I conclude that the Arminian righteousness and the righteousness that men have through their adherence to the Law of Moses or other own traditions were one and the same thing. A fair show in the flesh. This is not the Righteousness of God or Christian righteousness that the gospel of the Lord Jesus brought about. I concluded that men may begin well by faith in the Lord Jesus alone for salvation but then fall from grace into making them selves perfect according to religious tradition of men. They then persecute those who do not go along with them. It was as depicted in the Apocalypse, these religious people wer governed by a deceptive unclean spirit.

"And upon her forehead was a name written, MYSTERY, BABYLON THE GREAT, and THE MOTHER OF HARLOTS AND ABOMINATIONS OF THE EARTH. And I saw the woman drunken with the blood of the saints, and with the blood of the martyrs of Jesus. The spirit of the Mother of Harlots, MYSTERY BABYLON, was governing these men in the Philippines. Rev. 17 verse 5- 6.

I came to the conclusion that when we decide to do things our own way and not be directed by what scripture says, we leave our selves open to be the cause of another persons hurt and distress. This leaves to an opening for the devil to work and so we oppose the cause of the lord Jesus Christ.

It was for this reason the this idea to found Bierton Particular Baptist College was considered and is now open to student wishing to study the Doctrines of Grace.

GoTo: http://www.BiertonParticularBaptists.co.uk

Our Second trip to Baguio City and Benguet Provincial Jails

We visited both Baguio City and Benguet Provincial Jail in

December 2002 and after a number of visits by William Poloc to these inmates I baptized 22 prisoners who had been converted from crime to Christ in Baguio City Jail and also 8 souls in Benguet Provincial Jail and to that work. You may see the YouTube video relating to this mission

(Click here) Our Second Visit to Baguio City

William is committed and he continues to this day as an independent minister teaching the doctrines of grace (TULIP).

William Poloc our sent man at Benguet Provincial Jail

William Poloc talking to the Warden

Benguet Provincial Jail

William Benguet Provincial jail

Our Video's outlining the Work (Video)

Registration of Trojan Horse International

It was on the 16th January 2003 that I met a Particular Baptist pastor Ronaldo l. Lopez, at the Internet office in Muntinlupa City and we shared our experiences. H stepped in and assisted me in many ways and for which I am very thankful to this day.

I noted the day, as this was exactly 23 years to the day of my conversion from crime to Christ. With Ronaldo's assistance I registered our Trojan Horse international (TULIP) Phils Incorporation with the Securities Exchange in SEC Commission Building, EDSA, Greenhill's, Mandaluyong City,

Our Security Exchange Registration Certificate

Trojan Horse International (TULIP) Phils. Incorporated Registration Certificate.

(The necessary proof of our existence in the Philippines).

29 Missionary Visa Philippines

The first thing I needed to do was to secure a full time visa permit to continue my stay in the Philippines and mission work to the Jails. In order secure the necessary details I wrote to the Police in Fareham in the UK, Mr Ramsbottom, the pastor of Luton Bethel Gospel Standard Church, Mr Janes, one of our Trustees at the Bierton Church, Mr Crane our Church overseer from Lakenheath Strict Baptist Church and also Mr Peter Jacob an elder of the Portsmouth Gospel Church. This was in order to secure confirmation of my affidavit stating who I was and my credentials. I had to present evidence to the Philippine Authorities of my legitimate credentials.

Sadly but thankfully I received some help from the UK. Mr Ramsbottom replied to my request and so did and also Mr Janes but the sad thing was Mr Janes, one of our trustees of the Bierton Church, did not tell of the closure of our Bierton Chapel. Also Mr Peter Jacob due to the bad reports, which were spread in the UK about our work in the Philippines, refused to help in any way and would not confirm that I had attended their meetings and had been in good standing. I felt so alone and let down. I recalled at that time that it was this man, along with one of his elders and a so called lady Reverend that who opposed the first publication of my book Converted on LSD Trip.

I am sure the Apostle Paul felt forsaken, as I did when he wrote, For Demas hath forsaken me, having loved this present world, and is departed unto Thessalonica. 2 Tim 4 verses 10.

Help from the Chief Chaplain

The appointed Chief Chaplain for the Philippine Prison Ministries Rev. Monico Carany assisted me and with his direction and assistance of the Christian Missionary Services at Pasay City, I had to undergo medical and psychological examinations including X-rays, HIV test and intelligence tests, and as a result I was cleared and accepted with the Psychological Report. I was thankful for this as I had herd from the UK my mental health had been called into question. Just as they stated Jesus was beside himself and had a devil.

Medical and Psychological Examination

Date of examination 2nd April 2003.

Interpretation of findings

The subject possesses an average intellectual functioning and is able to express his thoughts and views. Has been noted to be responsive and open to social contacts. Observed to be work orientated and has a very positive outlook in life.

Emotionally, the subject manifests slight insecurities and loss. Evasive tendencies are relatively minimal.

Remarks:

Recommended.

My application was accepted and my admission status from a temporary visit under Section 9 (a) to Quota Immigrant Visa under Section 13 of the Philippines Immigration Act of 1940, as amended in my favor and granted to Rev. David Clarke a British National on the 10th April 2003.

It cost me in excess of Php 100,000.00 (£1000 GBP) to gather together and pay for all the required tests, examinations and documentation. The result was that I could permanently work, according to our Articles of Incorporation throughout the Philippines, as a missionary and return to the UK for two months of the year before having to return. It was some comfort to learn the results of this examination as I had heard that my sanity had been called into question and it had been rumoured that I was ill. The truth of the matter was I had incensed the religious carnal mind, in certain religious men, who were then moved by another set of principle other than that the gospel of our Lord Jesus Christ. I was thankful for the scripture record that told me this was a normal reaction from ungodly men. Then answered the Jews, and said unto him, **Say we not well that thou art a Samaritan, and hast a devil? Jesus answered, I have not a devil; but I honour my Father, and ye do dishonour me**. John 8 48-49.

...breath, with a low murmur, as she... she felt in...
...the conclusion... the meaning that my style...
...nature and... has been resolved up...
...matter, and until... that the previous...
...nothing... was... mentioned by another...
...vague... used in... 1530 Copies have...
...satisfactory in... little variety in... that the...
...result of the... matter... the Jesuit school...
...not stop the... that I... Scotus... and just a little...
...however, I have... hardly had time for my religious...
...discussion...

30 My return to the UK

The Closure of the Bierton Chapel

On my return to the UK, in July 2003 I spoke to Mr Crane, our Bierton church overseer. He informed me that the chapel had been closed for worship on the 22nd December 2002. I recalled noting that this was at exactly the same time that I was continuing my ministry, preaching and teaching the Gospel in Baguio City, where 30 souls had confessed their faith in the lord Jesus, and that being through the work of William Poloc, who was our sent man. As a result I baptized 30 souls who had been added to the Church, so confirming the ministry of William C. Poloc. I had baptized them in my capacity as a sent minister from the Bierton Strict and Particular Baptist Church.

Mr Crane suggested that I return to Bierton and reopen the chapel and he informed ne that the Association of Grace Baptist Churches LTD (South East), 7 Arlington Way, London EC1R 1XA, had taken on the responsibility of the churches property. They had taken the Bierton Church Trust Deed from the lawful Trustees, Mr Janes, Mr Martin, Mr King and Mr Baumber who had expressed they were too old to bare the responsibility of looking after the chapel.

It transpired that our Bierton Trust Deed had been lodged with one of our senior church members solicitors, which is a fact that is important when registering property with the Land Registry for the first time. They had recovered the Bierton Trust deed from the Solicitor of our church member when she died.

When I approached the Association of Grace Baptist Churches LTD to use our chapel for the ministry work they refused permission. This was because they wanted to sell the chapel and profit from the sale. They had hastily gone on with demolition work, contrary to the terms of trust, seeking to sell the Chapel, at a profit once they had acquired planning permission. Where as I had already negotiated and planned that summer to bring two Filipino Particular Baptist ministers to the UK to visit various churches and our chapel would have been the ideal solution for some of our meetings. The Association of Grace Baptists Churches LTD were not concerned or interested in carrying out the wishes and desires of the original church founders and church members of the day. To their shame.

They first of all denied that we were a Gospel Standard Church and my standing as a member of the Church. When I sent them a copy of my book, "The Bierton Crisis 1984" and letters of confirmation from Mr. Ramsbottom along with Mr. Cranes confirmation that Mr Crane had suggested and supported my request to re open the chapel, they tried to say I was no longer a member. This was despite my bringing to their attention the fact of our strict rules, in relation to cessation of membership ensured that I by default remained a member of the church along with Irene Mary Holloway and Mr A king. The truth was that I along with Irene Mary Clarke (now Holloway) were still church members as our membership continued. The Church never terminated our membership and Mr Crane confirmed this in writing and I had presented this information to the Association of Grace Baptists Churches LTD with my application to use our chapel.

When I stated that they were not the lawful trustees, as the Church had not elected them to that position, I was ignored. I asked them to confirm that the copy of the Trust Deed that I held was one and the same as the one they had recovered from our deceased church member, they refused my request. This was because the trust deed states who were the legitimate Trustees, how they are to be elected and the responsibility of church members.

324

Trustees were to be elected by the church and to be men who believed and supported the doctrines stated in the indenture. The reality was that the Bierton Church was a Gospel Standard Cause and had no association with Grace Baptist churches. The church would never have elected this Association to be its trustees because their beliefs were those of the London 1869 Baptist Confession, and not those of our Church, which was the Bierton Church and Gospel Standard.

Michael's Death and Burial

Michael sadly died in New Bilibid Prison on the 27th May 2005 and the **Association of Grace Baptist Churches LTD** refused to allow us to use our chapel for a memorial service of celebration regarding Michael's life death and conversion from crime to Christ.

Michael Exhorting Men on Death Row

To write their testimonies

Death Row New Bilibid Prison

Therefore because of this refusal of the Association to allow us to use our chapel, after all Michael was baptized in the Philippines, received by me and others as a Christian and was considered to be a member of the Bierton Church.

Our memorial service at our Bierton April 2005

Michael's Tomb Stone Bierton Chapel Chapel

Our memorial Service at the Bierton Chapel Cemetery April 2005

Michael in his Coffin

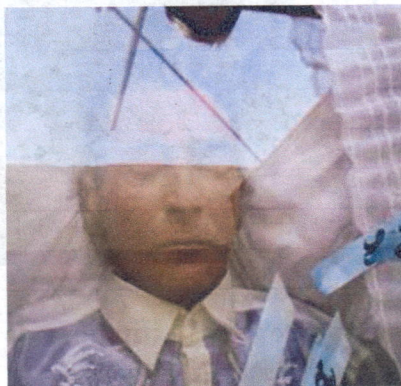

Michael Asleep

Michael Tomb stone or Plaque of Remembrance

He Being Dead Yet Speaketh

Association of Grace Baptist Churches LTD

The Association the ignored me and continued to deny my membership along with that of Mrs Irene Holloway.

David Whitemarsh

The Secretary of The AGBC Ltd

The Damning signature

16. Signature of applicant or their conveyancer	David S. Whitemarsh (Secretary)	Date	21.7.05

Note: Failure to complete the form with proper care may deprive the applicant of protection under the Land Registration Act if, as a result, a mistake is made in the register.

© Crown copyright (ref: LR/HQ/CD-ROM) 6/03

Here is the signature

The Association of Grace Baptists Churches LTD

The Association of AGBC LTD 7 Arlington Place

They acted therefore contrary to the trust that they claimed to hold. Just like the unjust stewards who killed the son of the husbandman in Luke's gospel, So they cast him out of the vineyard, and killed him. What therefore shall the lord of the vineyard do unto them? Luke 20 verse 15.

They then promptly sold the chapel to be a domestic dwelling, and pocketed the money. There is now no witness for the cause of truth in Bierton and the Association of Grace Baptist Churches LTD took all the money. A phrase has been coined in scripture, Acts 19 that refers to robbers of churches of which this Association had now become. Not only so, to cap it all, when the chapel was sold Michael's memorial stone was discarded.

I maintain that I am the lawful legal inheritor of our Bierton Churches assets, that the Chapel and all effects were stolen from me and that the monies that the Association of Grace Baptists Churches LTD, raised from its sale and Church books, should be rightfully returned to me so that the work that I was called to do a member of the Bierton Church may continue as the lord prospers. If there is any who would like to assist me in recovering the lost property I would value your help. Remember Abraham took his men and recovered lot from his trouble well her is a cause worth dealing with.

Spirit of Enmity

I believe the same spirit of enmity that I experience with this **same Association of Grace Baptist Churches, in 1982 (See Chapter 13)** was behind this move of the Association to take our chapel. Our legitimate Trustees had also changed their doctrinal beliefs and adopted the 1689 confession of faith and they like this Association. These too were opposed to us being a Gospel Standard cause. One of their objections to the doctrinal stand of the Gospel Standard is that we do not believe the Law of Moses is the rule of life for a believer. They say we are Antinomians. Yet in practice this Association are practical Antinomians as they have taken the away the Chapel of the Bierton Strict and Particular Baptists and sold it- **which of course is against the LAW.**

This kind of hostility, to our position as a Gospel Standard Baptists, is also spoken about in my book, "The Bierton Crisis", available from the publisher.

As I was still ignored so I decide to re publish The Bierton Crisis. When announcing the publication of, "The Bierton Crisis", I notified the Association of Grace Baptist Churches LTD of my intentions in order for them to respond in an appropriate way.

31 No place of rest for the sole of my feet

Gen 8 verse 9. But the dove found no rest for the sole of her foot, and she returned unto him into the ark, for the waters were on the face of the whole earth: then he put forth his hand, and took her, and pulled her in unto him into the ark.

Serious Errors Held By A Strict Baptist Minister

On my return to the UK I sought fellowship with like-minded believers, only to find more serious errors and practices were found amongst those who should have known better. A minister and Pastor of a Strict Baptist church in the south of England told me that I would not be accepted into membership by any Gospel Standard Church. This was because I had questioned his views on the Law of Moses .

And so in my case on my return to the UK unlike the dove of Noah I was not received back into the ark of church membership.

This was because I had stated to him that if he held the position he then he would have a problem with the Sabbath. I sought to be of assistance to him, as he would certainly find his belief in the Law of Moses a stumbling block to himself and also to others, if he taught those things. I wanted him to be honest with him self.

He informed me, in agitated tones, that my views would exclude me from membership of any Gospel Standard cause. I knew from my continued membership of the Bierton Gospel Standard Church that this issue was no isolated problem. And also I was the sole remaining member of our Bierton Church. I had returned to the UK, from mission work, and our chapel had been taken unlawfully and immorally, by the Association of Grace Baptist Churches LTD, and later sold. So what was I to do? And now I was told I would not be welcomed in and Gospel Standard Church. My response was one of dismay and hurt. So I decided I must write to this man as he was in serious error believing I could help him. His reply was far from satisfactory and less then gracious without any attempt to enlighten me to his un-scriptural position. Here is this mans reply:

The Ignorant reply from the Unnamed Minister

2nd December 2003

Dear David,

It is not my custom to answer letters of this nature. However, I have been persuaded by many friends to make this brief reply. I am thankful to be the recipient of your letter and not the writer.

David, the views that you hold on the Law and the Lord's Day are wholly wrong and derogatory to the person and work of Christ. I can assure

you that neither the church at B, nor the church at HE (of which I am a trustee), nor P, SS or hold your errors, and would never receive into church membership those that hold such notions. Furthermore, there is not one church on the Gospel Standard list that holds your views or would receive into church membership any that believed such none scriptural notions.

I have learned the hard way, David, never to enter into endless questions of this nature and soul destroying controversy that brings nothing but pain to the brethren and disturbs the peace of the churches, "But when ye sin so against the brethren, and wound their weak conscience, ye sin against Christ" (1 Corinthians 8:12). "But avoid foolish questions, and genealogies, and contentions, and striving about the law; for they are unprofitable and vain (Titus 3:9).

May God grant you light from his Word to turn from your errors? Please respect my wish not to publish my letter in any of your books. Yours sincerely: Un named Minister. How to deal with such correspondence.

This letter was in fact a reply to my letter that I sent to him in connection with the issue we were talking about. I had written to this minister seeking to help him as he had problems with the Sabbath. He had stated to me that I imagined strange things in connection with the gospel and so I wrote in order to establish a starting point to seek to resolve this difference of opinion and his problem. In fact his reply revealed gross errors on his part and demonstrated the need to defend the gospel truth.

My First Letter to: The Minister of Strict Baptist Church

This is the letter that I sent to this minister which resulted in his rejection of the me and the truth that I maintained and advanced.

Date: 18th November 2003-12-10

Dear Un- named Minister (By request)

I too hate controversy. So please let us not be contentious. The truth is given to us as light in order to shine in a dark place and I would not be faithful to its cause if I remained silent over an issue, which the scripture speaks so plainly about. I believe the distinction between Law and Gospel is a real distinction, which the scripture clearly speaks about. An argument, which rests upon a fact that one has held a view for 30 years and has contended over it, carries no weight when it opposes the plain teaching of scripture. A child who has no learning, in the school of the wise, but who believes the straight foreword words of scripture, is wiser than the men of this world who have read and studied all the works of many theologians.

This only would I learn of you received ye the Spirit by the works of the Law or the hearing of Faith. The contrasting statement in this instant is between works done to or according to Law or the hearing of faith, which is without reference to works done to Law. The Law in question is the Law, which came by Moses, and which was 430 years after the Gospel had been declared to Abraham. The Law here is the 10 commandments, which was delivered at Mount Sinai. I am not imagining this (as you have suggested) but quoting the plain teaching of Gods word.

Satan hates the truth and his ploy is to ridicule those who teach the truth. He will use underhanded methods to pick at the child of God by saying such things by saying ah! "That is your own imagination, you are wrong". This is because he hates the truth and does not wish the child of God to be free from the condemnation of the Law. But the child of God will be safe if he sticks close to the word of the Lord and he will not be confounded. The Law came by Moses but grace and truth by Jesus Christ. The Law came by Moses. Not Adam, Noah or Abraham. Those who say otherwise contradict the word of God. The epistle to the Galatians is very clear about this. All arguments to the contrary are wrong and it does not matter who argues them. I am not being contentious by stating what the Scriptures say, as this is the Word of God, without comment or alteration or explanation. The plain word states the Law, and by which I understand to mean the 10 Commandments, came by Moses but grace and truth by Jesus Christ.

This is without controversy and must not be gain said. Those who seek to change the plain meaning of these words are the ones causing contention and being controversial. They wrest the Word of God. The scripture does not say the Law came by Adam, or Noah, or Abraham, but by Moses.

The contention between the child of God and child of the bondwomen is foretold by the allegory of the two sons of Abraham Ishmael and Isaac. There was a contention then, so it is now. There will always be a contention between the spiritual man and the natural man. The Apostle makes the point that the one who contends for the Law as a rule of life is the natural man, or son born to the bondwoman, whilst the spiritual man is the heir of promise and the true son.

It is always the son of the bondwomen who will persecute the freeborn Son who is the seed of promise. This will always be the case. I am then going to ask you not to persecute me because I speak the truth, as stated here in this part of God's Word. There have been many books and many sermons spoken upon this subject and great minds have wrested with these issues. I maintain that it does not matter if the whole of the Christian world, and its writers or preachers were to opposed to the truth here spoken off, it will not alter the truth that the Law came by Moses but grace and truth by Jesus Christ.

The Law in all its glory came by Moses, to a people who had been chosen to be separate from all other people. It came to the Jew and not the Gentile. This Law, which came by Moses, excluded the gentiles from the covenants of promise. It did not include them.

Unless this can be agreed upon this straightforward statement of truth then we can go no further. There is no point in seeking to go further because if one seeks to alter truth in order to make scripture fit our system of doctrine and religious thinking then we will be deceived and not be those who rightly divide the word of truth.

I am open to discuss these issues with you, or with any one, but will not contend with you. It does hurt when you say it is my imagination when I recite the scripture. I know that I have a tender conscience and I would not wish to harm a child of God and if you are lead by the same Spirit you too would be grieved you if you know you hurt a child of God. I would never mean to hurt you, in any way so please do not get offended if I express that you are wrong on an issue of doctrine, that you mentioned and came up in discussion.

I am open to correction but this must be from the Word of God and according to it. I am very clear in my understanding of many scriptures and I am also aware that I am not clear on others. When I speak that thing that I know why do you find it strange that I can be so certain.

The problem that you have A----, with your view of Law, will be that is that of the Sabbath Day. The Sabbath according to Moses is the seventh day of the week (Saturday) not the first Day of the week. And this cannot be altered or changed. You have the problem of wresting the scripture if you try and alter the scripture to make it fit your view of Law and Gospel. I believe I can help you in this matter, by sharing with you the scriptures, but you will need to be patient with me and not get wounded with me or upset if you disagree with me. I would also ask you not to get personal with me by saying I have an imagination, which is wrong. I felt your spirit was wrong towards me in your retort at that point. Please forgive me if I came over to you like that, in such a manor.

Yours Sincerely

In the name of our Lord Jesus Christ. David Clarke. 18th

November 2003

Conclusion to the Response

of the ignorant reply of the nu-named minister

This method of response by this un-named minister to my genuine letter to is ungracious, un-scriptural and very hurtful. This is not the answer of God but that of a carnal religious man whose rule of life is the Law of Moses.

He advances no scripture truth to confirm his view regarding the subject of Law and gospel. It is as though his ears were Psalm 58 verse 5. His ears were stopped like a deaf adder and though I speak ever so scripturally, logically and with moral persuasion he would not listen. Therefore how can he respond to the truth? Then just as the adder he seeks bite. I was thankful for the promise in scripture that says, they shall take up serpents; and if they drink any deadly thing, it shall not hurt them; they shall lay hands on the sick, and they shall recover. Mark 16 verse 18.

This conduct and the way of response to me in my pilgrimage was that wrought by the Mother of Harlots. This being demonstrated by his persecution that began when he wrote stating that I would not be accepted into membership of any church, holding the scriptural views of the gospel of our Lord Jesus Christ.

No wonder he did not wish for me to publish what he wrote. He is a bully and wishes to give me a bashing metaphorically , behind closed door, and then seek to bind me to silence and then walk out of the room, pretending nothing had happened. Not so, as I am set for a defence and conformation of the gospel, and will not remain silent.

It is for this reason there is a need to teach the next generation of men the glorious truths of gospel of the Lord Jesus Christ. It is of paramount importance. This is the reason for the project that is now called the Bierton Particular Baptist College.

My response to the unnamed minister

I did not respond immediately to this letter but have left the matter for almost 10 years. The time however to has come to deal with these errors and other like errors.

Here is my response to that letter:

My observations and responses

To: Minister of the Gospel Strict Baptist Church Date: 18th November 2003

This letter suggests that such people who have views of the Lords Day and Sabbath day, as I do and teach, are wrong. To say he is like a weak brother like other are weaker brethren, and they have a tender conscience, is a subtle ploy of satan. That such views are hurtful to them and because they have a tender conscience towards the Lord and the their weakness must be considered by others is wrong. They cannot hear the truth. I believe this to be false. It is a deceit and the answer of Satan.

In this matter there is no problem, as no Christian would wish to offend the weak believers conscience, in the thing that he allows himself to do, and so cause a weak brother to stumble. I put it to the reader that this mans righteousness, the Un-named Minister is one of the flesh and so carnal and therefore not from Heaven. This man is seeking to bind the free to the bondage of Law, Sin and Death. The trial by fire will reveal this in due course. Let the Lord Jesus be the one to judge.

The reality is that such who assert their views on others as this man does, and insist we follow them are the ones who cause division. They say others must follow them and their way. This man is an elder and one who is the strong as Peter was, and the Jews who through bewitchment joined those who wanted to circumcise all believers. These were dogs. In fact dumb dogs. A dog without a bark is of no use to warn of approaching danger.

They caused the dispute by saying unless these converts be circumcised and keep the Law of Moses they cannot be saved.

And as such we are instructed to mark them that cause divisions and offences contrary to the doctrine, which ye have learned; and avoid them. Rom 16 verse 17. Paul and Barnabus had no small dissension and disputation with them. Act 15 verses 1.

Also When Peter came to Antioch, Gal. 2 11, Paul withstood Peter to the face because he was to be blamed. Paul and Barnabus had strong contention with him and rebuked him openly. This was because Peter had been carried away with the Jews dissimulation. So too, in this issue, the un-named Minister is wrong along with those who too dissimulate; as he caused the division as can be seen in his letter.

David is excluded from the privileges of a gospel church because he follows the Lord Jesus. And so the scriptures are fulfilled they that live godly shall suffer persecution.

To cap it all he thinks it right to beat me up metaphorically, behind closed doors, and then bind me to silence so as not to inform other of what he has done and said.

Set for a defence and Confirmation of the Gospel. I fell the time has come to earnestly contend for the faith once delivered to the saints. Grace be with you all in the name of our Lord Jesus Christ.

I Maintain The Scripture Teaches

The new man of grace is a new creation and he has a new nature whose motions are those of a good man. He also is possessed of his old nature that always seeks to dominate the new. Those who experience the new birth are those who were chosen by the Father, in Christ before the foundation of the world. They have been regenerated and are free to respond to the Gospel by believing in the Lord Jesus Christ.

Their right standing before God is based upon Gods act of Justification, where by the righteousness of the God man Jesus Christ is imputed to them, and in that righteousness they are declared just.

They are given the grace of faith to believe all the truth of God, and by faith have peace with God when they look too, and depend upon, the finished work of Christ, in his death. Who by it made full atonement for their sins?

The sentence of justification is passed upon the conscience of the believer as they rest in Christ and look to him for all their salvation. The Lord Jesus is their true Sabbath rest.

Therefore if any man be in Christ, he is a new creature: old things are passed away; behold, all things are become new. And all things are of God, who hath reconciled us to himself by Jesus Christ, and hath given to us the ministry of reconciliation; To wit, that God was in Christ, reconciling the world unto himself, not imputing their trespasses unto them; and hath committed unto us the word of reconciliation. 2 Cor. 5 verses 17

Now then we are ambassadors for Christ, as though God did beseech you by us: we pray you in Christ's stead, be ye reconciled to God. For he hath made him to be sin for us, who knew no sin; that we might be made the righteousness of God in him. 2 Cor 5 verses 20.

32 Bierton Particular Baptist College

Bierton Strict and Particular Baptists continues

I continue the ministry that I was commissioned too by our church, in 1982 and despite the fact that religious men have taken away our chapel. It has been decided to operate in a different way. All communication with the Bierton Strict and Particular Baptist's may now be directed to our office address 11 Hayling Close, Fareham, Hampshire PO14 3AE

This ministry continues in the form of the Bierton Particular Baptist College, which is an Open Internet Cloud facility. It is set up to teach and educate students wishing to educate themselves in Doctrinal and Practical divinity or theology.

Initially this will be in the form of an Access Course to Higher Education, To also teach men to preach the gospel of Christ, which will include historical and sociological studies. It is planned that our course of study will be underwritten by the Open University or a similar qualifying educational body. This will give graduating students educational status to continue their studies any where in the world.

The doctrinal basis for this college is the Articles of Religion of the Bierton Strict and Particular Baptist Society (Church), founded in 1831.

As the former Secretary of the church I still hold a copy of the original indenture relating to the founding of the Bierton Church and the minutes of our meetings, which can be read on our web site. This indenture specifies how the church is to elect its own trustees. The trust is a 1000-year trust, which commenced in 1832.

Our trustees failed in their responsibilities to the trust and our

Bierton Church Chapel, and property, have been disposed of and religious men have taken the inheritance, yet the work of preaching Christ to men goes on. I write and inform my readers all about this in my book, "The Bierton Strict and Particular Baptists, My Testimony and Confession." Alternatively: Set for the Defence and Confirmation of the Gospel.

Oliver Cromwell

Oliver Cromwell soon learned he had to train the men of England in the art of warfare to achieve his objectives. Likewise the Israelites needed help in their day of trouble. Remember the scripture:

Now there was no smith found throughout all the land of Israel: for the Philistines said, lest the Hebrew make them swords or spears:

So it came to pass in the day of battle, that there was neither sword nor spear found in the hand of any of the people that were with Saul and Jonathan:

I Sam 13 19.

Education And Teaching is the Way Forward

Since the Philistines have taken our Bierton Chapel this cannot stop the work of God. The Bierton Particular Baptist College is like the Open University, were students might partake in a disciplined course of study by distant learning. Leading to a degree of knowledge in Doctrinal and Practical Divinity. The basic foundation will be based upon the First London Baptist Confession of faith, 1646, 2nd Edition, and all associated learning will be treated. Including history, the social influences of the 17-century. Oliver Cromwell's cause in England and Europe. The study will include the works of men like John Bunyan, Dr, John Gill, Dr John Owen, Joseph Philpot, William

344

Huntington to name just a few.

Our Bierton Church articles of religion were written in 1831, which was before the Gospel Standard magazine was first published. However we aligned ourselves to the Gospel Standard Cause, in January 1981.

Those who know their history will be aware of all those conflicts and contentions that have arisen, so our philosophy is to start from the First London Baptist Confession, 1646, which is fairly comprehensive, and learn by examining these tenets and principles of truth by means of academic study and not indoctrination.

In our studied we will be treating the subject of the value and reliability of the Authorized Version of the bible, in order to ensure faithful reference to the Word of God.

A Note To Prospective Teacher

We welcome those who are being taught by the Lord to offer their services. We are sorry we cannot pay you. If you feel directed to offer your help we would welcome your application. Please send us an e-mail to that effect.

A Note To Prospective Students

We welcome those who feel they would benefit from a course of study. We know from experience the value of education for it is the truth that sets men free. Please send us an email with your request to enrol and enquiries regarding the curriculum.

Bierton Strict and Particular Baptists Members

I, David Clarke am the only remaining active member of the

Bierton Church. I am a sent minister of the Church and the full proof of my ministry are those 30 souls that I baptized in Baguio City Jail and Benguet Provincial Jail, in December 2002. This ministry activity being carried out by our sent man William C Poloc whose testimony is published in our book Trojan Warriors. This ministry being under my Directorship of Trojan Horse International.

Website Address for the College:

http://www.BiertonParticularBaptists.co.uk

E mail: SecretaryDolores@yahoo.co.uk

11 Hayling Close Fareham

Hampshire

PO14 3AE

United Kingdom

33 William C. Poloc's Work in Baguio City

Thankfully our work in the Philippines was not in vain and we can report that our man William Poloc is a sent minister of Trojan Horse International. This demonstrates that God has worked, blessing my ministry as a sent a sent minister from the Bierton Particular Baptist Church, in January 1981. This may be considered a vindication from the lord that I stood for the right things when at the Bierton Church, and in my contention with those in the Philippines, that turned from the way of grace to follow the traditions of men.

I tell the truth in my defense and confirmation of the gospel of the Lord Jesus Christ. A living proof of the truth that all things work together for good to them that love God and are the called according to his purposes. Rom. 8 verse 28. That the things that have happened to me have turned out rather for the furtherance and confirmation of the gospel.

News from the Philippines

Re: News Up date confirming the ministry

Wednesday, 28 March, 2012 1:32 From: "William Poloc sr" <williampolocsr@yahoo.com> To: "David Clarke" nbpttc@yahoo.co.uk

Dear David,

God's work here in the Northern Philippines bloomed most especially here in the city of Baguio. The Baguio Christ-Centered Church also multiplied with the following   d a u g h t e r churches and other ministries.

We have:

1 The Pilot- Christ-Centered Church,

2 The Kamog Christ-Centered Church.

3 The Christ-Centered-Church Theological School (TULIP),

4 The Christ- Centered Radio Ministry, The Christ-Centered Jail Minis

tries etc.). We'll, we are truly blessed by these works He has entrusted to us.

To God be the glory!

We are all doing great anyway and my family as well. Regards to everyone. God bless!!

In Christ,

William and Family Christ-Centered Ministries, Philippines

34 The Law and Gospel By F. L. Gosden

Preached at Gilead Chapel, Brighton, (This is just an extract fro the opening part to his sermon)

One Lord's Day evening 3 April 1946

"Great peace have they which love thy law: nothing shall offend them." (Psalm 119:165)

The law in the text is the gospel. The Law of Moses is a good law, holy and just; but it is not a law that sinners love. They reverence it, but it is an authority which can only curse them because they continue not in all things commanded, and shuts them up in prison; it can make nothing perfect; it leaves a sinner where it finds him; it brings him under its condemning power.

But the law of the text is the law of the gospel. The apostle James speaks of it as 'the perfect law of liberty.' It is perfect because it makes the comers thereunto perfect and because the Lord Jesus, Who is the sum and substance of it, is perfect-made perfect through suffering. The Law of Moses was a perfect law of bondage- the perfection of the Mosaic Law is the perfection of the justice of God exercised in the condemnation of sinners. The law of the gospel is the perfection of liberty.

'Great peace have they which love thy law.' There is a blessedness in this description of the gospel as being 'a law', for where there, is a law there is authority; and Oh, the blessedness of the authority of the gospel as contrasted with the terribleness of the authority of the law. The gospel is greater than the law-not by its abrogation or destruction, but in its fulfilment; its authority abounds over the law, for 'where sin abounded, grace did much more abound.' The apostle speaks of it in this way: 'For the law of the Spirit of life in Christ

Jesus hath made me free, from the law of sin and death.' He then goes on to speak of what the law, could not do. So that we see there are three laws, three authorities, three powers, three dominions spoken of. First, the law of the Spirit of life in Christ Jesus is the law of the gospel making one free, from the law of sin and death; secondly, the dominion of sin in our members. Then there is thirdly, the Law of Moses that is the Ten Commandments; and what this law could not do, 'in that it was weak through the flesh, God sending his own Son in the likeness of sinful flesh, and for sin, condemned sin in the flesh.' That is the authority, the power of the gospel. The apostle -said, 'I am not ashamed of the gospel of Christ': it is the power or the authority of God in a particular direction and to a blessed end; it is the power of God unto salvation in them that believe. Therein is the righteousness of God revealed, the righteousness of faith?

35 The Law and Gospel, by J.C. Philpot

I shall take the occasion to offer my thoughts on these three distinct points:

1 Why the law is not the believer's rule of life.

2 What is the rule?

3 Disprove the objection cast upon us that our views lead to doctrinal or practical antinomianism.

By a believer, I understand one who by faith in Christ is delivered from the curse and bondage of the law, and who knows something experimentally of the life, light, liberty and love of the glorious gospel of the grace of God. By the law I understand chiefly, though not exclusively, the Law of Moses. And by the rule of life I understand and outward and inward guide, by following which a believer directs his walk and conversion before God, the Church and the world.

It is very necessary to bear strictly in mind that we are speaking wholly and solely a believer. What has the law to do with a believer in Christ Jesus? Is he required by the revealed will of God to take the law as a guiding rule in his life? I answer, No; and for several reasons.

1 God does not leave us at liberty to take at will one part of the law and leave the other. It must be taken as a whole or left as a whole, for God has so revealed it. I cannot find in any part of God's Word any mitigation of its terms, or any halving of it, so that, according to the views of many divines who have written on the subject, we may be dead to it as a covenant, yet alive to it as a rule. The essential and distinguishing characteristic of the law is that it is a covenant of works, requiring full and perfect obedience, attaching a tremendous curse to the least infringement of its commands. If

then I, as a believer, take the law as my rule of life, I take it with its curse; I put myself under its yoke, for in receiving it as my guide, (and if I do not this it is not my rule,) I take it with all its conditions and subject to all its penalties.... The indispensable connection between a covenant and its rules is clearly shown in Gal. 5:1-6, where the apostle testifies to "every man that is circumcised, that he is a debtor to the whole law". It is idle to talk of taking the law for a rule of life, and not for a covenant; for the two things are essentially inseparable; and as he who keeps the whole law and yet offends in one point, is guilty of all (James 2:10), so he who takes but one precept of the law for his rule, (as the Galatians took that of circumcision,) by taking that one, virtually adopts the whole, and by adopting the whole puts himself under the curse which attaches to their infringement.

2 People speak very fluently about the law being a rule of life that think little of the resulting consequences; for amongst them is this, that its written precepts and not its mere spirit, must be the rule. Now, these precepts belong to it only as a covenant, for they were never disjoined by the Authority that gave them, and what God hath joined together let no man put asunder. To show this connection between the precepts and the covenant is the chief drift of the Epistle to the Galatians, who were looking to the law and not the gospel, and having begun in the Spirit, were attempting to be made perfect by the flesh. Read with enlightened eyes, this blessed Epistle would at once decide in favor of the gospel as our guiding rule of Christian conduct and conversation. Observe how Paul chides those who would so act: he calls them "foolish Galatians", and asks who hath bewitched them that they should not obey the truth (that is, the gospel),"before whose eyes Jesus Christ has been evidently set forth, crucified among them." He appeals to their own

experience and asks them: "receive ye the Spirit by the works of the law or by the hearing of faith?" He draws a line of distinction here between those works which are done in obedience to the law as a guiding rule, and that power of God felt in the heart which attends a preached gospel when heard in faith, and asks them under which of the two they had received the teaching and testimony of the blessed Spirit. But observe, further, now he bids them "walk in the Spirit" (Gal. 5:16). Now to "walk" is to live and act, and the rule which he here gives for this living and acting is not the law but the Spirit, and he tells them of the blessedness of this divine leading and guiding: "If ye be led by the Spirit, ye are not under the law": that is, neither as a covenant nor as a rule- that they were free from its curse as a condemning covenant, and from its commands as a galling yoke which neither they nor their fathers could bear (Acts 15:10). But to show them that deliverance form the law did not set them free from a higher and more perfect rule of obedience, he bids them "fulfill the law of Christ", which is love, a fruit of the Spirit and not produced by the law which worketh wrath and gendereth to bondage (Rom. 4:15; Gal. 4:24).

3 If we are willing to abide by the inspired Word of Truth we need to go no further than this very Epistle to decide the whole question. For in it we have laid down the rule according to which believers should walk, which is a "new creature" (or a new creation): "For in Christ neither circumcision availeth anything nor uncircumcision, but a new creature. And as many as walk according to this rule, peace be upon them, and on the Israel of God" (Gal. 6:15-16). Is the law or the Spirit's work upon the heart held our here as the rule of a believers walk? The law is strictly a covenant of works; it knows nothing of mercy, reveals nothing of grace, and does not communicate the blessed Spirit. Why, then, if I am a believer in

Christ and have received his grace and truth into my heart, am I to adopt for the rule of life that which does not testify of Jesus either in the Word or in my conscience? If I am to walk as a believer, it must be by a life of faith in the Son of God (Gal 2:20). Is the law my rule here? If it be, where are those rules to be found? "The law is not of faith". How, then, can it law down rules for the life of faith? If I wish to walk as becomes a believer with the Church, what help will the law give me there? To walk as such must be by the law of love as revealed in Christ and made known in my heart by the power of God. If I am to walk in the ordinances of God's house, are these to be found revealed in the law?

We give the law its due honor. It had a glory, as the Apostle argues (2Cor 3) as the ministration of death and condemnation, but this glory is done away, and why are we to look to it now as our guiding rule? The ministration of the Spirit, of life, and of righteousness "doth much more exceed in glory", and why are we to be condemned if we prefer the Spirit to the letter, life to death, and righteousness to condemnation? A rule must influence as well as guide, or else it be a dead rule. If you chose to be guided by the killing letter which can only minister condemnation and death, and we chose for our rule that which ministers the Spirit, righteousness, and life, which has the better rule? It is much to be feared that those who thus walk and talk have still the veil over their heart, and know nothing of what the Apostle means when he says: "Now the Lord is that Spirit, and where the Spirit of the Lord is there is liberty. But we all with open face beholding, as in a glass the glory of the Lord, are changed into the same image from glory to glory, even as the Spirit of the Lord" (2Cor 3:17-18).

But not only have we these deductions to influence the mind in rejecting the law as a rule for a believers walk, but also we have the
354

express testimony of God as a warrant for so doing. We read, for instance, "I through the law am dead to the law, that I might live unto God" (Rom. 7:4). As a believer in Christ, the law is dead to me, and I am to it. The Apostle has clearly and beautifully opened up this subject. He assumes that a believer in Christ is like a woman is remarried after the death of her first husband; and he declares that "she is bound by the law of her husband as long as he liveth, but if the husband be dead she is loosed from the law of her husband (verse 2). Of course the first husband is the law, and the second husband is Christ. Now adopting the figure of Paul's, may we not justly ask: Which is to be the rule of the wife's conduct when remarried, the regulations of the first or the second husband?

2. What, then, is the believer's rule of life. Is he without rule? A lawless wretch because he abandons the Law of Moses for his rule has no guide to direct his steps? God forbid! For I subscribe heart and soul to the words of the Apostle: Being not without law to God, but under law to Christ "(1Cor 9:21) (footnote- not under THE law, as our version; there being no article expressed or implied in the original). The believer then has a guiding rule, which we may briefly call -the gospel. This rule we may divide into 2 branches. The gospel as written by the divine finger upon the heart, and the gospel as written by the blessed Spirit in the Word of truth. These do not form two distinct rules, but the one is the counterpart of the other; and they are mutually helpful to and corroborative of each other. One of the promises of the New Covenant (Jer. 31:21-34; Heb. 8:8-12 compared) was: "I will write My law in their inward parts and write it in their hearts." This writing of the law of God in their heart, I need not tell you, is that which distinguishes it from the law of Moses which was written on tables of stone: and becomes an internal rule whereas the law of Moses was but an external rule.

This internal rule seems to be pointed out in Romans 8:2 where we find these words: "For the law of the Spirit of life in Christ Jesus has set me free from the law of sin and death." By "the law of the Spirit of life", I understand that guiding rule (for a rule in Scripture is frequently called a law; the word law in Hebrew signifying literally "instruction") which the Spirit of God, as communicating life, is in a believers heart. It is, therefore, the liberating, sanctifying, guiding influence of the Spirit of God, in his soul which, as a law or a rule, delivers him from "the law of sin and death"; by which I understand not so much the law of Moses, as the power and prevalence of his corrupt nature.

If this then be a correct exposition of the text, we have a guiding internal rule distinct from the law of Moses, and a living rule in the heart, which that never was nor could be; for it did not communicate the Spirit (Gal. 3:2-5) But this internal rule as being "the law of the Spirit of life", has power to lead all the children of God; for in the same chapter (verse 14) the Apostle declares that "as many as are led by the Spirit of God, they are the sons of God." This leading which is peculiar to the children of God and is an evidence of their sonship, delivers them from the law; for if we are led by Spirit we are not under the law" (Gal 5:8) either as a covenant or as a rule, for we have a better covenant and a better rule (Heb. 8:6). What is the main use of a rule but to lead? But who can lead like a living Guide? How can a dead law lead a living soul? The very proof that we are the children of God is that we are led by the Spirit; and this inward leading becomes our guiding rule. And is it not a disparaging of the guidance of the blessed Spirit to set up in opposition to His guiding rule a dead law and to call those Antinomians who prefer a living guide to a dead letter? This living guide is that holy, and blessed Spirit who "guides into all truth" (Jn. 16:13).

Here is the main blessedness of the work and grace upon the heart, that the leading and guiding of the blessed Spirit form a living rule every step of the way; for He not only quickens the soul into spiritual life, but maintains the life which He gave, and performs (or finishes- margin) it until the day of Jesus Christ (Phil. 1:6). This life is eternal, as the blessed Lord at the well of Samaria declared, that the water that he should give the believer should be in a well of water springing up into everlasting life (Jn. 4:14) It is then this springing well in a believer's soul which is the guiding rule, for, as producing and maintaining the fear of God, it is "a fountain of life to depart from the snares of death" (Pro.14: 27).

But lest this guiding internal rule be abused, which it might be by enthusiasm, and that they might not be left to substitute delusive fancies for the teaching of the Holy Spirit, the God of all grace has given to His people an external rule in precepts of the gospel as declared by the mouth of the Lord and His apostles, but more particularly as gathered up in the epistles as a standing code of instruction for the living family of God. Nor do these at all clash with the rule of which I have just spoken, but on the contrary harmonize entirely and thoroughly with it; for, in fact, it is one and the same rule; the only difference between them being that the blessed Spirit had revealed the one in the written Word, and by the application of that Word to the soul makes the other to be a living rule of heart.

Now there is not a single part of particle of our walk and conduct before God or man which is not revealed and unculcated in the precepts of the gospel; for, though we have not minute directions, we have what far excels all such unnecessary minutiae- most blessed principles enforced by every gracious and holy motive, and forming, when rightly seen and believed, a most perfect code of inward and outward conformity to the revealed will of God, and of all holy walk and conduct in our families in the church and in the world.

I would say that a believer has a rule to walk but which is sufficient to guide him in every step of the way; for if he has the eternal quickening's, teachings and leadings of the Spirit to make his conscience tender in the fear of God, and has a law of love written upon the heart by the finger of God; and besides this has the precepts of the gospel as a full and complete code of Christian obedience, what more can he want to make him perfect in every good word and work (Heb. 13:21). Can the law do any of these things for him? Can it give him life, in the first instance, when it is a killing letter? Can it maintain life, if it is not in its power to bestow it?

But it may be asked: Do you then set aside the two great commandments of the law: "Thou shalt love the Lord thy God" etc. and "thy neighbor as thyself"? No, On the contrary, the gospel as an external and internal rule fulfills them both, for "love is the fulfilling of the law." (Rom. 13:10). So this blessed rule of the gospel not only does not set aside the law as regards its fulfillment, but so to speak absorbs into itself and glorifies and harmonizes its two great commandments, by yielding to them in obedience of heart, which the law could not give; for the believers serves in the newness of the Spirit, not in the oldness of the letter (Rom 7:6), as Christ's freeman (Jn. 8:32) and not as Moses's bond slave. This is willing obedience not a legal task. This will explain the meaning of the Apostle: "For I delight in the law of God after the inward man: for the new man of grace, under the powerful influence of the Holy Spirit, delights in the law of God, not only for its holiness, but as inculcating that to do which fills the renewed heart and the inward delight -love to God and His people...

36 The Christian Relationship To Mosaic Law

By Philip Mauro

The Gentile Believer and The Law

We have said that the experience of the "wretched man" of Romans 7 is not the normal experience of a converted Gentile. It is, nevertheless, a sad fact that it may (and often does) become the abnormal experience of converted Gentiles, who, through ignorance of the great gospel truths revealed in Romans, or through the influence of Judaizing teachers and legal systems of theology, fall from their standing in grace, and seek justification, or the gift of the Spirit, through law-works. Hence the solemn warning of Galatians 5:4: "You are deprived of all effect from Christ, whosoever in law are being justified; you are fallen from grace." For as there were in Paul's day, so are there now, many who desire "to be of the law, understanding neither what they say, nor whereof they affirm."

So also the struggle of that "wretched man" becomes the experience of many unconverted Gentiles who, totally ignorant of remission of sins through faith in the blood of Christ.... are seeking perpetually (because seeking vainly) for and inclination of the heart to keep the Mosaic Law. The condition of such, if they be earnest and sincere in their desire to keep the law, is indeed "wretched" in the extreme.

It was needful, therefore, that, in addition to the revelation given in Romans 7 of deliverance for the believing Jew from the yoke of the Law, the Epistle to the Galatians should have been incorporated into the Word of God, in order to instruct and warn Gentile believers against putting themselves under that yoke.

In referring, however, to Galatians our object will be simply to seek the light it throws upon the conflict described in Romans 7. What we find in Galatians affords strong confirmation to the view that the experience described in Romans 7 is that of a conscientious unconverted Israelite, and not at all a "Christian" experience. In fact, the main object of the Apostle in writing to the assemblies of Galatia was to warn them against teachings, which would lead them into such an experience.

Galatians 2

In Galatians 2 Paul relates how he remonstrated with the Apostle Peter for compelling the Gentiles to live as do the Jews (v. 14). We may be sure that the matter in dispute is esteemed by the Spirit of God to be exceedingly important; otherwise it would not be brought to our attention in the form of a rebuke administered by Paul, the Apostle to the Gentiles, to Peter, the leader of the twelve. In this connection Paul draws the line sharply between Jews and Gentiles, saying: "We, Jews by nature, and not sinners of the Gentiles, knowing that a man in not justified out of the works of the Law, but out of the faithfulness of Christ, even we [Jews] have believed on Christ Jesus that we might be justified out of the faithfulness of Christ, and not out of works of Law" (vv. 15-16). And he adds: "For if I build again the things I threw down, I constitute myself a transgressor." That is to say, if he should set up the Law again as an obligation for himself, he would make himself a law-breaker. "For," he continues, "I through the Law died to the Law, that I might live to God." Here Paul again brings himself forward, as a typical Jew, and repeats in few words the doctrine elaborated in Romans 7. "I have been crucified with Christ, nevertheless I live"; or, as the Greek may be equally well rendered, "I am not any longer living, it is Christ that lives in me; and the life I now live in the flesh I live by the faithfulness of the Son of God."

It is possible for every believer to reach the place where he can make this saying of Paul his own. It involves death to sin and life to God in Christ, and the abiding presence of the Spirit of Him who raised up Christ from the dead. This verse obviously contains a condensed statement of the truth revealed in Romans 6 and 7 concerning the believer's death (as to his old nature) with Christ, and his living again in the supernatural life of the risen Christ. That new life is not lived under the Law of Sinai.

"I do not," says Paul, "make void the grace of God" (as Peter was doing by his dissimulation and by returning to the practice of Judaism) "for if righteousness comes through the Law, then Christ died for nothing" (v. 21).

Galatians 3

Having thus dealt with the case of the believing Jew, who had been delivered from the Law by means of Christ's death, the Apostle directly addresses the Galatians, who, being Gentiles, never were under Law, but began their relations with God in the Spirit. The Jew began his service of God in the flesh. For him, therefore, there might be found some excuse for continuing after conversion as a man in the flesh under Law, not exercising the liberty wherewith Christ had made him free. But for Gentile believers, who never were under the Law, but had the great advantage of beginning in the Spirit, to put themselves under Law and to attempt to be perfected in the flesh was the "senseless" action of those who had been "bewitched." "O senseless Galatians, who had bewitched you," that you should act thus after the truth concerning Christ crucified has been plainly put before you? "Are you so senseless? Having begun in the Spirit, are you now being perfected in the flesh?" (Gal. 3:1-3). It was indeed "senseless" in the extreme to undertake the perfecting in the flesh of the work that was begun in the Spirit.

The Apostle then refers to Abraham, whose faith was accounted to him for righteousness, and points out that the Scripture, foreseeing that God would justify the Gentiles out of faith, proclaimed that good news to Abraham, saying, "In you shall all nations (Gentiles) be blessed." (Gal. 3:8).

The Galatians are warned of two serious facts. First, Paul teaches that all who are of the works of Law (in contrast to those that are "of faith") are under the curse of the Law. Second, he asserts that the curse comes upon every one who continues not in all things, which are written in the book of the Law to do them. From this it follows that no one is being justified with God in virtue of Law: "For the just shall live out of faith; but the man that does those things (required by the Law) shall live in virtue of them" (vv. 10-12).

In view of this, it would naturally be asked, How does it come about that the Jews, who were placed under the Law, which none of them has kept, have escaped from the curse of the Law? The answer is, "Christ has redeemed us (Jews) from the curse of the Law, having become a curse for us." This statement manifestly applies solely to Israel, for the curse of the Law was never pronounced against the Gentiles. Hence Paul uses in verse 3:13 the pronoun "us." The contrast between Jews and Gentiles is again clearly marked by 3:14, which goes on to say that Christ was made a curse for the Jews in order that the blessing of Abraham might come on the Gentiles in Christ Jesus. The contrast between the curse of the Law, pronounced upon those who were under the Law, and the blessing of Abraham coming to the Gentile believers in Christ, is very instructive. And an additional result of the endurance by Christ of the curse of the Law is then set forth, namely, that we might receive the promise of the Spirit through faith.

The promise was made to Abraham and to his seed long before the Law was given. From this it follows that the Law, which was given 430 years after, cannot nullify the promise. If then the Law was not given for the purpose of adding anything to the promise, or of taking anything from it, why was it given? It was added for the sake of transgressions that is in order that the repeated transgressions of the Law by every Israelite might reveal the presence and nature of sin in the flesh, and show the futility of attempting to secure justification out of Law-works. Moreover, it was given, not as a permanent institution, but only "until the Seed should come to whom the promise was made." (3:19).

This statement shows that the period of the Law was strictly limited in time, as it was limited also in scope to the children of Israel. Its era did not begin until 430 years after God had begun to deal with Abraham, Isaac and Jacob and their descendants; and it ceased when the promised Seed died under the Law. The curse of the Law was exhausted when Christ was made curse by hanging on a tree (Deut. 21:23). Whatever God's purposes were with the Law, they were all accomplished when the promised Seed died on the Cross? Since that event even the Jew is no longer a man under Law, for by no amount of law keeping can he now secure the promised blessings of the Promised Land. The old covenant is entirely at an end (2 Cor. 3:7- 11; Heb. 7:13). The words on the Cross-, "It is finished" (in the original it is the single word "accomplished") included the purpose of the Law, which thereupon came to an end.

The temporary character of the Law as a Divine institution is further set forth, with great clearness, in verses 23-25. "Before faith came," says the Apostle, "we [Jews] were kept [or guarded] under Law, having been shut up to the faith which was about to be revealed. Wherefore the Law has been our pedagogue [tutor] up to Christ in order that out of faith we might be justified. But faith having come, we are no longer under a tutor." By noting the tenses of the verbs, as given in the above renderings, the sense will be readily and clearly apprehended. It is very clear indeed that these statements apply only to Israelites. The Gentiles were not kept under Law, but were left without Law. They were not "shut up" in any way, but allowed to follow the devices of their own hearts. They were not under a pedagogue, or under tutors and governors (4:2), for God had no dealings with them. God has called Israel His "Son" (Hosea 11:1; see Amos 3:2); and of Israel alone, of all the peoples of the earth, can it be said that they were under tutors waiting the time appointed of the Father.

After speaking in the first person of the Jews, the Apostle, addressing the Gentile Galatians, says by way of contrast: "For you are all the children of God through faith in Christ Jesus. For as many of you as have been baptized into Christ have put on Christ. There is neither Jew nor Greek." The contrast between the "we" of verses 24,25 and the "you" of verse 26 is very significant.

Some of the statements (in Galatians 4) are broad enough to embrace both Jews and Gentiles, for both were, before conversion, in bondage to the elements of the world; but the special bondage of the Jew - the yoke of the Law and the penalty of its curse - is also specifically mentioned. As the heir is "under tutors and governors until the time appointed of the father; even so we, when we were children, were in bondage under the elements of the world: But when the fullness of time was come, God sent forth His Son, born of a woman, made under the Law, to redeem those that were under the

Law, that we [Jews] might receive the status of sons. But because you [Gentiles] are sons, God has sent forth the Spirit of His Son into your hearts, crying, 'Abba Father.'" (4:2-6) The defective reading of verse 6 in the A.V. "And because you are sons," instead of "But," as it is in the original, hides the contrast between the case of the believing Israelite and that of the believing Gentile. The former needed to be redeemed from under the Law before he could receive the status of a son ("adoption of sons"); whereas for the latter there was no such need. The bondage of the Gentiles was a different kind of bondage. They, not knowing God at all, were in bondage to those who by nature are not gods (4:8); but the point we wish to examine is that they were not under Law at any time, and this point is very clearly presented in the passage we have been examining. (Editor's note: Randall Seiver has presented a better explanation of this passage in his book on Galatians "The Fullness of Time" available from Sound of Grace, Webster N.Y.

The Believer's State Is Not One Of Lawlessness

In emphasizing the important truth that the believer is not under the Law, because, if a Jew he was delivered from the yoke of the Law by the death of Christ, and if a Gentile he was never under the Law at all, must not obscure the important fact that the state of the believer is not one of lawlessness - far from it. What is spoken of in Romans 7, as "the Law" is the Law given to the Israelites through Moses? That Law was by no means a complete statement of God's requirements, though it was quite sufficient for the purpose of revealing the presence of sin in the flesh, for demonstrating the utter corruption of human nature, and for making manifest the exceeding sinfulness of sin. The teachings of Jesus Christ showed that the full requirements of God's holiness and righteousness are far above those of the Law of Moses. "You have heard that it was said by (or to) them of old, you shall not kill...But I say to you, whoever is angry with his brother without a cause, etc." (Matt. 5:21-48).

The believer of this dispensation is not living under the Law of Moses. That law was given for the regulation of the conduct of men in the flesh. The believer is "not in the flesh, but in the Spirit." (Rom. 8:9). He is not, therefore, in the sphere in which the Law of Moses was effective.

The child of God, though not under the Law of Moses, is "not without Law to God, but in-law to Christ" (ennomous Christou, 1 Cor. 9:21). He owns the risen Christ as His Lord, and judges that his entire life in the body is to be lived no longer unto himself, but unto Him who died for him and rose again (2 Cor. 5:15). Being in the Spirit he is to be governed by "the law of the Spirit" (Rom. 8:2). Being in Christ he is to "fulfil the law of Christ" (Gal. 6:2). This is a condition very different from that of the Israelite under the Law of Moses, and on a much higher plane. The life of the child of God is not a life hedged about by constraints and prohibitions, but a life of liberty in which he is free to follow all the leading of the Spirit, and all the inclinations of the new nature, which the Spirit imparts, to those whom He quickens. It is a life of freedom - not freedom to sin, but freedom not to sin. He who practices sin is the slave of sin; only the free man can refuse obedience to the demands of sin, and yield himself to God as one who is alive from the dead. The Word of God abounds in directions addressed to the children of God, by which their walk, while yet in the body, is to be guided and controlled. These directions are found in the commandments of Christ, and in the Epistles of the Apostle Paul, whom the risen Lord empowered to be the channel for the revelation of His special communications to and concerning the Church. And these directions are illustrated by all the Holy Scriptures, the things which happened to the Israelites

368

having been written, not for our imitation, but for our admonition (1 Cor. 10:11).

The believer has been called into liberty; and he is exhorted to stand fast in the liberty wherewith Christ has made him free (Gal. 5:1). Yet he is not to use his liberty so as to furnish occasions for gratifying the desires of his old nature (Gal. 5:13). Having been brought, through the resurrection of Christ, into the sphere of the Spirit, the believer is commanded to remain there; that is, to be occupied with and interested in the things of the Spirit. While so engaged he cannot at the same time be fulfilling the desires of the flesh. "This I say then, walk in [or by] the Spirit, and you shall not fulfill the desires of the flesh" (Gal. 5:16). "If you be led of the Spirit you are not under the Law" (Gal. 5:18).

Ephesians, which especially reveals the position of believers as quickened together with Christ, raised up (i.e. ascended) together with Him, and seated together in the heavenlies in Christ, abounds in practical directions for the believer's guidance in all his earthly relations. We...call attention to them in order to guard against the supposition that, because the believer of this dispensation is not under the Law of Moses, he is therefore in a state of lawlessness.

The main points, then, of the teaching we have been examining are these:

1. That the sufferings of Christ were incurred for the sins of His people, that is to say, the sins of those whom God justifies upon the principle of faith.

2. That the death of Christ delivers the believing sinner, whether Jew or Gentile, rom the servitude of sin.

3. That the death of Christ also brought the economy of the Law

to an end, and delivered all converted Israelites from the yoke of the Law.

4. That the resurrection of Christ brings all believers into the sphere of a new humanity, where there is a new life, whose Source is the risen Christ, which life is imparted by the Spirit of God to the believer while the later is yet in the mortal body.

5. That believers, though not under the Law of Moses, are governed by the Law of the Spirit of life in Christ Jesus, and are required to "fulfill the law of Christ."

37 The Sabbath By Gilbert Beebe

January 1, 1855

There is much said at the present day on the subject of a Sabbath day, as being of perpetual obligatory force on all mankind throughout all time. But in what part of the Scriptures they find a precept to that effect we are not informed. They certainly but seldom, if ever, refer us to the fourth commandment of the Decalogue; and we have supposed their reasons for not doing so were obvious.

1. Because we are expressly informed by Moses himself that, that very covenant, or law, was made exclusively with those Israelites who were all of them then present, and alive on the day that the ten commandments were presented to them from the Mount of God. It was a law which, had not been given even to the patriarchs, (See Deut. 5:1-4).

2. Because the fourth commandment required those unto whom it was given, to observe the seventh, and not the first day of the week, as the Sabbath of their God—because that God had rested from the work of creation on the seventh, and not on the first day of the week.

3. Because the children of Israel were by the fourth commandment required to observe the seventh day altogether differently from the manner in which professed Christians pretend to observe the first day. The children of Israel were to totally abstain from all labor, themselves, their wives, their children, their servants, and even their cattle; no fires were allowed to be kindled, no horses to be harnessed, no meetings to be attended, no Sabbath Schools to be kept, no collections for mission or other purposes, to be taken up on that day.

4. Because the penalty for a transgression of that precept, was altogether different from that inflicted by modern Sabbatarians for a breach of the Sunday laws of our own, or any other lands. That provided in the Jewish law, being death by stoning, and the laws of men only requiring fines and imprisonments.

5. The fourth commandment required those unto whom it was given to labor six days, including the first day, and the Sunday laws of our land forbid our obedience to that part of the fourth commandment which requires us to labor on the first day of the week.

We know of no partial obligation to keep the law. If the Sinai covenant, which was given exclusively to the children of Israel, is binding on the Gentiles to any extent, it must be binding in its full extent. An inspired apostle has settled this question beyond all reasonable dispute, "For whosoever shall keep the whole law, and yet offend in one point, he is guilty of all," (Jam. 2:10). And Paul to the Galatians, 5:3, shows who are debtors to keep the law. He says, "For I testify again to every man that is circumcised, that he is a debtor to do the whole law." But in searching the Scriptures, we can find none who are obligated to obey part of the law, or partly obligated to do the whole law. "Whatsoever the law saith, it saith to them that are under the law," and they are of course bound to go according to the letter of the commandment. The grand question then is, whether the whole Sinai law is binding on all men, and throughout all time? If so, then all are involved in the curse, and the salvation of any of the human family is impossible. For as many as are of the works of the law are under the curse; for all have sinned; and consequently by the deeds of the law, no flesh shall be justified in the sight of God.

The doctrine of redemption is very prominently set forth in the gospel; and Christ has not only redeemed his people from the curse, but also from the dominion of the law; and the apostle has made the emphatic proclamation to the saints, "Ye are no more under the law, but under grace." The inquiry then is reduced to this; How far are we obligated to keep a law that we are not under? When Paul found some of the brethren inclining to the works of the law, he was afraid of them, lest he had bestowed on them labor in vain, for they observed days, and months, and times, and years. In his allegory, (Gal. 4:21-27), Paul sets forth the old Sinai covenant, by the person of Hagar, the bondwoman, who could not be the mother of a free child. For this Agar is Mount Sinai, in Arabia, which answereth to Jerusalem, which now is, and is in bondage with her children. But Jerusalem, which is above, is free, which Jerusalem he affirms, is the mother of all those saints, who, as Isaac was, are the children of promise. In the second chapter to the Colossians, we are informed that Christ has blotted out the handwriting of ordinances that was against us, which was contrary to us, and took them out of the way, nailing them to his cross; and having spoiled principalities and powers, he made a show of them openly, triumphing over them in it. Let no man therefore judge you in meat, or in drink, or in respect to an holy day, or of the new moon, or of the Sabbath days, which are a shadow of things to come; but the body is of Christ. This language would seem to be plain enough for an ordinary Christian, taught of God. These ordinances of the old covenant were a shadow of things, which are realized in the body of Christ, or in the gospel church, which is his body, his flesh and his bones. We trace the shadowy import of the Sinai Sabbath to the body of Christ, or to the gospel church, and there we enter into that rest which was shadowed forth by the legal Sabbaths of the old covenant. The antitypical Sabbath, being found alone in that rest which remaineth for the children of God, and into which all those who, with a true and vital faith, believe in our Lord Jesus Christ, have entered, is clearly set forth in the New Testament, particularly in the third and fourth chapters to the Hebrews. This gospel Sabbath we understand to be the whole gospel dispensation; in distinction from the old covenant dispensation, and it begins severally with each believer in Christ, as soon as they truly believe in our Lord Jesus Christ; and are enabled to rest alone on him for their justification before God. We have neither the time nor the space necessary to show the analogy, which the typical Sabbath of the law bears to the rest, which is enjoyed by the saints in the gospel. A very few particulars must for the present suffice, and,

1. The old covenant Sabbath was given exclusively to the circumcised children of Israel, and to no other people; so the gospel Sabbath, or Rest, is given exclusively to the spiritual Israel, who are the circumcision which worship God in the spirit, rejoice in Christ Jesus, and have no confidence in the flesh.

2. The children of the old Sinai covenant were often charged with the sin of Sabbath-breaking, and that sin, with them, consisted in their performing on the seventh day, such labor as was only lawful for them to perform in the six days in which they were commanded to do all their labor. So under the gospel dispensation, the saints, by adhering to the abrogated institutions of the old working dispensation, observing days, and months, and times, and years; or by looking for justification before God by anything short of the blood and righteousness of Christ, do violence to the holy Sabbath of the gospel. As in the types, many of the children of Israel could not enter into rest, because of unbelief, so we find that our doubts and unbelief, which often press us down, render it impossible for us to enter into that rest which remaineth for the children of God.

Our own experience teaches us that when we doubt the reality of our interest in Christ, or the application of his promises to us, we are like the troubled ocean that cannot rest: we labor, and toil to do something ourselves, to reinstate ourselves in the favor of the Lord. When we feel cold, we are prone to kindle fires of our own, and to comfort ourselves with sparks of our kindling, and endeavor to walk in the light of our fire; but if we are truly the children of God, we shall for all this lie down in sorrow; for this Sabbath-breaking. No fires were to be kindled by the Israelites on that day. Nor will the Lord suffer us to warm or enlighten ourselves by any fires that we can make. Christians are commanded to forsake not the assembling of themselves together for the worship of God, and for their mutual edification. To obey the command, suitable times must be appointed for such meetings; the first, or any other day of the week, may be designated, provided that we attach no special sanctity to the time; and the first day of the week is as suitable as any other day. The apostles met frequently on the first day, and also on all the other days of the week, they were daily in the temple praising God, &c. So we conclude that the Christian church is at liberty to make her own appointments,

as to time—provided that she allows no man, or set of men, to judge her in regard to the time, and when she makes such appointments, each member is in duty bound to attend the appointment, unless providentially detained.

As Christians we have no right to observe any day religiously in obedience to human legislation; either Sabbaths, first days, or thanksgiving days; because God has forbidden that we should allow any man to judge us in these things. We require no human legislation on the subject. The order and decision of the church is more effectual with the saints than all the pains, penalties and fines, ever imposed by the rulers of the darkness of this world. Let us observe the admonition of the apostle, and "Stand fast therefore in the liberty wherewith Christ has made us free; and be not entangled again with the yoke of bondage."

The Sabbath of the Jews required no grace in the heart, no spiritual emotion of the new man, to qualify those to whom it was given, to observe it. Their service was in the oldness of the letter, and theirs was a worldly sanctuary, and carnal ordinances. Any circumcised Jew, whether a believer or an infidel could abstain from labors on the seventh day, and that was all that was required of them. But the antitypical, or gospel Sabbath, requires faith in Christ; for none but believers can enter into that rest which remains, for the people of God. The hour has is come and the true worshipers must worship God in spirit and in truth. Not only the Scriptures of the New Testament declare it, but the testimony is corroborated by every Christian's experience. Christians know that they cannot believe only as the Lord gives them faith; and equally well do they know that they cannot rest unless they believe.

When faith, which is of the operation of God, is given, the recipient requires neither the thunder of Sinai, nor the arm of secular legislation, to incline him to keep the christian sabbath of Gospel Rest. The starving soul requires no coercion to incline him to eat, nor does the weary, heavy-laden soul require legal enactments to drive him to his rest. As the Sinai Sabbath required the carnal Israelite to abstain totally from servile labor, so the gospel Sabbath requires the spiritual Israelite to cease from his work, and trust, and rest alone on Christ, for his justification and acceptance with God. As the Sabbath-breaker under the law was to be stoned to death, by all the children of Israel, so the legalist who would attempt to drag the ceremonies of the legal dispensation into the gospel church, or to

376

justify himself before God by the works of the law, is to be stoned, (not with stones literally, but with the smooth stones from the brook of gospel truth), by all his brethren, until his legal spirit yields up the ghost.

Those who have no higher conception of a gospel Sabbath than to suppose it consists in the literal observance of one day out of seven, have yet to learn

that "Whom the Son makes free, are free indeed."

----

38 Appendix Publications of David

1. The Bierton Crisis 1984, which deals with my joining and secession from the Bierton Strict and Particular Baptist Church. This is available on request and not published.

2. Mary, Mary Quite Contrary, which deals with the rise of women seeking positions of eldership in churches. In this I deal with scriptural teaching regarding Marriage, divorce and remarriage and in particular what the scripture taught concerning male and female relationships.

3. Converted on LSD Trip 1st Edition. This deals my conversion from crime to Christ until Michael's conversion and our work in the Philippines

4. Trojan Warriors, This contains the story of Michael's conversion and our mission to the Jails of the Philippines. It contains 66 testimonies of converted criminal from crime to Christ all from New Bilibid Prison.

5. Before the Cock Crows. This deals with the successes and troubles that we experienced on our missions to the Philippines, showing the doctrinal and practical errors that we encountered, and suggestions how to avoid them.

6. Converted on LSD Trip 2nd Edition. This is the whole story relating to Michael and I and the range of difficulties that I experienced since leaving the Bierton Church. I deal with Marriage, Divorce, Imprisonment, travel abroad, preaching in the Jails of the Philippines.

7. The Bierton Crisis. This is a published version of my first book but with the names removed for the sake of confidentiality.

8. **The Bierton Strict and Particular Baptists**, My Testimony and Confession; Set for a Defence of the Gospel. This is a complete work relating to my call, joining the Bierton Church and being sent as a minister including my secession for the Bierton Church. My work in taking the Gospel to the Philippines and the establishment of our Trojan Horse International (TULIP) Phils Incorporation. To the sending of William Poloc and him founding churches in Baguio City.

DC 2012